BRITAIN IN PICTURES

BRITISH ADVENTURE

COMPANION VOLUMES

THE BRITISH COMMONWEALTH AND EMPIRE
FIRST PUBLISHED 1943   REPRINTED 1945

IMPRESSIONS OF ENGLISH LITERATURE
FIRST PUBLISHED 1944   REPRINTED 1945

THE ENGLISHMAN'S COUNTRY
FIRST PUBLISHED 1946   REPRINTED 1946

NATURE IN BRITAIN
FIRST PUBLISHED 1946

The Editor is grateful to all those who have helped in the selection of illustrations, especially to officials of the various public Museums, Libraries and Galleries and to all others who have generously allowed pictures and MSS to be reproduced

BRITISH ADVENTURE

INTRODUCTION BY NIGEL TANGYE

EDITED BY W. J. TURNER

WITH
48 PLATES IN COLOUR
AND
120 ILLUSTRATIONS IN
BLACK & WHITE

COLLINS · 14 ST. JAMES'S PLACE · LONDON
MCMXLVII

PRODUCED BY

ADPRINT LIMITED LONDON

Copyright. All rights reserved

PRINTED IN GREAT BRITAIN BY
CLARKE & SHERWELL LTD NORTHAMPTON
ON MELLOTEX BOOK PAPER MADE BY
TULLIS RUSSELL & CO LTD MARKINCH SCOTLAND

BRITISH

ADVENTURE

CONTENTS

INTRODUCTION

THE word "adventure" embraces a company of great words. Courage, tenacity, selflessness, faith, these are some of them. But its most potent ingredient cannot be put into one word. It is the spirit of the volunteer for hazardous tasks ; for adventure implies a voluntary acceptance of a course of action, or a wilful initiation of a plan, that must involve risk.

Man has this capacity for adventure within him from the moment he is born. In a young child it is expressed by his seeking to climb out of his play-pen in order to explore the mysteries of the nursery. Adventure in this form hardly reflects credit on the child because his reasoning powers are not sufficiently developed for him to count the cost of his adventure in terms of potential risk. When the child has grown to a little boy, his startled parents may see him precariously perched on the swaying branch of a tree, in which case they have reason to congratulate themselves on begetting a boy with spirit.

As childhood gives place to adolescence, and adolescence to manhood, the spirit of adventure tends to be restrained, if not displaced, by caution. Adventure is sought because of an insistent fire within the soul of a man, but the fire is often smothered by reason, which draws attention to the dangers ahead and counsels safety first.

It can, however, hardly be disputed that these islands have bred more men and women of adventuresome spirit in relation to population, than any island or continent one may choose. Throughout our history the urge for adventure has proved stronger than the primary instinct of self-preservation, with the result that we have painted a large proportion of the map red, we go faster on land, sea and water than anybody else, we climb nearer the top of the highest mountain in the world than anybody else, and we undertake to fight the tyrant without, if necessary, any allies to help us. We show, in fact, an inexhaustible capacity to reach for the unattainable and then catch a firm hold of it.

Our attitude toward adventure is a puzzle to men of other lands. To them it is frequently illogical. To us, too, if we think about it, it is also illogical. But we admire the spirit in a man who attempts the impossible, and whether he has as much stupidity as spirit does not really matter.

Some fifteen years ago, a delightful gentleman arrived at the London Aeroplane Club at Stag Lane and said he wanted to learn to fly. He soon proved to be the worst imaginable pupil. He showed no vestige of aptitude whatever. But he persevered, and because of his enthusiasm and his friendliness, the instructor persevered, too. Finally, after a record total of hours' instruction, he went solo.

No sooner had he done so than he bought his own Moth aeroplane. This caused some alarm to the Club members as it gave him a measure of independence and it was inconceivable that he could ever make a safe pilot. But the shock caused by his acquisition was nothing to his casual announcement that the reason he had been learning to fly was so that he could conquer Mount Everest *alone*. His plan was to land a little more than half way up the mountain (as far as his secondhand Moth could take him) and climb the rest of the way.

There are, of course, unlimited arguments to show that such a feat is impossible. There are, for instance, certain Laws of Nature that even adventurous Britons cannot overcome. But no facts, no arguments, could deviate him from his plan, or impress the faintest doubt on his conviction that his mission was feasible.

His first attempt to fly to India got him no further than the far hedge of the airfield. He hit it and wrecked his aeroplane. He had it rebuilt. His next attempt was successful and, to everyone's astonishment, he found his way to India.

It was in India that he encountered obstacles that not even his dauntless spirit could overcome. Bureaucracy forbade and prevented him from flying toward the Himalayas. He therefore cast aside his aeroplane and started to walk up the great mountain alone. His body was found at a considerable height some time later by one of the great expeditions.

This exploit, it might be thought, could better be termed a stunt than an adventure, and therefore unworthy of notice; but the solitary climber of Everest sought no press interviews, contracted with no newspaper. He had an urge within him, akin to that of the great explorers even though it was misguided; and it was the recognition of this spirit of adventure that caused those who had known him to mourn his loss and overlook the eccentricity of his purpose. Admiration for his adventuresome spirit predominated over feelings of disdain for his stupidity. Would that have been the case in other countries ?

On this day that I write there is another example of the British pride in adventure. There is an account in the newspaper of four lads who "stole" a motor boat from Ramsgate harbour with the intention of reaching France. They were quite inadequately provided for the journey with the result that, several days after they had set out they were rescued in the last stages of exhaustion. Their adventure included being struck one night by a steamer that failed to spot them. This incident had the effect of severely damaging the boat.

One would imagine that the reaction of the owner would be anger at the damage caused to his property. Not a bit of it. This was his comment on the incident : "I cannot help admiring the pluck of the boys—setting off to sea in such a small craft, and apparently with little food and petrol. That, after all, was the spirit of the little ships at Dunkirk." And the boys themselves, while they were yet prostrate in hospital, averred that in spite of their experience they still wanted to join the Merchant Navy.

Thus we see that adventure does not have to be successful to evoke the admiration of the public, nor does it have to be of importance in its aims. It is enough if the spirit of the individual assumes the shape of courage. The direction in which he chooses to travel is of secondary interest.

Furthermore, the failure of a mission touches the heart even more than its success. We are bound to admit the logic of Hitler in 1940 when he scoffed at us for turning the retreat at Dunkirk into a victory. Scott's tragic failure to reach the South Pole before Amundsen, and the loss of his party, fills a place in our hearts much bigger than if he had been successful. And the vision we have of Mallory and Irvine "going strong" through the swirling mists up toward the summit of Everest, never to return, is one that inspires us more than if they had been successful.

It is this legacy of inspiration that makes adventure so doubly worthwhile. Physical and material achievement are among the prizes success awards, spiritual inspiration for those that follow over the years is the treasure that even failure brings.

"A fire burnt in him and caused his willing spirit to rise superior to the weakness of the flesh." Norton wrote this of Mallory, and it is something that can be said of each and every one who deliberately follows the path of adventure. But if we read this as meaning that the conquest of the flesh and its insistent demands by the spirit is something that is easier for them than it is for us more humble mortals, we should be wrong. I have yet to meet a man who knows no fear. The finer the spirit of a man the finer the example that he sets and the less will he betray his fears. Hence we imagine that men who voluntarily accept hazardous tasks are blessed with a disregard for danger that we do not possess. It is not so. Physically and mentally they are made the same as we. Their bodies are prone to the same pains, their minds suffer the same anxieties, but what they do have that we do not have is something that comes from within, something which we are all able to summon but which most of us are too weak to do anything about but admire its qualities in others. It is the transcendent power of the spirit to stifle "self." To summon this power the individual must fight gigantic battles within himself, and no sooner has he gained one victory than he must fight another. Reason, hunger, love of life, the insistent call of home, all these build themselves into vast obstacles which he must fight and surmount and which, with the profligacy that nature bestows on physical things and temptations alike, rear themselves before him again as soon as he has overcome them.

Varied are the material rewards for these giants among men. They range from the little bronze Victoria Cross to a stack of charts of hitherto uncharted lands.

I suspect, however, that the spiritual rewards given for adventurous attempts and achievements are very similar. All of us touch on them sometime in life. It may have been after winning a race at school, or striking the demon bowler for six. It may have been after a hard day's work in the fields, or even as you rise from your desk after wrestling with visions and petrifying them into words to your satisfaction. At these moments you are acutely aware of the goodness in life, the cares and problems are but shades, and you feel a sense of mystical wisdom, an elemental awareness of Being; and you delight in the strange exaltation which, for some minutes, surrounds you.

The giants, to whom I have referred, must sense these things a thousand-fold and, because of the magnitude of the tasks that have evoked them, must surely be awarded the gift of storing their exaltation so that they draw on it at will and refresh themselves.

In the pages that follow are accounts of "British Seamen," "British Polar Explorers," "British Merchant Adventurers," "British Soldiers," "Britain in the Air" and "British Mountaineers." The common strain that runs through all of them is adventure. In all but "British Mountaineers" there is a practical goal of one sort or another. Mountaineering, however, is confined almost entirely to a test of spirit and stamina, so that the reward to the mountaineer is mainly limited to the spiritual gain which we have been considering.

Richard Jefferies in *The Story of My Heart* gives us an idea of what that gain is :

"Moving up the sweet short turf, at every step my heart seemed to obtain a wider horizon of feeling ; with every inhalation of rich pure air, a deeper desire. The very light of the sun was whiter and more brilliant here. By the time I had reached the summit I had entirely forgotten the petty circumstances and the annoyances of existence. I felt myself, myself . . . I was utterly alone with the sun and the earth. Lying down on the grass I spoke in my soul to the earth, the sun, the air, and the distant sea far beyond sight. I thought of the earth's firmness—I felt it bear me up ; through the grassy couch there came an influence as if I could feel the great earth speaking to me. I thought of the wandering air—its pureness, which is its beauty ; the air touched me and gave me something of itself.

I spoke to the sea ; though so far, in my mind I saw it, green at the rim of the earth and blue in deeper ocean; I desired to have its strength, its mystery and glory. . . . I turned to the blue heaven over, gazing into its depth, inhaling its exquisite colour and sweetness. The rich blue of the unattainable flower of the sky drew my soul towards it, and there it rested, for pure colour is rest of heart. By all these I prayed; I felt an emotion of the soul beyond all definition . . . I prayed that I might touch to the unutterable existence infinitely higher than deity."

Such is the reward that Nature gives to those with the courage to probe her secrets.

NIGEL TANGYE

BRITISH
MERCHANT ADVENTURERS

BY

MAURICE COLLIS

RALPH FITCH: MERCHANT-TRAVELLER
(*fl.* 1583-1611)

WHEN Queen Elizabeth came to the throne in 1558, her dominion extended only over England and Ireland. Her subjects were few, poor, and backward, and were in grave danger of being subjugated by Spain. But for a reason no one can entirely explain, they were animated by a spirit for which there was no warrant in the size of their territory and their reasonable prospects. This spirit was a compound of pride, love of liberty, and resolution. They were quite sure they could do as well as or better than the great states of the Continent. The Portuguese and the Spaniards during the previous half-century had discovered Asia and the Americas, and with the Pope's sanction had divided between them the vast trade of these continents. These discoveries had enormously enriched them, and Spain planned to found a united Catholic order in Europe under her king. But the idea of Spain ruling the world seemed nonsense to the English because man for man they felt themselves superior to the Spaniards. In riches and possessions, however, they were a long way behind them. The realisation of all this, and the determination to change it, caused an uprush of the national genius, which showed itself in every department of life.

II

The Government was inclined to lag, to talk of prudence. Elizabeth was a very cautious woman. Philip II's power was formidable on paper. But the people wanted fighting and adventures. Without the Queen's sanction, many privateers were fitted out and preyed on the Spanish trading galleons. Drake was the most famous of such buccaneers. He sailed round the world in a ship the size of a small schooner, arriving home with half a million pounds' worth of loot, as much as the whole revenue of the Crown for a year.

But this was not business, and the merchants of London and other cities, some of whom had long been combined for trade in Europe under the name of the Merchant Adventurers of England, were very desirous of straightforward settled trade with the East. In the twenty-third year of the reign they resolved to send out men to report on what could be bought and what sold in Asia. These travellers were to go via Syria and the Persian Gulf, because the Portuguese, who, in the division, had taken the Eastern trade and used the Cape route, would have tried to sink intruders who went that way. Moreover, in 1580, Portugal had been united to Spain, the arch-enemy of England, and Spain's enemies were now Portugal's.

So in February, 1583, a party of merchant-travellers set out. They were financed by a particular syndicate, called the Turkey Company, which was backed by a charter from Queen Elizabeth. Among them was Ralph Fitch of London. "Her husband 's to Aleppo gone, master o' the Tiger," says the First Witch in *Macbeth*, and it was to that identical place they first went and on that very ship. Travelling thence overland they came to Basra, at the head of the Persian Gulf. Some of the merchants remained there, but Fitch and three others were deputed to proceed to India. They had a letter from Elizabeth addressed to Akbar, the Great Mughal. But at Ormuz, an island at the mouth of the Gulf, from which they planned to slip across the Arabian Sea, they were arrested by the Portuguese, who had a fortress there.

The charge was heresy, but the reason, of course, trade jealousy : the Portuguese knew the English had come to make enquiries. So as heretics they were sent prisoners to Goa, the capital of the Portuguese Indies, where an Inquisition existed and a Grand Inquisitor. This Inquisition was notoriously severe, more cruel and terrifying than the Inquisition of Spain.

Besides the prison of the Inquisition, there were two other notorious prisons in Goa known as the Salle and the Al Jabir. It was in one or other of these that Fitch and his three companions were confined. Both were filthy underground dungeons in which galley-slaves and common male-factors of all races were crowded together, in stifling heat and without sanitation. Bad as English prisons were at that time, they were pleasant places in comparison. But by good fortune a member of the Jesuit College at Goa happened to be an Englishman. This was Father Stevens, the first of this nation known to have set foot in India. Thanks to him, they were released on bail after a month and took a house in the city.

JAHANGIR DRINKING WINE UNDER A CANOPY

Indián painting by Manohar

MAP OF ASIA BY J. BLAEU, 1622

THE MARKET PLACE AT GOA IN THE SIXTEENTH CENTURY
Engraving from Linschoten's *Itinerario*, 1579-1592

The Goa they saw was at the height of its prosperity. It was the most beautiful city which any Western nation has ever built in the East. The palaces and churches were in Spanish baroque. As admirable as any in that style in Europe, they seemed more enchanting set in a tropic landscape. Gorgeously dressed, the Portuguese, both high and low, attended by Indian or African slaves, paraded the main streets, saluting each other with the extravagance of actors in melodrama. The shops were packed with all the products of the East. Fitch noted the luxury and splendour, little dreaming that one day his countrymen would build greater (though less beautiful) Indian cities. After five months, no further proceedings having been taken against them, the Englishmen asked for the return of their bail money. "The Viceroy made a very sharp answer," writes Fitch in the narrative of his travels, "and sayd wee should be better sifted before it were long, and that they had further matter against us." This alarmed them, and when they heard privately that they were to be given the strappado, a torture where you were hoisted by ropes tied to the wrists and then suddenly dropped a distance so as to dislocate the arms, they fled secretly one early morning. Travelling across the continent they made their way to Fatehpur Sikri, the wonderful red-sandstone city which Akbar had just built. There they saw the Mughal Court at its greatest moment, but were not given formal audience by the Emperor and so were unable to deliver Queen Elizabeth's letter. Probably as mere travelling merchants they were not qualified for that honour. Moreover, they had no presents. Nevertheless, one of them, Leeds, a jeweller, was given employment at Court on a good salary.

It was at this point that Fitch decided to undertake the journey on which his fame rests. He would go to Burma. No Englishman, as far as is recorded, had ever been to that country. Parts of it were well known to Portuguese

15

adventurers, free-lances and mercenaries who sold their services, often as artillerymen, to the Burmese Kings. Two Italian travellers, Frederici and Balbi, had visited Pegu, the capital, and published memoirs. But it may safely be said that very few people in England knew anything of the kingdom, nearly twice as large as France, which lay between India and China.

In September, 1584, Fitch started alone. Taking boat on the Ganges he floated down to Hugli in Bengal, a Portuguese settlement independent of the Viceroy of Goa, situated near the site of the present city of Calcutta, noting as he went the products of the countryside. From Hugli he passed into Chittagong, where, embarking on a Portuguese ship—the Portuguese here were more buccaneers than merchants—he sailed along the coast of the Bay of Bengal till he reached one of the mouths of the Irrawaddy. Ascending that river to Bassein he transferred to a small boat and in ten days came by tidal riverways to Pegu.

For an Elizabethan, Burma was a strange, incomprehensible place. The Mohammedan and Hindu religions of India were understood to the extent that the followers of the first were called Moors and of the second Gentiles. But no European could have said more of the Buddhism of Burma than that it was a kind of paganism. A great deal of what Fitch saw was, therefore, wholly unintelligible to him. He had not the smallest notion of Burmese history.

The reigning king was styled Nanda Bayin, the son of Bayin Naung, whom the Portuguese called Braginoco, as if he were some paynim knight in Ariosto. And indeed he had been a galloping high-coloured personage who had united all Burma and conquered Siam. He died at sixty-six, leaving ninety-seven children. By him was laid out on a grand scale a new city of Pegu, which was filled with the loot he had taken from Siam. There his son, Nanda Bayin, now sat, the most important monarch in all the territories which lay between the domain of Akbar and of Wan Li, the Son of Heaven. But neither of these two Emperors, particularly the latter, would have admitted him to be more than a barbarian.

For Fitch, however, he was a great king. Pegu was so much bigger than London. "Pegu is a citie very great, strong and fair," he writes, "and very populous, and is made square and with very faire walles, and a great ditch round about it full of water, with many crocodiles in it. It hath twenty gates. The streets are the fairest that ever I saw, as straight as a line from one gate to the other, and so broad that tenne or twelve men may ride a front thorow them. The king's house is in the middle of the city," he goes on, and describes a wooden palace, gilded and carved, before the gate of which were the elephant stables, where stood hundreds of black and four white elephants.

These particular white elephants were the most valuable part of the loot taken by the King's father, Bayin Naung, from Siam. At different periods in the world's history different things are valued and for different reasons. In

16

THE INHABITANTS OF PEGU AND THE MOLUCCAS
Engraving from Linschoten's *Itinerario*, 1579-1592

sixteenth-century Burma the four white elephants were worth so much that
not all the wealth of the country could have bought them. The only other
comparable object in Pegu was a tooth of the Buddha, which had been
procured by treaty from Ceylon. But here some doubt existed, for the
Viceroy of Goa declared that he and the Archbishop had destroyed the
veritable tooth when it fell into Portuguese hands after a battle. They had
done so because they believed it to be a potent relic of the Devil.

Fitch went to see the white elephants. Visitors were allowed in on payment of half a ducat. He saw their gilded stable and watched them eat
from gold plate. He also watched them having a bath in the river. As they
walked to the bank, their attendants shading them from the sun with para-
sols, a band played ; and when they came out of the water there was a
gentleman in court robes ready with a silver basin to wash the mud off their
feet. Fitch saw all this, but he did not know that they treated the white
elephants in this way because of the belief that the soul of a future World
Saviour in its long upward transmigration was lodging in each animal. As

17

to black elephants, there were thousands of them trained for battle, in which they played the part of tanks in modern warfare.

Fitch did not aspire to be received by Nanda Bayin, but he saw him giving audience attended by his *She-min* or Ministers and saw petitioners *ski-ko*, a prostration very similar to the Chinese kotow. He also saw the King riding abroad "with a great guard and many noblemen," sometimes on an elephant, at others in a palanquin. And he heard of his great treasure of rubies, sapphires and spinels. Yet he perceived his weakness : "This king hath little force by sea, because he hath but very few ships." That was the mortal weakness which eventually was the ruin of Burma. Fitch's real business, however, was to observe the trade, and in his account he gives a

AN INQUISITION SCENE AT GOA IN THE SEVENTEENTH CENTURY
Engraving from Dellon's *Relation de l'Inquisition de Goa*, 1688

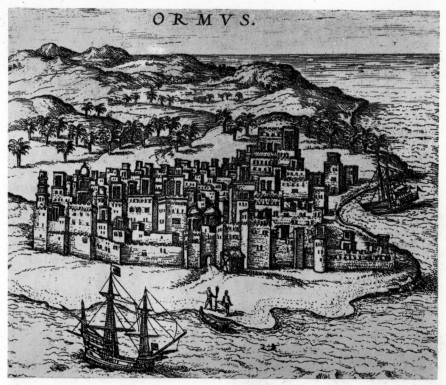

ORMVS.

VIEW OF ORMUZ
Engraving from H. Braun's *Civitates Orbis Terrarum*, 1588-1594

list of the chief commodities as well as the foreign goods for which there was demand.

After visiting Rangoon and the Shwe-dagon pagoda—his description of the latter might stand for it to-day—he left Pegu for Chiengmai in Northern Siam, never dreaming that one day the capital where he had seen such riches and state would be a country town administered by an English official. The writer of this book has often been there, and seen the remnant of the great walls and the crocodile moat.

When he had investigated the trade at Chiengmai he returned to Pegu and took ship to Malacca near Singapore, where the Portuguese had a fortress which commanded the Straits. On the way he passed Martaban, Tavoy, Mergui and Junkseylon, palm-fringed little ports where the wind always blows, and in one of which, Mergui, a hundred years later so many Englishmen were to be massacred, as will be related further on. Having noted the vital importance of the Straits of Malacca for a maritime power

19

trading to the Far East, he returned to Pegu and at last set his face for home, travelling by sea to Ceylon, thence up the west coast of India to Cochin, then to Goa, where he was careful only to remain three days, and so on to Basra, Babylon, Mosul, Aleppo and "by God's assistance safely to London."

He had been away eight years and except for his narrow escape at Goa had had no misadventures. He had travelled some twenty-four thousand miles by sea and land, mostly alone, and at a period when travelling of the kind was extremely dangerous, yet he was neither robbed nor shipwrecked. He had acquired a mass of first-hand information of the greatest importance, which, when it was sifted by the merchants of London, led to the founding nine years later of the East India Company, the great organisation which in the course of two hundred and fifty years was to acquire for England almost all the towns he had visited. In 1611 he died and is buried in St. Catherine Cree in Leadenhall Street, a most remarkable man, hardly known, because what he accomplished was more solid than brilliant ; because he was over-shadowed by the many dramatic figures of the Elizabethan era ; and because the little he wrote of himself and his travels was modestly worded and hardly hinted at the multitudinous perils through which he had passed unhurt.

THE WHITE ELEPHANT OUTSIDE THE PALACE AT AMARAPURA
Capital of Burma in the early nineteenth century
Lithograph from Yule's *Mission to the Court of Ava*, 1855

SIR THOMAS ROE
Engraving by Vertue after Miereveldt

SIR THOMAS ROE: MERCHANT-AMBASSADOR
(1580-1644)

THE East India Company was a monopoly. By the Royal Charter of 1601, the right to trade in the Eastern seas was reserved to its shareholders. At the time monopolies were a normal way of encouraging trade, though there were plenty of men to say that an Englishman had an inherent right to trade freely wherever he liked. But it was reasonably contended for the monopoly of the Eastern trade that only a body which had not to face competition and was protected by the Crown could hope to pay its way in the face of the dangers and obstacles inherent in an attempt to force English trade in the face of Portuguese opposition.

21

The first ship sent by the Company to India did not arrive there until 1608. It was commanded by William Hawkins and put into Surat, the chief western port of the Mughal's dominion. Hawkins journeyed to Agra, the imperial capital, to solicit permission to open trade, Jahangir having recently succeeded his father, Akbar. He remained in Agra for three years. The Emperor granted leave to trade at Surat, but the Portuguese, who were strongly represented at court by Jesuits, succeeded in obtaining the cancellation of this grant and the virtual expulsion of Hawkins in 1611.

The Company tried again. In 1612 Thomas Best managed to come to an agreement with the imperial officials at Surat. But it was a very limited and insecure arrangement. The Company wanted a charter of rights from the Emperor himself which would place English commerce on a firm and enduring basis. To effect this the Jesuit diplomats at the court of Agra must be confronted by an English diplomat as clever as themselves. Accordingly it was decided to send, with King James's sanction and credence, an ambassador to Jahangir.

For this entirely novel and most difficult appointment the Company selected in 1614 Sir Thomas Roe, a man of thirty-four years of age, who was a Member of Parliament and had made a voyage of discovery to South America. His grandfather had been Lord Mayor of London. The plan was for him to go to the Indian capital, take up his residence there, get the better of the Portuguese Jesuits and foster and expand the trade which had been tentatively begun. James gave him a letter addressed to Jahangir. He was to press for a treaty of free trade between the two countries. It was known that the Court of India was a splendid court and that to impress it Roe would require money and presents. But the Company was not in a position to do very much. His salary was fixed at £600 a year, a sum equal to at least £5,000 nowadays, but the incomes of the big people at Jahangir's Court ran into tens or even hundreds of thousands. Moreover, his staff was not very brilliant. A chaplain and a doctor on £50 and £24 per annum were supplied, Roe himself having to pay the wages of the rest of his retinue from an annual grant of £100. Later he records in his diary how ashamed he was of his clothes. The Mughals were dressed in the most dazzling manner. "Five years' allowance would not have furnished me with one indifferent suit sortable to theirs," he writes. But important though clothes and presents were at the Court of India, they were not everything. Intelligence, firmness, courage, an engaging address, had their effect there as everywhere else. And Roe was a very intelligent man, of indomitable courage, with great charm of manner. Anthony à Wood calls him a scholar and a gentleman. But he was also a very subtle man of affairs. He arrived at Surat in September, 1615.

The Mughal dominion in India was analogous to the Mongol dominion which Marco Polo saw in China three hundred years before. In both cases nomad horsemen of Mongolian type inhabiting the vast steppe between

By courtesy of Mrs. Morris

AN INCIDENT IN THE WARS BETWEEN THE SIAMESE AND BURMESE

A 17th or 18th century painting by a Siamese artist

A MALAYAN VILLAGE

Coloured aquatint from T. and W. Daniell's *Picturesque Voyage to India by the Way of China*, 1810

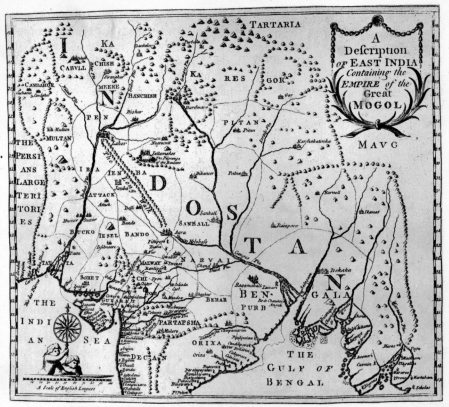

A MAP OF THE TERRITORIES OF THE GREAT MUGHAL CONTEMPORARY WITH ROE
Engraving from Edward Terry's *Voyage to East India*, 1655

Manchuria and the Caspian had left their pastures and taken possession of an old agricultural empire. The nomads of Genghis and Kubilai were largely barbarians, and the Chinese civilised them. The Mughals, however, had acquired a tincture of Persian Moslem culture before they entered India. There were, moreover, already Indian Moslem states, for similar nomads had been raiding the sub-continent for six centuries. The Mughals conquered these as well as the Hindus, the inhabitants proper of the country, whom they were careful to leave in the enjoyment of their religion and customs. The Court itself was a sort of colonial version of the Court of Persia ; the tone was nominally Moslem but in reality sceptic, and its literature, painting, calligraphy and ceremonial were derived wholly from Persian models. Besides art, sport held an important place, hunting, shooting, hawking and polo being considered the proper relaxations of a gentleman. The women had lost the freedom of the steppe and were confined in harems

25

guarded by eunuchs. Brahmanical India went its own way outside. There were Hindus, however, in the civil service, and there were Hindu women in the imperial seraglio. As Jahangir's mother was a Rajput, he was half Hindu. His father's, Akbar's, mother had been Persian. Thus the original nomad blood in the royal house was much diluted. Educated though the Court was, its information was limited. It did not realise that Europe, though poor and backward in many ways, had recently made scientific discoveries of great promise. Nor had it a proper conception of the new importance of sea power. But in these respects it did not differ from the far grander and more sophisticated Court of China.

Roe had not a good reception at Surat. The Governor, a man called Zulfikar Khan, was a nominee of Prince Khurram, Jahangir's favourite son and the future Emperor. This prince, with Jahangir's Empress, the famous Nur Jahan, one of the most remarkable women in Indian history, was the head of the Court faction which favoured the Portuguese. Zulfikar Khan, therefore, made difficulties when Roe announced that he desired to proceed to the capital. However, the Emperor, on learning that an ambassador from the King of England had come with new presents—Jahangir had a mania for novelties—gave orders for him to be sent up. The Court was then at Ajmere, two months' journey inland. Roe arrived there on 13 December, 1615, having met *en route* that astonishing eccentric, Tom Coryat, a London writer, who had walked to India as a diversion !

Roe had decided on the line he should take. He must stand on his dignity as an ambassador, refuse to bend, refuse to bribe, show that an envoy of his rank was very different from Fitch and Hawkins, put his case with patience, expound the advantages of trade with England, declare there was plenty of room for both English and Portuguese, and work so that reason and common sense should prevail. It was from Portuguese animosity that he had most to fear. But he was fortified by the reflection that Portugal's position in Eastern waters was not so strong as it had been. If it came to a fight, he knew the British could beat her armadas. The Dutch had recently appeared in Indian seas and were also bent on breaking her monopoly. But Roe did not want it to come to a fight. That would annoy the Mughal and, moreover, cause such expenditure that the trade would pay no dividends for years. If humanly possible he must carry through his mission by diplomacy.

On 10 January he was received in audience by Jahangir. The Emperor sat in a gallery overlooking a wide courtyard full of people. Roe was conducted through the crowd to a rail enclosing a space for men of a better class, where he made a reverence towards the Emperor in the English Court manner. Thereupon he was led across this first enclosure into a second, which was raised somewhat and well carpeted. This was full of courtiers and men of quality. Here he made a reverence again and was taken on until he stood immediately below the balcony, not a high one, on which Jahangir was seated. As he made his third reverence, sweeping the carpet with the

26

REPUTED PORTRAIT OF NUR JAHAN, WIFE OF JAHANGIR
From a Manuscript in the Bodleian Library

plume of his hat, the Emperor bade him welcome with pleasant informality. Roe thereupon handed up King James's letter and some presents. Jahangir seemed very pleased. He talked affably through an interpreter, enquiring after Roe's health, which had not been good, and offering to send him his own physician. No business was discussed. At the end of the audience Roe was congratulated by some of those present on his reception, which had been, they said, more gracious than any accorded to ambassadors from Turkey or Persia.

But he was a very long way from obtaining his desires. The clique headed by the Empress and the Heir Apparent was by no means pleased that the Emperor had received him. He himself did not understand at that time the composition of the Court parties, and was more optimistic than the real facts warranted. Jahangir's affability had less importance than appeared because Nur Jahan dominated her husband. Moreover, Jahangir did not regard him as an ambassador from a monarch of equal rank. He considered King James no more than the petty king of a remote island.

Among the presents were a coach, a virginal and a sword. Jahangir had asked Roe's musician, Thomas Armstrong, to play on the virginal there and then and was so intrigued by the music that he took him into his employ. From where he sat he could not see the coach well, for it was outside the courtyard, but that evening he went down and got into it and commanded his men to draw him about. Later, at ten o'clock at night, he sent for Roe to show him how the sword should be worn, and "marched up and downe, draweing yt and flourishing." Jahangir was nearly always drunk by 10 p.m.

For the next week or so Roe remained at his lodging, for the fever he had caught returned. He was homesick and low, and felt a strong distaste for the people with whom he would have to negotiate. Writing to his friend, Lord Carew, on the 17th, he said: "This is the dullest, basest place that ever I saw."

On the 24th, restored to health and spirits, he attended the Emperor's Durbar, as the levee held from the balcony was called. When Jahangir caught sight of him, he beckoned with his hand. Roe had a clock with him, and this he presented. Clocks at that time were not manufactured in the East. Ricci, the Jesuit, made a good impression with one in 1600 at the Court of China. They represented that first application of Western science and mathematics to practical mechanics which afterwards was to give Europe such overwhelming power. But, of course, Jahangir had no inkling that from the little mechanism ticking under his hand would grow engines which one day would strike down all Asia. He was pleased and said bluntly, "What do you want of me?" "Justice," replied Roe, and he detailed certain pressing injustices under which the English traders lived at Surat, particularly how they were robbed and insulted by the local officials. Jahangir immediately issued orders for the remedying of these abuses. In the months that followed Roe patiently pursued a negotiation that became drawn out into years and was not concluded until September, 1618, three years after he had landed in India. When he understood what he calls the "pace of the Court," that is, the strength of the various parties, and was sure that he could always obtain a hearing from the Emperor, who had got to like him, he cleverly decided not to force the pro-Portuguese faction into open hostility by persuading Jahangir to pass orders over its head, but to try and win it over by fair argument, while letting it be known that if he were refused justice against all reason he would appeal to the Emperor. Asaf Khan, the

Empress's brother, was the person with whom he dealt directly. This lord was very rude at first, but Roe never abated an inch of dignity, and when on one occasion he was summoned by Asaf Khan and kept waiting deliberately, he sent him in this tart message: "If your greatness were no more than your manners you would not dare to use me so." It paid to stand up to the Mughals.

The final settlement was not exactly the treaty between Jahangir and King James which he had come to get, but it was a satisfying compromise. He obtained a public declaration by the Emperor of his amity towards the East India Company at Surat. The merchants were given liberty to trade freely, to live in a rented house on shore, to govern themselves and to bear arms when they went abroad in the city. No payments beyond the normal dues were to be demanded of them. The Portuguese were invited to cooperate in an open trade.

A settlement is best judged by its actual results. This one had the effect of giving the East India Company enough security to carry on its trade with profit, an advantage that sufficed to lay the foundations of the power which eventually enabled the British to supplant the Mughals as lords of India.

THE ENGLISH QUARTERS AT SURAT
An eighteenth century engraving

29

SAMUEL WHITE: MERCHANT-INTERLOPER
(1650-1689)

AS we have seen, the East India Company was a monopoly. To be more precise, it was a royal monopoly, deriving from the King's prerogative and not from statute law. By the time of Charles II public opinion had turned more and more against royal monopolies. Indeed, by then it had been held by the judicature that the King had no power to grant them inside the realm. In 1683 a test case was brought to determine whether he could grant them outside the realm, with special reference to the East India Company's monopoly in Asia. It came before the notorious Judge Jeffreys and he found for the Crown.

This verdict was very pleasing to the Company's shareholders, a small clique of about forty persons closely connected with the Court. A few years previously their stock was valued at £1,700,000, on which the dividends averaged 22 per cent. Jeffrey's verdict guaranteed their future profits. But it is one thing to lay down the law and another to enforce it. To prevent Englishmen who were not shareholders in the Company from trading in Asia was impossible. From the beginning there had always been men who refused to recognise the Company's monopoly and sailed east in their own ships. Claiming that they typified the spirit of independence which was England's glory, they called themselves Free Merchants, though by the members of the Company they were dubbed Interlopers. The most remarkable of these Interlopers was Samuel White.

Samuel White started life as an employee of the Company, sailing east in 1675 on board one of their ships, the *Loyal Subject*, in the capacity of mate. Sixty years had passed since Roe had set the Company on its feet at Surat. During these years it had drawn level with and then passed the Portuguese, as far as India was concerned. The Dutch, by taking Malacca, had also got the better of them, and proceeded to lay the foundations of what is now the Dutch Empire of Java, Sumatra and the adjacent islands. After the Dutch came the French, who established a small trade with India and were interesting themselves in the possibilities of Siam. These events almost eliminated the Portuguese and resulted in the trade to and from Asia being mostly handled by the English and the Dutch. Surat remained the headquarters of the East India Company, which had acquired subsidiary trading settlements at Bombay, Madras, Hugli and certain intermediate ports. Its policy was unchanged. "Our business is only trade and security, not conquest," wrote Sir Josiah Child, President of the Court of Directors at this period. Conquest, indeed, was out of the question, because the Mughal Empire, though it had passed its zenith, was still very strong. The trade consisted in the buying of cotton goods in India, for cash or in exchange for English manufactures. But there was another trade, known as the country trade, the

VIEW OF SIAM
Engraving from le père Guy Tachard's *Voyage de Siam des Pères Jésuites*, 1688

exchange of commodities between the various countries inside Asia. The Company was not interested in that trade, which was carried on by the local inhabitants and the Interlopers. But the employees of the Company were allowed to engage in it for their private profit in a half-open partnership with the Interlopers. Thus, there existed a good deal of give and take between the East India Company and the Free Merchants. As long as the latter confined themselves to the country trade and made no attempt to compete in the London cotton market or embarrass the regular trade by agreements with native rulers contrary to its interests, their activities, though not officially recognised, were winked at.

This was the world, these were the possibilities, to which Samuel White had arrived when the *Loyal Subject* landed him at Madras in 1676. As an employee of the Company he had a ridiculously small salary, £10 a year, with the prospect later on of promotion and private trade. If he did not die of fever or dysentery he might hope to return to England in ten or fifteen years with a modest fortune. But White was not a person for whom the modest, the safe and the slow had any appeal. He wanted a large fortune in a hurry and he was prepared to run desperate risks to obtain it. The interloping

31

trade gave a man of his character, vehement, enterprising and without scruples, exactly the opportunity which he required. And an opening happened to be ready for him, for his brother, George, was established as a Free Merchant at Ayudhya, the capital of Siam.

At that time Ayudhya was an important centre of the country trade, for it was the emporium where Chinese and Japanese goods were exchanged for Indian goods. The trade route was from Canton by sea to Ayudhya ; thence overland to Mergui, a port on the eastern shores of the Bay of Bengal and in Siamese territory ; and so across the Bay to Masulipatam, some two hundred miles north of Madras. Samuel White took an early opportunity of visiting his brother, travelling to Mergui and thence to Ayudhya.

The East India Company had agents in Ayudhya, as had the Dutch and French companies. There were also many Free Merchants. The King of Siam, Phra Narai, was a man of vision. Unlike the Great Mughal and the Son of Heaven, he seems to have grasped the significance of the European irruption into Asia, and to have argued that if he could westernise his army and increase his wealth by trade with Europe, he would make Siam the most powerful kingdom in the Indo-Chinese peninsula, able not only to resist her Asiatic rivals, but to face the danger of European, particularly Dutch, encroachments. To achieve this he must get the assistance of a European state. He did not trust the Dutch and this left him the choice between the English and the French.

When Samuel White reached Ayudhya the King was beginning to enlist Englishmen in his service, and George White had no difficulty in procuring for his brother an appointment as captain of one of the King's ships plying between Mergui and Masulipatam. This was in 1677, and for six years Samuel White sailed backwards and forwards across the Bay of Bengal, delivering the royal cargo—it was elephants—and trading on his own account. Meanwhile a friend of his brother George, a Greek adventurer called Constant Phaulkon, had attracted the King's attention. He was a man of enormous talent and ambition. To the King he seemed the very person to carry out the new policy. He was appointed Minister and soon became the most powerful figure in the kingdom. On his advice the King decided to look to France rather than to England for the arms and military assistance he required. Time would elapse before these could materialise and it was decided to take certain preliminary steps with the help of the English Interlopers in the Siamese service.

Accordingly, White was sent for in 1683, created Mandarin and made Shabandar of Mergui, an appointment which combined the duties of a Superintendent of Trade and a Commissioner of Maritime Affairs. He was instructed to fortify Mergui and get together a fleet of armed merchantmen, so that when the French arrived Mergui would already be a port of the first importance on the Canton-Masulipatam trade route, a base where the French ships could anchor and from which, with their assistance, Siam

A VIEW OF THE NEW GOVERNMENT HOUSE, CALCUTTA, BUILT IN 1802
Coloured aquatint by J. Clarke and H. Merke after Moffat, c.1807

A VIEW OF KUTRA MOSQUE BUILT BY MIR JAFFIER AT MURSHIDABAD

Coloured aquatint from William Hodge's *Select Views in India*, 1786

could dominate the Bay of Bengal. The plan was a direct threat to the East India Company, whose ships commanded the Bay and its approaches.

In accepting this appointment White placed himself in a situation which was bound sooner or later to bring him into conflict with the East India Company. But his eyes were fixed entirely on the fortune which his new appointment would enable him to make as an Interloper. He did not care whether he hurt the Company or not, nor had he the slightest intention of working as the faithful servant of the King of Siam. Mergui was a week's journey by forest track and river from Ayudhya, and he calculated that supervision would be lax and that he would be free to pursue his private ends without interference.

As soon as some of the armed ships which he was authorised to build or purchase were available, he placed them under the command of English Interloper captains and, declaring an unprovoked war on Burma and Golconda, an Indian kingdom independent of the Mughal, without the knowledge or sanction of the Siamese Government, proceeded to seize all ships belonging to those states which were encountered in the Bay of Bengal. Then, manning the prizes with his own crews, he sent them to ports in Sumatra or the Persian Gulf, where their cargoes were sold as his private property. For two years he continued to prey on native shipping in this manner without being called to account by the Siamese Government. His profits enabled him to remit home £15,740 and to keep by him a trading capital in cash and jewels of a like amount, a total which nowadays would be equivalent to at least £150,000. Besides this commerce with other people's property, he made very free with the money granted to him by the Siamese treasury, for he embezzled the entire sum allotted for the fortification of Mergui and, by maintaining a garrison which only existed on paper, was able on pay-day to credit himself with their wages.

Public opinion in the Siam of the date was not very vocal, but such was the indignation in Mergui at his contemptuous disregard of his duty that complaint was made to the Government and he was recalled to Ayudhya in 1686 to explain the charges against him. He survived the enquiry through a combination of circumstances. Phaulkon stood by him, partly because he seems to have had some share in White's profits, and also because George White, now in England, was acting for him there. Moreover, he knew that, brilliant though his position was, it was also precarious, because the Mandarinate disliked his policy, believing that if the French secured a hold on the country it would lose its independence. White, he thought, could be trusted to support him against a possible rebellion. He therefore quashed the enquiry proceedings and sent him back to Mergui with increased powers. This convinced White that he had little more time in which to enrich himself. In a heart-to-heart talk with Francis Davenport, his secretary, he said one day: "To tell you truly, I am not without strong apprehensions that his Lordship stands but in a slippery place and in case he once slips how can I expect to keep my footing. I am resolved to make Hay while the Sun shines and so be in readiness for any Revolution that may happen."

On arrival at Mergui he moored below his house a new frigate he had built called the *Resolution*, and began loading it with money, jewels and a rich cargo, so that he could escape to England at a moment's notice. But another, and a more formidable, danger was looming on the horizon. The East India Company had come to the conclusion that he must be suppressed. As a private individual he had obliged them by putting trade in their way but his depredations in the Bay had upset their official commerce. Moreover, he was now associated with Phaulkon's French policy. If the French established themselves at Mergui, immediately opposite Madras and on the route to the Far East, the whole position of the Company was potentially threatened. They therefore procured from James II, who was a large shareholder, an order recalling White from service with the Crown of Siam, and sent a frigate called the *Curtana* to Mergui, commanded by a Captain Weltden, whose orders were to bring White to Madras, there to stand his trial.

The *Curtana* arrived at the bar of Mergui on 23 June, 1687. Then began a strange drama. White knew that to go to Madras with Weltden meant ruin and possibly death on a charge of piracy or treason. To fight Weltden would also be a capital offence, for which, if he escaped afterwards to England, he could be arrested and tried. To flee to Ayudhya was equally desperate, as Phaulkon's régime was now tottering : he would be murdered there. The dilemma was appalling, but he saw a way out.

Weltden was very poor and he began by offering him a chance to make money. Getting friendly with him in this way he persuaded him that the charges of piracy and treason were malicious and that he was a much wronged, worthy gentleman. He also professed perfect willingness to go to Madras.

Meanwhile he had told the Siamese Council at Mergui that Weltden had come to seize their town and secretly encouraged them to resist. It was arranged that they should send fire-boats down on the tide and burn the *Curtana*. So friendly, however, did White appear to become with Weltden that the Siamese thought he was tricking them and must have bought his own immunity by promising to deliver Mergui to the English. They therefore decided, in addition to burning the *Curtana*, to kill him and the numerous interloping Englishmen who had settled in Mergui. The attack took place on the night of 14 July, 1687. White narrowly escaped death by taking refuge in the *Resolution*. His house was burnt and some eighty Englishmen were killed. But the fire-boats failed to set the *Curtana* alight and both ships cleared the port in safety.

White then persuaded Weltden that the Siamese attempt to murder him was proof of his loyalty to King James. Weltden, quite convinced of his innocence, believed him when he said he would accompany him to

Madras, and became so lax that White was able to give him the slip one day and sail for England with all his treasure.

He got there long before any news of his recent doings at Mergui had reached the Company's Directors. Moreover, James II had just fled the realm and William and the Whigs had come in. The Whigs had always been opposed to royal monopolies. White saw his chance : he would anticipate any charges which the Company might subsequently bring, by himself suing them for damages to the extent of £40,000. But he died suddenly in May, 1689, before the case came on. Phaulkon had lost his life the previous year in the expected revolution.

Mary and Susan, White's daughters, succeeded to the fortune.

A SIAMESE MANDARIN
Engraving, 1691

ROBERT CLIVE: MERCHANT-SOLDIER
(1725-1774)

THE next date is 1744, for it was on 1 June of that year and at seven in the evening that Robert Clive landed at Madras to take up his appointment as clerk to the East India Company on a salary of five pounds per annum. He was aged nineteen, of neurotic temperament and subject to fits.

During the sixty-six years which had elapsed since White defied the East India Company, it had undergone a change in constitution but not in policy. The agitation against it, of which White's petition to Parliament was a part, culminated in a resolution of the Commons in 1694 that "all subjects of England have equal rights to trade in the East Indies, unless prohibited by Act of Parliament." The trade being thus thrown open, the Interlopers founded a rival Company. It was discovered, however, that this was not good business. Neither Company prospered. Accordingly, in 1708 the new Company became fused with the old, with the result that, since the combined shareholders were now fairly representative of all interests, the united Company was no longer a harmful monopoly. As to its policy, that remained trade and security, not conquest. Though its trading ports at Bombay, Madras and Calcutta were fortified to resist attack from the sea by European, and from the land by Asiatic, adventurers, they were in all other respects no more than emporiums for the exchange of English manufactures and Indian cotton goods. They served, moreover, as settlements on the way to China, where the Company also had its factory and agents. The story of its progress at Canton cannot be told here. Suffice it to say that by the middle of the eighteenth century England had in peace-time a secured trade route via the Cape eastwards to the opposite side of the globe. The wealth, knowledge and opportunities which this afforded led during the century to the discovery of Australia, New Zealand and Oceania, and

38

eventually to that migration overseas of the British people which produced the phenomenon of the new British Empire—the old British Empire having come to an end with the loss of the American colonies. The first step towards the founding of that Empire was the change of policy from peaceful trading to territorial expansion which force of circumstances obliged the East India Company to make at the very time when Clive landed in India. He was fated to put the new policy into execution, and his success was so much greater than was expected that the conquest of all India followed inevitably. Clive's arrival was concurrent with an event of the first importance. The Mughal Empire, which to Roe had seemed so imposing, was breaking up. The officials who governed its provinces were turning into independent princes and were making war upon one another. The imperial administration, essential to trade, was ceasing to function. In what manner could the Company steer a peaceful way through such dangerous perplexities ? Before it had decided how to protect itself and its dividends from the threatened anarchy, the Company of French merchants trading to India showed the way. At the head of them was a man very different from the cautious English merchants. He was an adventurer, and instead of merely strengthening the fortifications of the French emporium at Pondicherry and hoping for the best, he resolved to take sides in the scramble for kingdoms which was beginning in that part of India and, by backing a successful claimant, obtain from him concessions which would make the French, not the English, the leading merchants in India. This forced the East India Company to abandon its old policy. If it were to survive it must fight the French and their partisans, and it must support rival partisans. It continued to believe that the fight was only for trade and security, but actually it was for the mastery of India.

Two years after his arrival Clive was transferred from the commercial to the military side. He had been a queer and homesick clerk, but now found he possessed a natural aptitude for soldiering. In 1747 he was made ensign, in 1749 lieutenant, and by 1752, aged twenty-seven, had become captain. He was noted for coolness in action and for that feeling for the rhythm of a battle which has always been the mark of the born military leader. It was largely thanks to the military genius of this young man that the Company got the better of the French, and by 1753 secured for the throne of the Carnatic (the area of the coast where Madras and Pondicherry were situated) a prince favourable to English interests.

The Directors would gladly then have returned to their former trading and sent Clive back to his desk but, having once become entangled in Indian politics, they found it impossible to extricate themselves. In 1756, Suraj-ud-Dowlah, who had the position of Nawab or Viceroy of Bengal, though actually he was independent of the Empire, descended upon the Company's settlement at Calcutta, defeated the garrison, burnt the town, and shut up one stifling night of June a hundred and forty-four of his English prisoners

39

in a barrack cell, 18 by 14 feet, where most of them suffocated. It seems he was instigated to attack by the French, whose settlement at Chandernagore was near Calcutta. The catastrophe roused the merchants of Madras, and after long confabulations they decided to send an expedition to retake Calcutta.

Clive, who had just returned from a year's leave in England, was appointed to command it. He was only thirty-one years of age, but his services in the Carnatic campaigns had been so distinguished—his defence of Arcot had made him a hero—that the Directors in London had procured him a colonelcy and given him a seat on the Madras Council. The expeditionary force was composed of six hundred white troops and one thousand sepoys. Clive felt that he had been entrusted with a task of great moment. Though the other members of the Council had no idea that to restore the situation in Bengal would mean more than a return to the safe trading they had previously enjoyed there, he had an intuition that he was about to make history. "This expedition, if attended with success, may enable me to do great things," he wrote to his father ; and to the London Committee he declared : "I flatter myself that this Expedition will not end with the retaking of Calcutta only."

It certainly did not end with the retaking of Calcutta. That was a small matter, for the Nawab, having reduced it to ruins and not expecting an English counter-attack, had left few troops in the neighbourhood. But when he heard that Clive had re-occupied it, he marched against him with an immense force. Clive would have had no chance at all if Suraj-ud-Dowlah had been a viceroy of the Mughal Empire in its prime. But the Prince represented no one but himself, and his government and generals were corrupt and cowardly. Painfully aware that he might be displaced by a rival at any time, he had no confidence in his troops. When the Indians reached the gardens near the town, Clive penetrated their lines in a thick mist at dawn and alarmed them so much that the Nawab opened negotiations, offering to recognise the English return to Calcutta.

But Clive saw that this would be no permanent settlement. The Nawab and the French of Chandernagore were in league and, if the expedition were withdrawn, the Nawab could not be trusted. To make Calcutta safe two measures were necessary, the destruction of the French and the replacement of Suraj-ud-Dowlah by another prince ready to further British trade, as had been done in the Carnatic. Accordingly he attacked Chandernagore and took it, thereafter entering into a correspondence with Mir Jaffier, the Nawab's uncle, who was offered the throne for his help. Mir Jaffier had not the smallest respect for his nephew and declared that if Clive marched on the Nawab's capital of Murshidabad he would join him with the forces under his command. Murshidabad was some hundred and fifty miles north of Calcutta. To attack it with 613 European foot, 91 half-castes, 10 guns and 2,100 sepoys—for such were the exact forces at Clive's disposal at the

SOUTH-EAST VIEW OF TRICHINOPOLY, MADRAS
Coloured Aquatint by Thomas and William Daniell, 1798

moment—was a wild imprudence. The Nawab's army consisted of 15,000 cavalry, 35,000 infantry and 53 heavy guns, mostly served by French gunners. Mir Jaffier had promised to come over, but had given not the smallest guarantee of good faith. Defeat meant not only the annihilation of the expedition but a second sack of Calcutta, perhaps a second Black Hole. But Clive marched.

At a place called Katwa, seventy miles up the road, he expected to find Mir Jaffier and his men. The Prince, however, failed to keep the appointment and Clive had to decide whether to cross the Hugli, which at that point lay across his path, and with that large river in his rear, which the approaching monsoon would cause to flood, press on against an army sixteen times the size of his own and sitting comfortably in front of its entrenched base. Against the advice of his officers and the whole experience of war he decided to cross.

At Plassey, a large mango grove twenty miles further on, he suddenly was confronted with the Nawab's host. The battle which ensued has been the subject of much writing since that June day nearly two hundred years ago, but no one has succeeded in fully explaining how Clive won it.

41

Perhaps the chief reason was that it did not occur to the men of the old Thirty-ninth (the modern Dorsets), who formed the bulk of Clive's white troops, that they could be beaten.

When the battle was won and Mir Jaffier saw it was safe to cross over, he joined Clive, and together they took Murshidabad. He was installed as Nawab and in the vast area of Bengal, the gateway to upper India, the British found they could do what they liked. The Directors still cherished the hope of returning to plain business, but the native administration went to pieces and eventually they were obliged to substitute their own, which in the course of a century was gradually extended over the rest of India.

After the prodigious stroke of Plassey, which is one of the decisive battles of the world though only twenty-three men were killed on the British side, the rest of Clive's life was a series of misfortunes. He had gone out to India as a merchant with the object of making money and now turned his attention again to this matter. Mir Jaffier paid him £160,000 down for his help, and he acquired jewels worth a million pounds in modern values. Moreover, he secured a great estate in Bengal so that on his return to England his income amounted to £40,000 per annum, a fortune which he declared was no more than a "genteel competence," for it might have been much larger if he had taken full advantage of his opportunities.

Had he retired into private life with his money all would have been well enough. But, having been created a peer, he sought to make himself felt in the Government. He was no politician, however, and in 1764, seven years after Plassey, accepted the Presidentship of the Council of Calcutta. There he tried to prevent the employees of the Company from enriching themselves by corrupt practices which the weak native Government was unable to stop. He failed because his colleagues declared that he with his large fortune had no right to restrain them. This caused a return of his neurosis and he became again subject to fits. "It grieved me beyond measure," wrote at this time his friend Carnac, "to see a Person endued with such extraordinary firmness oppressed in his spirits as to exceed any degree of hysterics I was ever witness to." In this state he returned to England in 1767.

There his enemies engineered an attack on him, nominally on moral grounds but really from malice. He was charged with having abused his position after Plassey by acquiring enormous wealth. For two years he was subjected to an inquisition by a Select Committee of the Commons, and though in the end he was allowed to keep his fortune, and his great services were acknowledged, the strain had been too much for his nervous temperament and he committed suicide at the age of forty-nine.

To-day his statue stands on the steps of the India Office looking down upon St. James's Park. Though no adequate biography of him exists, he is one of the best known of England's worthies, largely because Macaulay wrote an essay about him which is read in all schools.

MODE OF TRAVELLING IN AFRICA

Coloured aquatint by I. Clark after W. Hutton. From W. Hutton's *Voyage to Africa*, 1821

A JAVAN IN COURT DRESS

Coloured aquatint from Raffles's *History of Java*, 1807

MUNGO PARK: MERCHANT-EXPLORER
(1771-1806)

THE four previous sketches have suggested how Asia was opened to international commerce. The case of Africa was very different. In the late eighteenth century nothing was known at first hand of any part of the tropical interior of that continent. There were rumours of a river called the Niger and that it crossed Africa near the 15th parallel, but no white man had ever seen it. Some believed it to be the Senegal or the Gambia ; others argued that it was a tributary of the Nile or of the Congo ; others again declared it to be the Congo itself, for no large river had been observed to fall into the sea between the mouth of the Gambia and of the Congo. Timbuktu lay somewhere on its banks, a fabulously rich city, roofed, it was declared, with solid gold.

The Mediterranean coast of Africa had, of course, always been known, and the other immense coasts to the Cape and up to the southern end of the Red Sea had been explored by the Portuguese in the sixteenth century on their way to India.

Later, when the plantations in the West Indies and in America developed, it was learned that the Moslem inhabitants of Africa were prepared to sell negro slaves to Europeans. From the time of Elizabeth onwards the English engaged in this slave trade. Through agents stationed principally near the mouth of the Gambia they established touch with the Moslem slavers, who marched down their living merchandise from the interior to the ships waiting to carry it across the Atlantic. This export, together with a little ivory and gum, was the extent of the African trade for two centuries.

Towards the end of the eighteenth century, however, men began to argue that the great African continent must yield many other profitable commodities. For instance, it had long been said to be rich in gold. But these were rumours which only exploration could verify. Timbuktu, the alleged centre of the continental trade, must be reached. If it lay on the Niger, then the course of that river must be traced.

With these objects in view, the African Association was founded in 1788, a year after Wilberforce had begun his crusade against slavery. The first man to be sent out by this body was a Major Houghton, but he died in 1791 before reaching the Niger. His place was taken by Mungo Park, the subject of this chapter.

Park was born in 1771, the son of a small Scottish farmer of the vale of Yarrow. A quiet, studious and earnest youth, he worked his way up to a degree in medicine at Edinburgh University and sailed to Sumatra as surgeon on an East India Company's ship. On his return he was introduced to Sir Joseph Banks, the founder of the African Association, and shortly afterwards agreed to go and search for the Niger. At that time he was only twenty-four years of age.

At the beginning of the diary which he kept of his travels, he gives both the objects of his journey and a glimpse of his own modest and resolute character. "If I should perish in my journey, I was willing that my hopes and expectations should perish with me ; and if I should succeed in rendering the geography of Africa more familiar to my countrymen, and in opening to their ambition and industry new sources of wealth and new channels of commerce, I knew that I was in the hands of men of honour, who would not fail to bestow that remuneration which my successful services would appear to them to merit."

In June, 1795, he reached the Gambia and lodged in the house of a Mr. Laidley, a slaver who lived at Pisania, some distance up the river. The village was no more than a clearing in the vast forest beside the steaming tidal water, and there he waited till the rains were over, learning Mandingo, the most useful negro language.

In December he set out for the unknown interior, riding a horse, wearing a blue coat and a top-hat, and accompanied by two negro servants. His course was eastwards, through the dominions of independent negro kings, amiable, greedy, ridiculous ruffians. The first of them was Almani of Fatteconda, on whom he called to pay his respects on December 21. This potentate was fascinated by his blue coat and umbrella and obliged him to offer them both as a present. As Park penetrated further, this kind of robbery became more ruinous, until King Tiggity Sego took three-quarters of what remained to him on the plea of customs duty. Rapacious though they were, however, these pagan monarchs plundered him without malice and he was perfectly safe in their dominions.

But further east there lived less manageable rulers, the Moslem sultans who preyed on the Pagans. After crossing the upper waters of the Senegal he entered their territories. These Sultanates had been founded centuries before by Arabs from the Mediterranean littoral, who by intermarriage with the indigenous negroes had become a race of half-castes, rather similar in appearance, says Park, to the mulattoes of the West Indies. In character they were like the worst type of Arab, malicious, cruel and ferociously bigoted. Park's method of securing the good will of kings on his route was always to make them presents, but on entering the domains of Sultan Ali of Benaun in March, 1796, he was arrested by minions of that prince before he had had time to take this precaution. "Ali was sitting upon a black leather cushion, clipping a few hairs from his upper lip, a female attendant holding up a looking-glass before him," records Park. "He appeared to be an old man, of the Arab cast, with a long white beard : and he had sullen and indignant aspect." Park was abominably treated by him and his people, being detained a prisoner, robbed of all he possessed, subjected to every indignity which malice could devise, and given only one small meal a day.

46

MUNGO PARK
Miniature after Henry Edridge

As an example of his miseries, one scorching night in May, having been harshly refused water, he crept out to the cattle troughs where "kneeling down, I thrust my head between two of the cows, and drank with great pleasure, until the water was nearly exhausted, and the cows began to contend with each other for the last mouthful." In these trials Park exhibited an extraordinary patience and mildness, neither resisting his cruel treatment nor repining, being seemingly upheld by some inner certainty that he would reach the mysterious river of his dreams.

Not till the end of June did he escape from this grievous servitude, being aided in some measure by Ali's wife, Fatima, who had been won by his handsome face. Prim to a degree though he was, Park moved the hearts of many women in Africa.

Thanks to Fatima he was able to escape with his horse, his servants and his clothes, which now consisted of two shirts, two pairs of trousers, two handkerchiefs, two waistcoats, his riding boots, cloak and top-hat, in the lining of which were concealed his notes. He had no valuables of any kind with which to pay his way, but undaunted, indeed dauntless, he headed on

47

A VIEW OF ALI'S TENT AT THE CAMP OF BENAUN
Engraving from Mungo Park's *Travels*, 1816

for the Niger, now reported to lie some 250 miles to the south-east. Here the land was desert and very soon he was suffering terribly from thirst. His horse could carry him no further, his servants had deserted him and he fell to the ground exhausted, expecting death. "I cast," he writes in his stilted way, "a last look on the surrounding scene, and whilst I reflected on the awful change that was about to take place, this world with its enjoyment seemed to vanish from my recollection." A sudden thunderstorm saved his life. Revived, he pressed on, and at last on 21st July, "looking forwards, I saw with infinite pleasure the great object of my mission—the long-sought-for majestic Niger, glittering to the morning sun, as broad as the Thames at Westminster, and flowing slowly *to the eastward*. I hastened to the brink, and having drunk of the water, lifted up my fervent thanks in prayer to the Great Ruler of all things, for having thus far crowned my endeavours with success."

That the Niger flowed east and not west cleared up one point which had been long in doubt. But where did it flow to ? Did it turn south to the sea or go on across Africa to join the Congo or the Nile ? With unquenchable spirit Park went on alone to find the answer to these questions. Actually he was about 1,800 miles from the Niger mouth, which is concealed in a delta of mangrove swamps in the Gulf of Guinea.

A VIEW OF A BRIDGE OVER THE BA-FING OR RIVER NIGER
Engraving from Mungo Park's *Travels*, 1816

After walking about a hundred miles along the north bank he saw that it was hopeless to proceed, for he was entering again a Moslem Sultanate, where imprisonment and slavery inevitably awaited him. "Worn down by sickness, exhausted with hunger and fatigue, half naked, and without any article of value by which I might procure provisions, clothes or lodging . . . I was now convinced that the obstacle to my further progress was insurmountable." He turned back with a heavy heart, for he learnt that he was only twelve days' march from Timbuktu.

The hardships on his journey back to the coast were much greater than on the way out. On 25th August he met a band of robbers. He still possessed his horse, his top-hat, and the clothes he stood up in. The robbers only left him a shirt and trousers, "but, as they went away, one of them threw back my hat, in the crown of which I kept my memorandums, and this was probably the reason why they did not wish to keep it," he writes, meaning that they thought the writing was magic and unsafe to tamper with.

Lying helpless and alone in the tropical forest, five hundred miles from the nearest European settlement, Park was nearer giving up hope than on any previous occasion. "But at this moment," he records in a characteristic passage, "the extraordinary beauty of a small moss in fructification irresistibly caught my eye . . . Can the Being, thought I, who planted,

D

49

watered and brought to perfection, in this obscure part of the world, a thing which appears of so small importance, look with unconcern upon the situation and sufferings of creatures formed after His own image?" This reflection comforted him and, certain that all would be well, he got on to his feet and trudged on. He was not disappointed, for the negroes at the next village treated him with kindness.

His diary now becomes of particular interest. He joined a gang of slaves, who were being marched down to the coast, and his account of what he saw is strangely moving. At no part of his narrative, however, does it occur to him to denounce slavery as an institution. He is sorry for the slaves, but accepts their state as part of the nature of things. Though a man of the highest character, mild-mannered and pious, the humanitarianism of his great contemporary, Wilberforce, would have seemed to him over-enthusiastic.

On 11th June, 1797, he reached Pisania and Mr. Laidley, who had long given him up for dead, and in October was safely home in England. In 1805 the African Association sent him out again, this time in command of a well-equipped party. But three-quarters of his companions were dead of fever and exhaustion before he reached the Niger, this time by another route. There the remnant embarked in a canoe and followed the river past Timbuktu and for a thousand miles, until, while still some 800 miles from its mouth, they were all killed by tribesmen at the rapids of Boussa. Not until thirty-three years later was the mouth located.

As the nineteenth century passed, the whole interior of Africa was mapped and partitioned. The slave-trade was abolished, the Gambia region becoming for that reason impoverished; the Negro kings and Moslem Sultans lost their independence; new sources of wealth and channels for commerce, openings for European ambition and industry, were, as Park had hoped, developed. Central Africa for the first time in its long dark history was brought into contact with the centres of civilisation and entered upon a course the end of which is not in sight.

SIR THOMAS STAMFORD RAFFLES
Engraving from D. C. Boulger's *Life of Sir Stamford Raffles*, 1897

THOMAS STAMFORD RAFFLES:
MERCHANT-ADMINISTRATOR
(1781-1829)

HAD the scheme of this book permitted, the adventures of the British in America might have been illustrated by some typical career. That not being possible, it should be noted at least that when on 19th October, 1781, Cornwallis surrendered to Washington at York-town, the British dominion in America came to an end. England was thus thrown back upon the territories and trading points she had acquired in Asia. These, as we have seen, pivoted upon India and reached on to China through the Malayan straits which the Dutch had made the centre of their trade operations.

Suddenly Napoleon strode upon the scene. He annexed Holland out-right in 1810, and so acquired the Cape of Good Hope, Ceylon and the great islands of Sumatra, Java and Borneo. India was thus encircled and it was his grand plan to drive the British out of that continent by an advance based on the Dutch possessions. To spike that plan it was decided in June, 1811, to seize Java, the strategic centre of his whole operation. The

51

Governor-General of India was then Lord Minto, and he led the expedition in person. His secretary was Stamford Raffles, a young man of thirty.

Raffles was born off Jamaica on 6th July, 1781, on board a merchant-ship of which his father was master. He was brought up in London, and at the early age of fourteen a clerkship was secured for him at the East India House, the London headquarters of the East India Company, as his family was too poor to support him longer. In this humble appointment he displayed much assiduity and continued his education out of office hours. In 1800 he was promoted to a post worth £100 a year and, continuing to impress his superiors by his extraordinary industry, was appointed in 1805 Assistant Secretary on a salary of £1,500 a year to the Governor of Penang, a trading-port on an island off the Malay Peninsula, which the Company had recently acquired by arrangement with the local Sultan. Here again he became remarkable for his unceasing toil and the exceptional interest which he took in everything which concerned the country. By 1810, though only twenty-nine years of age, he was considered the greatest authority on that part of the world. In manner he was amiable and high-spirited, and his character was essentially humane and lovable. These qualities and qualifications attracted the attention of Lord Minto, and thus it was that he became the Governor-General's personal assistant in the expedition to Java, an appointment which carried him into the great world-stream of the Napoleonic war.

The British taking of Java in 1811 from the Dutch and French was an analogous operation to the taking in 1941 of Syria from the French and Germans. It was effected in three months without much difficulty, the British casualties being 633, and the Franco-Dutch 7,000. Raffles was then appointed Lieutenant-Governor of Java.

His administration of the island was very remarkable. He was, it should be remembered, in the employ of the merchants of the East India Company, whose first preoccupation was to secure dividends. It is true that in India, after Clive had opened the way to political dominion and Warren Hastings had organised a civil service which reflected British ideals of law and justice, the Company had advanced a distance beyond the strictly commercial point of view that had been its strength in early days. Responsibility for the native inhabitants was there admitted. But outside India, in Penang, for instance, the only duty of the Company's officials was to foster trade. It was therefore quite remarkable that Raffles in his administration of Java should have set himself with indefatigable zeal to improve the condition of the islanders. Indeed, he was the first outside India to put into practice the new principle of trusteeship for backward races, then hardly accepted or understood beyond the small body of reformers and humanitarians of whom Wilberforce was the principal. In this respect he differs from Park, who, though humane by temperament, saw no compelling reason why the oppression of the weak was unworthy of the England for whose glory he died. In 1814,

A RONG'GENG OR DANCING GIRL
Aquatint from Raffles's *History of Java*, 1817

writing of the work of the officials he had appointed, Raffles says : "Placed in situations which, but a few years ago, were considered only as affording a fortune to the individual . . . they have without exception felt the honour and character of the British nation prompt them above every selfish consideration and in six months enabled me to effect a revolution which two centuries of Dutch administration could scarcely dream of." In a memorandum dated 1810 he had written that the Dutch policy in Java was "a more cold-blooded, illiberal and ungenerous policy than has ever been exhibited towards any country, unless we except the conduct of the European nations towards the slave-coast of Africa." But Raffles' principles cost money, and as the Directors were business men and not humanitarian reformers, they were by no means enthusiastic about him and his idea that the primary object of his government should be the welfare of the Javanese.

The fall of Napoleon put an end to Raffles' work in Java, for Holland, as one of the main pegs in the European balance, had to be restored to her

53

original position, and in consequence all her overseas possessions except the Cape and Ceylon were returned to her. This was a great blow to Raffles, who on the termination of his appointment took leave and returned to England. Though coldly received by the magnates of the East India House, he was welcomed by the scientific world as an oriental savant, for during his eleven years in Asia his intellectual curiosity had driven him to make extensive studies in the botany, zoology, art and history of Malaya and Java. He had brought back with him, moreover, part of his collections, and his contributions to knowledge were received with such acclaim that society lionised him, until finally the Prince Regent bade him to a levee and, "expressing the high sense he entertained of the eminent services he had rendered to his country in the government of Java," made him a knight. This obliged the India House to look on him with more favour, and in 1817 he was appointed Lieutenant-Governor of Bencoolen, a small possession of the Company's on the west coast of Sumatra.

The situation in Sumatra was this. The Dutch held the south end of the great island. The rest of the thousand miles of its length was ruled by small Sultans. Bencoolen was a mere trading post. Raffles and his newly-married wife, fresh from the excitements and delights of the London season, found themselves in a deadly little hole, "the roads impassable, the highways of the town overrun with rank grass, the Government House a den of ravenous dogs and polecats." However, this was the sort of thing that stimulated Raffles. He conceived almost at once the idea of making Bencoolen the capital of Sumatra, of inducing the Sultans to accept him as overlord and of developing the country for the benefit of its inhabitants. So extraordinary and indefatigable a man was he, that he might well have accomplished this feat, had not the Dutch become alarmed, for they knew Raffles well and did not doubt that his personality would suffice to bring the Sultans under English influence. This would have meant for all practical purposes the loss of Sumatra, though under the peace settlement the whole island had been declared their sphere. Accordingly they took steps to extend their effective occupation and to put every difficulty they could in the way of British commerce throughout the whole region of the Islands. This policy ran counter to the trade agreements embodied in the peace settlement and profoundly disturbed the Directors at home. They blamed Raffles' forward policy and complained to Canning, who on his side had been assailed by protests from the Dutch Government. Canning and his colleagues were more concerned with maintaining the stability of Europe and the friendliest relations with the new kingdom of the Netherlands than with the expansion of British trade in rivalry with the Dutch in Java. So Raffles was censured and told to confine his activities to the routine business of Bencoolen.

But a man of genius cannot be kept down. If you confine him in one direction he breaks out in another. Raffles was determined that British interests in the Islands should not be eclipsed and he appealed in a masterly

INDIA HOUSE, LONDON : THE SALE ROOM
Aquatint from Ackermann's *Microcosm of London*, 1808

despatch to Lord Hastings, the new Governor-General of India, against the disastrous view of the Cabinet. Hastings was not a small-minded man. Raffles' wide vision fired his imagination and in 1818 he invited him to Calcutta.

To the Marquess, Raffles explained what had long been in his mind. From Bencoolen it would be impossible to cope adequately with the Dutch. A new British post must be found, not on Dutch territory but yet in the strategic centre of their island group, some position that commanded the straits of Malacca, the waterway to China. There was such a place. The Dutch had overlooked it. It was a small island at the extreme tip of the Malay peninsula, where once had stood the ancient city of Singapura. The island belonged to the Sultan of Johore. If he were induced to sell it, a city could be built there which, ideally situated both for trade and defence, would assure British commerce throughout the Far East.

Raffles had an irresistible way with him and the Marquess was fascinated. "Sir Stamford, you may depend upon me," were his last words as he speeded him on his way to Singapore. The negotiations with the Sultan of Johore were carried through rapidly and at the beginning of 1819 the British flag was hoisted on the island.

55

Then the storm broke. When the Dutch heard that the Englishman they feared more than anyone else in the East had broken from his Elba at Bencoolen and found an unguarded spot inside the fence they had striven so hard to make impenetrable round their preserve, they were furious. For a moment it looked like war. It was rumoured they would sail in and take Singapore, which was garrisoned by a mere handful of soldiers under a major. The Directors in London quailed. That incorrigible Raffles ! Why had they allowed him to go East a second time ? Why had they not long ago recalled him to England ? The Foreign Office heartily shared their opinion. Raffles' action might plunge all Europe into war ! Lord Hastings received several very nasty letters, but though the authorities in London expressed their displeasure in the plainest terms, they were afraid in the end to over-rule their Governor-General and left the matter to his discretion.

But Hastings to his eternal glory stood by Raffles. He did not believe the Dutch would fight and airily declared that "we could but expect that in the event of our securing a station which would baffle the injurious policy of our neighbours, they would not fail to impugn our right to take possession."

He was right. The Dutch did not fight. The storm blew over. In 1824 Bencoolen was ceded to them on their recognising Singapore. The place had become a city almost in a night. In the first year its population reached 5,000 ; by 1824 it was 30,000. The foundations of the citadel, upon which the defence of India and of Australia was to depend, had been well and truly laid. Nay, more, by a twist of fate it would be to that same strong place that a hundred and seventeen years later the Dutch themselves would look for the protection of their Island Empire.

When he had accomplished this his crowning work, Raffles prepared to return home. But some power was jealous of his immortal fame and dealt him blow after cruel blow. First, three of his children suddenly died, and he with his wife fell gravely ill. When he did set out, the ship went on fire and he lost all his property, including his immense oriental collections. After he was settled near London, the India House basely demanded £22,000 from him on account of salary paid in excess many years before. And three months later, aged only 45, he fell dead of apoplexy.

BRITISH
POLAR EXPLORERS

BY

ADMIRAL SIR EDWARD EVANS

FOREWORD

WHEN, at the age of twenty, I joined the stout little whaler, *Morning*, as Second Mate, to take part in the first Antarctic Relief Expedition then being fitted out to search for and carry stores, coal, and extra clothing to Captain Scott wintering somewhere in the South Polar regions, I had read a good deal about British Polar explorers. If asked for a dozen names of my countrymen who had penetrated into the Polar Seas, I should have replied, "Frobisher, Davis, Hudson, Franklin, Ross, Parry, Nares, and one or other of the Markhams." As I knew less about those who had sailed the Southernmost seas, I should have added, "Cook, Biscoe, Balleny, and Ross"; and, thinking it over, this list was as good as any. One might add to-day, Jackson, who sailed north in the *Windward*, Gino Watkins for the Arctic, and Scott, Shackleton, Mawson, Rymill and Ryder, the first Antarctic explorer to win the Victoria Cross.

In a book depicting the British Polar venturers in so short a space, one would be foolish to attempt to portray the achievements of more than half a dozen, or eight at the most, and for this purpose I propose to take my favourites for what I think they have done. Unfortunately, early Polar pioneers wrote unimaginatively and recorded too little of what they saw, experienced and achieved. Look at the illustrations and colour plates in *Scott's Last Expedition*, and at Ponting's masterpieces in *The Great White South*. And not being myself one of the greater gods of Polar exploration,

I can still, at the age of sixty, conjure up and admire Captain Scott, and Shackleton, and Dr. Wilson, artist, peacemaker and great Christian gentleman. It seems only a few months ago since I felt that strong, sincere handshake from Captain Oates far away in 87°35' S., when my part in the longest sledge journey on record had been played, and I bowed and went my way.

It has been my privilege to know Fridtjof Nansen, Roald Amundsen, and Riiser-Larsen, the three Norsemen whom I call "the Last of the Vikings." I owe my own Polar aspiration to that father of modern Antarctic exploration, Sir Clements Markham, and I also knew and admired Admiral Sir Albert Markham, who showed such kindness to the first Antarctic Relief Expedition when our little ship came to Sheerness ; Admirals Egerton and May and one or two other naval men entitled to wear the white ribbon for Polar exploration ; Borchgrevink, the Norwegian leader of Sir George Newnes' *Southern Cross* Antarctic Expedition ; Pirie ; Mossman ; Rudmose Brown ; and last, but not least, my friend William Spiers Bruce, who led the Scottish expedition which sailed just after the little *Morning*, under Captain Colbeck, took me south in the first Antarctic Relief Expedition. Bruce, like Mawson, was a scientist explorer, and certainly deserves that salute to adventurers which I have accorded at some length to the eight Polar leaders whose expeditions I have written about. Bruce played an important part in the international campaign of modern South Polar exploration, in which Scott, the Englishman, Charcot, the Frenchman, De Gerlache, the Belgian, Drygalski, the German, Nordenskjöld, the Swede, and last, but most modern of all, Byrd, the American, all contributed and co-operated to find out for civilisation as much as they could about that six million square mile area of "billow and breeze, mountains and seas," as well as glacier and barrier and bleak lonely plateau, which comprise Antarctica.

In these pages you will find a simple sailor's appreciation of his favourite squires and knights of the Polar Seas.

MARTIN FROBISHER

BRITISH North Polar explorers seem to have had as their principal objective the discovery of a North-West Passage—a grand idea—which would be a short cut for our merchant ships from the Atlantic to the Pacific and to the China Seas ; and Martin Frobisher must be given the credit, I think, for giving birth to this bold notion.

As far back as 1576, this intrepid seaman sailed northward with "one tall ship and two small barques" and succeeded in discovering what he believed to be a strait, which he named after himself following the fashion of Elizabethan sailors. This was really a bay running into Baffin Land, but Frobisher believed that it cut through the middle of Greenland. On this first voyage of his he discovered and named Meta Incognita which is separated from the North American mainland by what is now known as Hudson's Strait. Frobisher took back with him pieces of black ore which were greedily examined by English merchants and "company promoters"— and believe me we had some then, and we also had some aliens in our midst ready to exploit us. One of these, a *soi-disant* Italian alchemist, claimed that he had obtained gold from one of the specimens. Largely due to this dud claim, Frobisher was placed in command of an even bigger expedition which he fitted out in 1577, and sailed for Meta Incognita to seek and bring back cargoes of gold-bearing ore.

It is interesting to read his instructions for this second expedition.

"Geven to our loving friend Martin Farbusher, gentleman, for orders to be observed in the Viag [Voyage] now recommended to him for the North West parts and Cataia.

(1) First you shall enter as Captaine Generall into the chardge and governement of theis three vessells, viz. the *Ayde*, the *Gabriell* and the *Michell* with all that appertaineth to them whatsoever."

The instructions go on to tell him "(yf yt be noe hindrance to your viadge) to set on land upon the coast of Freezeland vj. of the condemned persons which you carrie with you with weapons and victuells such as you may convenientlie spare," etc. Frobisher is also directed to visit Hall's Island, "being in the entrance of the supposed strait, which we name Farbusher's Strait, discovered by yourself this last yeare in your journey thitherwards." Frobisher is enjoined to pay special attention to the matter of keeping his vessels in company, and to punish sharply any wilfulness or negligence as an example to the rest.

Frobisher took with him miners for this digging for gold and instructions tell him that, if the miners do not yield the substance required and hoped for, he is to proceed with his entire expedition, less the *Ayde*, "towarde the discovering of Cataia." Frobisher is required to behave himself and cause his ship's company to do the like, and warned to consider his own safety when he has to have conference with the people that he may meet; he is enjoined to behave towards such people in a manner that may give least cause of offence and to win both friendship and liking. But the commercial aspect is never lost sight of, and he is told that if the ore is of that quality and quantity looked for he must laden his ships with as much as possible, while leaving out other superfluous things. It is also suggested that he might bring home three or four, at the most, of the people of the Great Unknown. Whilst endeavouring to do so, Frobisher was wounded by an arrow and nearly lost his life.

Had Frobisher not been bound by his instructions, he would no doubt have done far more valuable exploring. Nevertheless, he brought back a great deal of information concerning the Eskimos whom he met. It is on record that he built for them a house as like as he could make it to an English home, with the idea of ensuring the good will and friendship of these tough little people for expeditions to come. Actually the remains of this house were found by the American explorer, Hall, in 1860. We owe to this Elizabethan seaman the impulse to explore the frozen North and our first knowledge of the customs, habits, and character of the little people of those far latitudes. An unsolved mystery is linked with his name, the existence or not of West Friesland in latitude 58°, which was said to lie between Iceland and Greenland and to be touched by Frobisher in his search for Greenland's gold. Later explorers talk of "stormy deep waters covering this sunken land of a hundred towns," and many people, one of them sailing about its supposed position, describes the locality as "valleys of dreadful soundings, and peaks of tremendous and destructive contact." We are indebted to Frobisher for a lively, if somewhat terrifying picture of the Arctic pack ice, which has baffled so many stout-hearted seamen and crushed so many sturdily-built ships. In his records he wrote, "the force of the yce was so great, and likewise so rased the side of the ships, that it was pitifull to behold, and caused the hearts of many to faint."

JOHN DAVIS

FOLLOWING in the wake of Frobisher's enterprises, came a fine Devon seaman, John Davis, who sailed forth from Dartmouth under the patronage of the Merchant Venturers of that part of England. Davis, who was a constructive thinker, planned ahead and was thus able to make three Arctic voyages in the years 1585, 1586 and 1587.

He had, to begin with, two ships called the *Sunshine* and the *Moonshine*. Captain Davis himself commanded the *Sunshine* and on this first voyage worked a considerable distance along the west coast of Greenland or Desolation Land, as he named it. His greatest geographical discovery was that grand, if somewhat stormy stretch of water which he named after himself, Davis Strait. The northern part of this twelve-hundred-mile-long sea is now known as Baffin Bay, and where it narrows between Ellesmere Island and far North-West Greenland, it is called Kane Basin or Kane Sea. Various strips in the northern narrows which extend almost to 83° of latitude have been named by later explorers, Smith Sound, Kennedy Channel, Hall Basin, Robeson Channel; but Davis Strait, which includes the whole, is by far the greatest strait in the world. Davis also located, on the west of Greenland, Gilbert's Sound and the lofty, steep-to island called Sanderson's Hope, very nearly in 73° North. But attributable to John Davis's voyages from a commercial outlook was the foundation of the great cod fishery industry on the banks off Newfoundland, besides considerable information concerning whales which contributed to the foundation of the whaling

ESKIMOS
Aquatint by J. Lyon, from Captain Parry's *Journal*, 1821-1824

industry. As Davis's ships did not face the rigours of the Arctic winter, there is nothing remarkable about the powers of endurance of himself and his ships' companies, but to have sailed his heavily-sparred vessels through unknown ice-beset waters, to have landed on the Greenland coast as frequently and fearlessly as he did, is anything but a mean achievement.

John Davis made friends with and learnt a very great deal about the Eskimos, and having heard from Frobisher and other adventurous spirits a good deal about the natives of the North, he included amongst his ships' companies a sprinkling of musicians, with the idea of charming these queer little people. And so wherever Eskimos were met with, the "band call" was sounded, and old English folk-tunes played. Davis secured a distinct success through his foresight. What fun it must have been to see his mariners and himself dancing in the summer snows, and on the harder palaeozoic rocks and jet-black and green slates, which must have shaken with their bear-like prancings! John Davis was a good observer, and from what he learned on his first voyage he employed further devices to extend his Eskimo friendships, for in 1586, when he again sailed North, his fleet consisted of the four ships *Sunshine*, *Moonshine*, *North Star* and *Mermaid*. A proper *entente* was now cemented, for, realising how nimble and strong were the Eskimos, he brought along good wrestlers, more musicians and some agile runners and athletes. Edith Elias in her valuable *Book of Polar*

61

Exploration has described this occasion as one of the earliest records of an English team going abroad ! Music, dancing and sport have done far more for international friendships than dry lectures and Foreign Office pamphlets ever have, and in John Davis's day there seems to have been none of that manœuvring for position which is part and parcel of most bureaucrats' and modern emissaries' make-up. Davis benefited by Frobisher's example, but he seems to have been much more human and to have had a greater horizon of thought in the explorer's sense. He writes concerning the wrestling-matches and races and high-jumps, "Our men did overleape them, but we found them strong and nimble, and to have skill in wrestling, for they cast some of our men that were good wrestlers."

All this time progress was being made, and sketch surveys were being carried out by these Northern voyagers, who learnt to taste and enjoy the flesh of seal and walrus and to admire the grandeur of the Arctic and to become familiar with the sight of gigantic delicately-hued icebergs, lit and coloured by the Arctic sun. Davis Strait, with its winds and currents and sometimes heavy seas, tried out our early seamen far more than our later naval explorers who had the advantage of steam under which they could work through open water leads, where manœuvring under heavy topsails and topgallant sails was indeed a trying business, and often an extremely dangerous game. Beating to windward in narrow waters, under sail, meant all hands on deck to man the braces and constant working at the helm which often left the steersmen in a bath of sweat, however cold and bitter was the breeze. Foodstuffs in those days had not been studied from a scientific standpoint, and the health was the health of the hardy. Scurvy was only too often in evidence ; men's gums grew spongy from malnutrition, teeth loosened and fell out ; dysentery made wrecks of sailormen, and surgery was very primitive. Snow-blindness in the summer months, with its ex-cruciating eye pains, must likewise have tried them to the utmost. Never-theless, the lure of facing the unknown and penetrating further into the realm of the Great Ice Queen had its excitements and attractions. No wonder John Davis ventured a third time into these little-known seas.

He had no difficulty in getting together a crew, for men who had once served with him always wanted to enter again, and his shipmates seem to have shared his enthusiasm for discovery, but when he urged the west-country merchants to continue to finance him, they shook their heads. They had lost heart because their expectations of great profits had not been ful-filled. Davis wrote sadly, "All the westerne marchant-adventurers fell from the action." London gave him a better reception, thanks to the efforts of his unfailing friend, William Sanderson, a merchant prince who took a practical and intelligent interest in exploration and geographical research, and, supported by a sufficient number of adventurers in London, Sander-son made it possible for Davis to fit out his third expedition in Dartmouth. At midnight on the 19th May, 1587, his small squadron comprising the

WHALING
Woodcut from J. van der Brugge's *Journael*, 1634

Sunshine, *Elizabeth* and the little clincher *Ellen* sailed out of Dartmouth before a fresh north-easterly gale and made its way in company until Greenland's icy mountains were sighted, with the loom of glaciers between the peaks.

Now Davis was determined to make this voyage pay its own expenses with a view to inducing sea venturers of Britain to continue their efforts. He had deliberately prepared the *Sunshine* and the little *Ellen* for the fishery business, and among the crew were many expert fishermen. These blue-eyed, somewhat inarticulate folk gave trouble from the beginning because they had embarked for a fishing voyage and not for searching out new, uninhabitable lands ; and so in June, when the squadron had anchored in Gilbert Sound, John Davis made a decision which can only be described as heroic. He separated the sheep from the goats, as it were, and sent the fisherfolk, properly commanded, in the larger ships, *Sunshine* and *Elizabeth*, to the fishery. With the bold, intrepid souls who were ready to sacrifice their lives if need be for their leader and for further exploration and discovery, Davis continued, to his lasting credit, in the clincher-built pinnace *Ellen* of barely twenty tons. Sailing for a couple of hundred miles up the north-east coast of Baffin Land to nearly 70° North, he encountered what that fine old historian Sir Clements Markham always referred to as the "middle

63

pack." This heavy belt of 8-foot ice was too much for the little *Ellen* to withstand, so Davis coasted along its southern edge until, in longitude 55° West, he was able to alter course to the northward whilst his excited and interested crew gazed upon new islands lying off what he called the "London Coast," being the west coast of Greenland. He had scarcely been away from pack ice since he parted from the bigger ships, and he and his officers had plotted coast-lines and inlets and named them after their patrons and aristocratic friends—"Lord Lumley's Inlet," "Warwick's Foreland," "Cumberland Gulf," "Cape Walsingham," "Exeter Sound," "Mount Raleigh," and so on. But the high light of this enterprise was named after the steel-true William Sanderson, who indeed was the best type of English merchant and shipowner and, indeed, we have some of these even to-day! Davis called the mighty, cliff-girt islet which marked the most northerly point that this great explorer reached, "Sanderson His Hope." Indeed it was the leading mark of Sanderson's hope of a navigable North-West Passage. The little crew of the *Ellen* were tremendously impressed with this discovery. Its island summit is 850 feet above sea level, narrow ledges traverse the cliff side, and Davis's men saw hundreds of thousands of guillemots rear their young upon them. When disturbed they flew out in dense clouds, circled the *Ellen* two or three times and then returned to their young. Davis's journal records on the 30th June, 1587, "No ice towards the North but a great sea, free, large, very salt and blue, and of an unsearchable depth." That night the little pinnace was obliged to alter course to the west owing to a strong northerly wind having sprung up, and a few days later progress was finally checked by a "mighty bank of ice." This prevented Davis from exploring the strait further north.

The third Arctic voyage of John Davis was the most hazardous and interesting of all. He found whirling tide-races and very heavy over-falls, which would have been alarming enough to those in big ships. His crew landed energetically whenever they could and found deer, gray hares, and plenty of animal life, also fish, white bears and whales in "great store." Reindeer and foxes and most of the Arctic birds are referred to in his narratives, and last, but not least, we are indebted to this really great explorer for his descriptions of the superstitions and mode of life of the Eskimos, their tents and kayaks (or seal-skin canoes) and for a vocabulary of their language. Sir Clements Markham says that "Davis converted the Arctic region, from a confused myth into a defined area . . . He not only described and mapped the extensive tract explored by himself, but he clearly pointed out the work cut out for his successors. He lighted Hudson into his Strait. He lighted Baffin into his Bay. He lighted Hans Egede to the scene of his Greenland labours . . ."

Davis of the North, like Cook and Scott and others of the South, by his dauntless gallantry and enthusiasm lit a beacon for British explorers to be guided by.

SIR MARTIN FROBISHER, c. 1538-1595
Oil painting by Cornelius Ketel
By courtesy of the Curators of the Bodleian Library

WHALE OR GREENLAND FISHERY

Coloured engraving by E. Kirkall after T. Baston, c.1720

By courtesy of the Parker Gallery, London

HENRY HUDSON

HENRY HUDSON'S first recorded voyage, when he set sail from Gravesend, was to add an illustrious chapter to the story of the icy northern seas. He sailed in the *Hopewell* on a May day in 1607, and made his way northward towards the bleak coast of Greenland, using the passage between Iceland and Jan Mayen Island. He experienced balmy weather and smooth sailing, sighting countless whales and rejoicing at his rapid, unimpeded progress, until somewhere about 75° latitude a sudden change occurred ; thick weather and piercing cold was the prelude to sighting new lands. The decks of the *Hopewell* became coated with ice, as did the rigging and sails, a biting north-east gale beat the little ship back, and not until the weather cleared could Hudson make sure of the forbidding coast-line and mountainous land, the loom of which his crew had seen and reported. Actually, Hudson's landfall was well up the east coast of Greenland, in the region of King Oscar's Fjord, as we now know it ; and the very high, snow-covered mountain summit must have been the "Peak of God's Mercies." Hudson, after his instructions, should have sailed more directly towards the Pole in his search for a North-West Passage, and he lay well to the westward of his course ; he was always in some ways a rebel and scarcely ever kept to the letter of his sailing directions, but, as Cleland wrote of him, "He possessed the combinations rare enough of talent, invincible courage, patience and fortitude under suffering, daring, enterprise tempered by prudence, promptness and decision, united with calm reflection, sagacity, fertility of invention, strong common-sense, combined with enthusiasm and vivid imagination, the power of commanding other minds, joined to gentleness of manner and ready sympathy." What more could one want ? Despite his virtues and good qualities, however, Hudson appears to have been a very indifferent navigator, and in consequence there will always be a mix-up as to who discovered what, and when, in the Arctic Ocean in Elizabethan, Stuart and even later times.

Close in to the coast a great number of birds was observed, but Hudson was lucky enough to escape meeting the shore ice—which became such a deterrent to later voyagers. Working to the north-east, his vessel was sorely tried by a series of fierce gales often accompanied by thick weather, and then he met plenty of pack and found seals galore and polar bears whose flesh they ate *ad nauseam*. Mapping, as best he could, the trend of the Greenland coast, more high land was viewed and somewhat sketchily charted, and almost in latitude 80° he bore east and visited Spitsbergen, the discovery of which is more generally credited to Barents. To an educated member of the crew named Pleyce was given the duty of keeping the ship's journal, according to which, on the 27th June, "about 1 or 2 of the clock in the morning we made Newland [Spitsbergen or, to give it its proper modern nordic name, Svalbard] . . . this day at noon we were in 78° and we stood along the shore." The ship was then caught in the pack and carried some small distance into an icy fjord.

In early July, after tantalising setbacks due to fog, pack ice and gale, Hudson stood away to the southward, but soon again met adverse conditions until the luck changed, and on the 12th July at midnight, Collins, the bo'sun, sighted (in what we now know as Whales' Bay) a tongue of land which Hudson christened Collins' Cape, after the man who first sighted it. The Bay was so full of whales that they actually hampered the ship. To Hudson may well be ascribed that great stimulus to whaling which subsequently became one of our great industries of the North.

Towards the end of July, Hudson gave up exploring the Spitsbergen coast, and turned west again for Greenland, with the idea of returning to England, via the north of Greenland and south again through Davis Strait. He very nearly met his end on his way back to the Greenland coast, the *Hopewell* being nipped and almost crushed in the ice. This is a startling experience and to watch heavy ice-floes over-riding one another and being forced up by pressure, and to listen to the grinding and crunching of the floes and the thunderous noise as they fall apart and down, is enough to make man look to his Creator for support, as most Polar explorers own that they have done.

The passage to the north of Greenland was abortive, and Hudson returned home, passing close to the southern part of Spitsbergen and returning in mid-September to the Thames. His employers were disappointed, but nevertheless he commenced a second voyage in April next year, sent by the same company, with the object of finding a North-East Passage which would shorten the route to China. He had with him quite a small company (a dozen men and two cooks) and sailing up the coast of Norway he soon met with misfortune through the cold incapacitating some of the crew. Rounding the North Cape and coming into a very high latitude whilst sailing towards Nova Zembla, he met heavy pack on which were numerous bears and seals, with whales blowing in and about the ice, and, *mirabile dictu*, two men, Hils and Raynor, set eyes on a mermaid, "who played for a moment on the surface of the sea and then, with a flourish of her fishy tail, disappeared in the cold depths." Hudson's account states that she looked earnestly upon his men until the sea overturned her. He says that, "From the navil upwards her back and breasts were like a woman's . . . her skin very white, and long hair hanging down behind of color black." In her going down his men saw her tail which was "like the tail of a porpoise and speckled like a mackerel." Well, other reputable seamen in these times have often sighted and described the great sea-serpent—perhaps ye rumme of Jamaica has helped to embellish mariners' tales, both ye anciente and ye moderne!

This North-East Passage attempt was sorrowfully abandoned, but Hudson did not at once give up. His men landed in Nova Zembla once or

68

twice and brought back a motley collection which included whale-fins, mosses, flowers and other vegetation and two pieces of a cross. They also brought eggs aboard, some of which they cooked, and also plenty of driftwood which, it seems, came from the American coast, and had bearing on the flow of the Gulf Stream. Hudson's little company displayed plenty of physical energy. They found numerous walrus and geese, and Hudson's records are full of descriptions of fish, birds, and animals. Thwarted by the pack ice, Hudson gave up all hope of passing between Newland (Spitsbergen) and Nova Zembla—he might, had he only known it, have worked south of the latter and won through to the Kara Sea. Still, with his boat, a fair-sized river was explored for several leagues, and he found the Arctic fox and deer, walrus and wild-fowl in abundance.

This second voyage was a not inglorious failure, and after an unsuccessful search for Willoughby Land, he made a landfall in Wardhus, Lapland, and then somewhat sadly turned homeward, returning to the Thames on the 26th August. Once again he disappointed his employers, who offered him then no further chance of continuing his explorations.

Finding the coffers of the English merchants closed to him, Hudson sought patrons in Holland, and making a decided impression upon the Amsterdam Princes of Commerce and also upon a Belgian Croesus, one Balthazar de Bouchéron, conference followed meeting, discussion, support, opposition and compromise, and resulted in the Amsterdam directors of the East India Company despatching Henry Hudson on his third Arctic voyage in 1609, in a yacht named *Half Moon*, with a crew of sixteen Englishmen and Dutchmen. From the standpoint of Arctic exploration, this voyage yielded very little. His crew, or at least a part of it, was soft—used to employment in the tropics; trouble started when cold discomfort commenced, and Hudson's third Arctic sailing was scarce worthy of the name.

Hudson's fourth and last voyage was undertaken in the *Discovery* (or *Discoverer*) in the year 1610. Once again his crew was poorly chosen, and included a dissolute fellow named Henry Greene, a vicious and mischievous incorrigible. Hudson was in Iceland by the end of May and battling off the southern end of Greenland in July, during which month he had his first sight of Labrador whence he worked to the westward and northward through the ice-fields, discovering and exploring new islands, forelands and capes. Hudson computed the Strait which bears his name to be some three hundred leagues in length, and when he emerged he came into the broad waters which open into Fox Channel to the northward, and that splendid inland sea which we now know as Hudson's Bay.

The whole story of this last voyage is spoiled by trouble, disloyalty, altercation, violence, mutiny, scurvy and death. Juet may have been the villain, but Greene was a devilish mischief-maker, and so apparently the first ship to winter in the Northern ice had her grand story spoiled. The *Discoverer* wintered in a little basin under most disorganised conditions aboard, food ran short or some ate more than their share, and when, next June, Hudson left his unhappy winter quarters and again encountered ice and was stopped by it, open mutiny followed and an angry group of malcontents eventually turned their Commander, with his little son and others, adrift in an open boat and sailed away.

Of all the stories of British Polar explorers, Hudson's story is the least palatable. In spite of what Cleland wrote about him, he must have had some serious defects in character. Whatever made him include that odious fellow Greene in his company, one cannot say—Edgar Mayhew Bacon, writing of Hudson's voyages, says, "Hudson's relations with Greene would alone furnish material for a romance or a tragedy." Anyway, Greene was the evil genius who thwarted Hudson's ambition and almost turned to naught his cherished plans and bravest efforts. Juet, an old Limehouse seaman, was the next-worst man in the ship, and Hudson's stupid choice of this proved scoundrel causes one to attribute truly bad judgment to him. Hudson undoubtedly had, or developed, other defects, besides being a poor navigator ; his own records in his later voyages lacked the value and preciseness of the earlier ones. His organisation and control in the last voyage seem to have been extremely poor, the provisioning and issues thereof contributed mainly to the open mutiny which broke out when the *Discoverer* freed herself from her winter quarters. The crew were worked up into fury with Hudson because he had cut an entry into the hold by which he had secret access to the provision store. A second cause of the mutiny was Hudson's order that the crew's sea-chests should be broken open and any food secreted in them brought to him. Prickett, a writer and untrained supercargo, a Puritan withal, seems to have got wind of the mutiny and endeavoured to quell it by peaceful persuasion. He failed however, and on 21st June, 1611, the Master, Henry Hudson, was attacked as he left his cabin by the most wanton in the crew, his arms pinioned by Greene and one Wilson, in particular, and then the "shallop" or launch was hauled alongside, and Hudson forced brutally into it. With him were driven his son, John Hudson, Widowes (or Woodhouse), a mathematical student ; and Ladley, Faner, Moore, King, and Butt, seamen ; and the carpenter, Philip Staffe, who volunteered out of sheer loyalty and sense of right. Greene and Juet were loth to let Staffe go, but in the end they allowed him and let him take his carpenter's chest and tools.

It must be noted that five of the castaways were too sick to be of use and thus we find Henry Hudson, "grave and worn by months of hardship and anxiety," his eyes burning with impotent rage, seeing the invalids so cruelly marooned. Hudson took this cowardly business with calm and dignity, and his self-control so impressed the mutineers that they crowded on all sail as though chased by some fearful enemy. It takes little imagination to picture Hudson's men dying one by one, starving, frozen and forsaken. What a story, what blackguard business, how unlike the seamen of our time !

SIR JOHN FRANKLIN, 1786-1847
Lithograph by Negelen after J. H. Maguire

JOHN FRANKLIN

JOHN FRANKLIN commenced his career as an Arctic explorer in 1818, having been chosen to command the *Trent* which, with the *Isabella*, *Alexander* and *Dorothea*, was being despatched by the Admiralty on an expedition to discover a North-West Passage from Hudson's Strait via the north coast of America to the Pacific Ocean. Included in the plans of the expedition was the attainment of the Pole. The detailed instructions

71

directed the *Isabella* and *Alexander* to proceed north via Baffin Bay, whilst the *Trent* and *Dorothea* were to go by way of Spitsbergen.

The squadron left the Thames on the 25th April, 1818, the *Trent* and *Dorothea* keeping company as far as Spitsbergen, meeting stormy weather and a fair amount of ice. They anchored for a while in one of Spitsbergen's northerly harbours and then in early June skirted the edge of the pack into which they were subsequently driven by the wind, being for some time beset with ice. Both ships were at one time in danger of being crushed and the *Trent* was lifted some feet by a gigantic ice mass under her keel. After vain attempts to warp and tow the ships out, they found themselves drifting southward through the open water leads, faster than they could press north, and Captain Buchan who commanded the expedition gave up all attempt to force the pack, freed the two ships and got clear in time to face a strong gale and heavy seas. Then with thick, hard ice to leeward and the gale increasing in violence, the ships under reefed topsails were headed back into the pack. The *Trent* was very nearly lost after broaching to ; but Franklin set more head sail, the ship's head paid off and she drove well into the pack, where she appears to have lain fairly snugly until the gale abated.

The gruelling on the edge of the pack ice caused so much damage to the *Dorothea* that after anchoring in a bay on the north coast of Spitsbergen, the two crews doing their best to repair the extensive damage to the ship, became necessary for the *Dorothea* to turn homewards in such a bad state that her consort was forced to accompany her.

Next year, 1819, the Admiralty fitted out two further expeditions with the *Hecla* and *Griper* under the command of Lieutenant Parry, and the second in one of the Hudson's Bay Company's ships under Franklin. Leaving Parry to proceed up Baffin Bay and endeavour to reach the Pacific through whatever channel he could navigate, Franklin was to proceed overland from the north-west shore of Hudson's Bay, across a great tract (now the North-West Territory) to a point on the shore of the Arctic near the outflow of the Copper Mine River, thence eastwards along the coast with a view to linking with Parry and his ships, who were to be on the lookout for the overland expedition. Franklin, with Dr. Richardson and two midshipmen, Back and Hood, two seamen who had served in the *Trent* and four boatmen from the Orkney Isles, left York Factory at the mouth of the Nelson River in the beginning of September that year, with portable boats or canoes, following as well as they could the line of lakes and rivers which should take them to the Great Slave Lake and the Copper Mine River itself.

After six weeks' really tough going, Franklin arrived at Fort Cumberland, but was disappointed to find that the trappers, guides, and helpers that were supposed to be available to help him were not forthcoming owing to commercial rivalry and jealousy between the North West Company and the Hudson's Bay Company. Meeting very cold weather, Franklin, who went ahead with Back and one boatman, left Richardson and Hood to bring the

A RELIEF PARTY IN SEARCH OF SIR JOHN FRANKLIN
Coloured engraving by Baxter

stores and provisions along as soon as the river was navigable. Franklin, with a couple of dog sledges to carry his stores and equipment, made his way to Fort Chipewyan on the shores of Lake Athabasca and spent a long and most uncomfortable winter there.

The two who brought the stores along rejoined their leader at Fort Chipewyan next summer, and pushed on to Fort Providence where, at last, they obtained the assistance of Canadian guides and hunters, with three women, and some children. Soon after this a few Indian hunters and trappers came to their aid, and, crossing bleak, rough country, they reached Winter Lake and the Copper Mine River, where they set about building winter quarters. Franklin named these "Fort Enterprise." An early winter, with bitter cold and driving snow, stopped them from gathering a sufficient food supply in the shape of reindeer meat, and it became necessary for Back to leave his leader and make his way all the way back to Fort Chipewyan to bring food to the advance base. Back, on this trip, travelled more than eleven hundred miles on snow-shoes, going without food for two and even three days at a time in a temperature as low as 50° below freezing-point and protected at night by only one blanket and a deerskin.

On June 14th, 1821, when Franklin was about thirty-five years old, his expedition left Fort Enterprise for the Arctic Sea, with nineteen companions, two large canoes and several sledges, and a fortnight later they launched their little craft on the Copper Mine River, down which they travelled for a fortnight, when they sighted the sea from a hill top. A week later they were afloat in the Arctic Ocean !

Now, proceeding eastward, sailing and paddling along the ice-flanked coast, with the frailest imaginable canoes, charting bays and inlets as he went, and naming them all, John Franklin travelled over 550 miles when, at the rightly-named Cape Turnagain, South of Victoria Island, and almost in 70° North, with pemmican sufficient for three days' food ration and very little else in the way of food-stuffs, he was forced to turn back. He made a short cut by way of Hood's River, while it led in the right direction, and then across country after breaking up his canoes and rebuilding them.

This last part of the journey ranks with the worst in history. Hungry, bruised, exhausted and often sick, their rations of necessity grew smaller and smaller each day until they were fortunate enough to kill a musk-ox and enjoy their first decent meal for three days. Owing to two of the Canadian voyagers losing their self-control whilst they were following the party, the last canoe was deliberately dropped and left behind, and only by building a willow raft to carry them over, and a kind of painted canvas canoe, were they able to re-cross the Copper Mine River and make their way back to Fort Enterprise. By November some of the party had died of starvation. One of the midshipmen had been murdered by an Indian named Michel and Dr. Richardson had avenged his death by shooting the murderer with a pistol. When Franklin and his companions were almost at their last gasp, relief came—Indians bringing supplies in, just and only just in time. They owed their lives to Midshipman Back, who was responsible for the relief expedition, and in May 1822, after a rough march home, Franklin won back to York Factory. He reached England in October, after a three and a half years' absence, and a land and water journey in far northern Canada of more than 5,000 miles.

Franklin's second overland journey under the auspices of the Admiralty commenced in 1825. Having with him Dr. Richardson and Back with a party of specially selected men who had preceded them to New York and the eastern end of Lake Huron, a very ambitious overland march was commenced. Meantime, the *Blossom*, a stout little ship, commanded by Captain Beechey, Franklin's old first lieutenant, proceeded via the Pacific and Behring Strait to Alaska, with the intention of working along the Arctic coast of the American continent to the eastward and if possible meeting Franklin, who was to march westward from the mouth of the Mackenzie River. This Great White Trail to the north-west was full of excitement, hardship, and danger of the sort that Franklin and his comrades seem to have almost enjoyed. Working along the north Canadian and Alaskan coast and often held up

PASSAGE THROUGH THE ICE, JUNE 1818

Coloured aquatint from Sir John Ross's *Voyage of Discovery*, 1819

THE NORTH POLE

Imaginary sketch by Sir John Ross, 1777-1856

by ice and fog, Franklin mapped new coast-line for nearly four hundred miles after leaving the Mackenzie River mouth, yet, due to the lateness of the season, he had to turn again eastward and so failed to contact Captain Beechey in the *Blossom* at Icy Cape.

The September equinox found his party back at Fort Franklin, where they wintered fairly comfortably, and then after charting more than 1,200 miles of new coast-line, and adding considerably to our scientific knowledge of the North, Franklin won proper if somewhat tardy recognition for his labours and retired from the field of Polar exploration for nearly twenty years. After governing Tasmania and serving in important naval commands, he again took up Arctic work about the time of his fifty-ninth birthday, and with the 370-ton ex-bomb vessels, *Erebus* and *Terror*, already famous for their two Antarctic voyages, he once more sought the North-West Passage. There were about 140 officers and men in Franklin's last expedition, the *Erebus* commanded by Franklin, while Captain Crozier commanded the *Terror*, as he had done in Antarctica—himself a fine character and a resolute explorer. These two ships, making their way via Baffin Bay and Lancaster Sound, worked through Wellington Channel to latitude 77° N. and returned by the west side of Cornwallis Island to Barrow Strait and southward to the easternmost bluff of Victoria Island, very near to the Magnetic Pole. They wintered actually at Beechey Island in 74° 43′ N., longitude 91° 39′ W.; but being beset with ice since 12th September, 1846, they passed a second and very cruel winter. Various sledging expeditions were undertaken, but, of course, the disaster which terminated Franklin's final Arctic enterprise left us with incomplete records. Actually, Sir John Franklin died on the 11th June, 1847, by which time his expedition had sustained a loss of nine officers and fifteen men. Captain Crozier now assumed command and the crews surviving faced a third winter, the ice failing to break up.

The *Erebus* and *Terror* were deserted on the 22nd April, 1848, when Captain Crozier landed, with 105 members of the two ships' companies, and attempted a march over the ice-floes to safety. What a terrible march it was, too. Cairns and relics (some of the cairns found on King William Island had records in them), a boat with two skeletons discovered near Cape Crozier, and the effects, instruments, clothing and equipment picked up with an amazing collection of articles by members of over thirty search and relief expeditions, notably by McClintock and Lieutenant Hobson, indicated that Captain Crozier had endeavoured to make for the Great Fish River, which he evidently meant to ascend. Hardship, famine, and that dreaded enemy of the explorer, scurvy, defeated Crozier's purpose. Crozier seems to have reached the entrance of the Great Fish River, and we are indebted to Eskimo statements to link up and piece together the story of this disastrous expedition, every one of whose members perished. We know nothing of the final sufferings and the fate of these unfortunate seamen, but their work and their hardships were not in vain any more than Captain

Scott's and his companions were—they died for science and geographical discovery and for the honour of our Nation. Sir John Franklin's spirit must have hovered over another gallant explorer, a Norseman, Roald Amundsen, who actually completed the North-West Passage in the little motor-sloop *Gjöa* during 1903-1906.

The foregoing briefly summarises Franklin's last expedition. It must be remembered, however, that whilst he was Governor of Tasmania, Captain Parry, R.N., and others, notably two officers of the Hudson's Bay Company, had added a great deal to the map of the Arctic regions thereabouts, from Icy Cape in Alaska to the Parry Islands and Melville Sound. The Hudson's Bay Company have spent very great sums in their Northern explorations and surveys, and quite recently came the account of the *Saint Roch*'s making the North-West Passage—from west to east. This, by Sergeant Henry Larsen and a few companions, in a Canadian Mounted Police Patrol ship of only eighty tons, is likely to rank with some of the greatest achievements of British and other explorers of the Frozen North. However open the season, however light the obstacles and setbacks, Henry Larsen and his fellow craftsmen in 1942 did it and placed their little ship in the same category as Amundsen's famous motor-sloop *Gjöa*.

Both these were armed screw-propelled square-rigged vessels—suitable enough for their work but overburdened with superfluities.

Franklin, unlike Hudson, was well and loyally served—perhaps too loyally, for his officers and crews seem to have obeyed orders blindly and overloaded their sledges to an extent that made naval Arctic expeditions appear ridiculous to men like Nansen, Scott, Amundsen and merchant-seamen explorers like Shackleton and Colbeck. Great cumbersome boats were dragged along over the ice, whereas the Canadian canoe or Eskimo kayak might well have sufficed for sledge journeys. The sledges themselves were too heavily constructed and the officers even took unwieldy telescopes strapped over their shoulders, apart from silver plate and heavy iron cooking-pots and stoves. All the same, Franklin's stout-hearted, muscular seamen put up a good enough record of marches, as did the selected crews of the many search expeditions that followed in the wake of the *Erebus* and *Terror*.

In 1902, Sir Clements Markham told me that Franklin was twenty years too old for the exacting work of Arctic exploration. Scott was forty-three when he died and he had lasted through as rigorous a time as any and shewn up as well in his last expedition as he had in his *Discovery* days when he was in the early thirties. If asked, I should give thirty-five as the best age for Polar activity and endurance, and Franklin's sixty-one years must have tried him sorely after the second winter when his ships were beset in the pack. Had Franklin only known it, he might after his first winter have worked round to the eastward of King William's Island and steamed through Simpson and Dease Straits in fairly open water, passing into Dolphin and Union Straits, and so completed the North-West Passage.

VIEW OF THE ICE ISLANDS
Engraving from Anderson's *The Whole of Captain Cook's Voyages*, 1781

THE GOLDEN LINK: JAMES COOK

BRITAIN'S greatest and most famous navigator, Captain James Cook, ranks, to my mind, *facile princeps* of our ocean voyagers, and his discoveries towards the end of the eighteenth century are remarkable in that his surveys are sufficiently accurate to leave the charts that he made often unaltered by modern surveyors, who are aided by the electric telegraph to fix their longitude by meridian distances and by instruments like 6″ theodolites, which can fix latitude to seconds of arc. Since, in his boyhood, this steadfast navigator, son of a Yorkshire farm labourer, traded up and down the Norwegian coast in the Whitby-built ships, *Freelove, Three Brothers* and *Maria*, it is possible that he crossed the Arctic circle, which cuts through Norway very well south of Narvik and the Lofoten Isles. We know that he crossed the Antarctic circle in December 1773 and February 1774 in the good ship, *Resolution*. Cook, therefore, just enters his name in the title of this book and is the link between North and South Polar Explorers since he voyaged in the Arctic and Antarctic seas. In fact, he pushed his way through the pack ice and managed to reach latitude 71° 10′ South in longitude 107° West on the 30th January, 1774, after earlier experience in the ice of the Southern seas, where pack may be met within 60° and icebergs in as low a latitude as 37°. And that is why I have named this all-too-brief mention of James Cook's voyages, "The Golden Link."—And now some account of British South Polar explorers.

JAMES CLARK ROSS

CAPTAIN James Clark Ross was an explorer of more than ordinary scientific attainments. He had, under Captain Parry, already located the North Magnetic Pole, although to Albert Markham falls the honour of actually reaching it. But Ross had besides enriched himself by acquiring considerable Polar experience in the Arctic, and this helped him fit out the specially strengthened *Erebus* and *Terror*, which ships sailed from Chatham on 25th September, 1839, to circumnavigate the Antarctic Pole and carry out an ambitious magnetic survey, on a genuinely scientific expedition. The Admiralty, thanks largely to Lord Minto, the First Lord Commissioner at that time, was at great pains to provision and supply the ships in the most generous manner, and everything taken was of the best.

Ross commanded the *Erebus*, and Commander Francis Crozier (who later lost his life in the ill-fated Franklin expedition) her sister ship, the *Terror*. The vessels were about 350 tons, and their crews each consisted of sixty-four officers, scientists and seamen, some of whom, notably the assistant surgeon of the *Erebus*, were to become men of distinction.

Sailing via Good Hope to Kerguelen, that and other sub-Antarctic islands were visited and scientific observations made. Ross then came to Hobart, Tasmania (or Van Diemen's Land), where he established a magnetic observatory and was well looked after by the Governor, Sir John Franklin, the Arctic explorer. He sailed southward on 12th November, 1840, and sighted his first iceberg in 63° 20′ S., and soon afterwards the two ships passed a chain of bergs, some of great size and height. Ross was surprised at their uniformity of shape ; he called them "tabular" icebergs and noted their perpendicular cliffs and their lack of "colour and variety of form" which distinguished them from the beautiful Arctic bergs. By December 29th he was sighting whales in great numbers—black whales, hunchbacks, sperms and rorquals.

The first week of the year 1841 found the two ships in the pack ice, and Ross learned of its great extent, variety and nature. His splendid leadership inspired his staff to make first-class records of all that they observed. And what with new species of birds, skua gulls, dainty white ice petrels, brown-backed and little black petrels, and clumsy giant petrels who ate so much that they could not always "take off" from the ice fields, his zoologists soon had their note-books filled. And then came the seals and penguins. New species were discovered and a rare seal with a goitre-like neck was found and named after Ross himself. But all this interest in animal life and crustaceans and fish and pack ice faded into insignificance when the high mountains of a new land were shown all towering in a magnificent panorama of glistening white and blue.

Ross named this great white icebound land, Victoria Land, after his young sovereign. The wonderland of mountain ranges and the mighty and

A GALE IN THE PACK, JANUARY 1842
Lithograph by Davis, from Ross's *Voyage of Discovery*, 1839-1843

majestic peaks had names bestowed upon them like Admiralty Range, and Mount Minto, Mount Sabine, and Mount Herschell, after important ministers, scientists and leading peers of the day. The capes and bays, islands and seas were reserved for the lesser luminaries, like Cape Crozier, Cape Bird, Wood Bay, McMurdo Bay (Sound) and so forth. The *pièce de résistance*, Ross Island, he named after himself, and the two volcanoes, one 13,000, and the other 10,000 feet in altitude, he christened Mounts Erebus and Terror.

Ross charted Victoria Land accurately enough, and his men landed on the Possession Islands. He discovered what will always be one of the world's greatest wonders, the Great Ice Barrier, that frozen Sahara which we now know to extend for five hundred miles and more southward. He sailed almost four hundred miles eastward along it and named that also, the "Ross Ice Barrier."

The *Erebus* and *Terror* worked eastward as far as 200° (or 160° West longitude) charting the barrier-cliff for almost the whole of its length, taking deep-sea soundings and magnetic and hydrographic observations, and industriously recording everything they saw and giving thereby such a true picture of Victoria Land, Coulman Island, Franklin Island, Beaufort Island, the Great Ice Barrier, and the ice conditions of the Ross Sea, that Ross's first Antarctic voyage gave later explorers an "Open Sesame" to Antarctica's heart.

What his sailors must have endured, trimming yards as the two ships manœuvred mostly under full sail, one can scarcely imagine, and when recounting how on 6th April, Ross returned to Tasmania's beautiful River Derwent and was again greeted by Sir John Franklin, it is befitting to set down his words, ". . . to call forth our gratitude to God for his guidance and preservation during the arduous and hazardous operations in which we have been engaged . . ."

After refitting in Tasmania, Ross sailed south again at the end of 1841 and continued his glorious work. On the 13th March, 1842, in one of those terrible gales that South Polar explorers all know, the ships passed through a chain of bergs under such hazardous circumstances that the greatest writer of tempestuous sea-lore would have difficulty in describing what the two ships endured—sails torn from the bolt-ropes, sheets of icy water crashing on to their decks, topsails in holes, and cool bravery which can never have been exceeded. The ships collided, the *Erebus* lost her bowsprit and presented a woeful spectacle with her broken spars and damaged rigging.

After much dangerous sailing in the Antarctic when their furthest south latitude, 78° 10′, was reached, and the Barrier further explored, Ross headed northward and eastward, and finally anchored in Port Louis, East Falkland Island, where he hauled up his ships to repair them, and then in lower latitudes and warmer seas he completed his magnificent scientific voyaging, and made his way back to the shores of old England which were sighted on the 2nd September, 1843, after four years' absence.

Ross succeeded in locating the South Magnetic Pole in 75° 5′ S. and longitude 154° 8′ E. and certainly repaid the country in full for the cost of his expedition. He ranks as one of our greatest scientific seamen-explorers.

SCOTT

ROBERT FALCON SCOTT, like John Davis, was a Devonshire man with no previous Polar experience. Strongly supported by Sir Clements Markham, President of the Royal Geographical Society, he was selected to command the National Antarctic expedition of 1901. He had specialised in torpedo and was serving as First Lieutenant of the *Majestic*, flagship of the Channel Fleet, when he obtained his promotion to Commander. Apart from being a brilliant naval officer, he had the keen brain of a first-class scientist, and the literary ability which has so often been denied to the British Polar explorer. Moreover, he had an exceptional way of appreciating any situation quickly and properly. Looking back over a period of forty years I would class him as one of the three cleverest men I have ever met. Directly he received his appointment he made himself felt, and whether in building the *Discovery* and fitting her out on the Tay, in selecting her staff or her stores and equipment, Scott's judgment seems to have prevailed.

HUT POINT FROM OBSERVATION HILL
Water colour by Dr. E. A. Wilson, 1911

Scott very soon mastered the early history of Antarctic exploration ; Weddell and Biscoe and Balleny's tracks were imprinted on his brain ; he always looked on Weddell's high latitude of 74° as a remarkable achievement, and when following in Ross's wake more than half a century later, he added vastly to that explorer's magnetic, hydrographical and geographical surveys. Scott sailed from the Thames in July 1901, with a very well chosen company, which included Shackleton, whose name, after Scott's, is perhaps the best known of the modern Antarctics. He had that lovable gentleman, artist, zoologist and doctor of medicine, Edward Adrian Wilson, with him, and Skelton, who was to become Engineer-in-Chief of the Navy ; Armitage, who had already served in the Arctic, and such naval men as Evans, who accompanied Scott to the Pole itself, Wild, who became Shackleton's second-in-command, and Lashly and Crean, who made the 1,500-mile sledge journey of his last supporting party.

Leaving Port Chalmers, New Zealand, on Christmas Eve 1901, Scott said good-bye to civilisation for more than two years, and steered south to the gales, fogs, bergs and pack, which he negotiated skilfully in his strong little ship. Entering the Ross Sea, he sighted Victoria Land after obtaining a deep-sea sounding of 1,480 fathoms, which told him that he was on the verge of the Antarctic land plateau, and heralded his first look at the Antarctic continent, whose peaks he could clearly distinguish more than 100 geographical miles away. The *Discovery*, after forcing her way through a heavy band of pack ice, entered Robertson Bay, and Scott landed at Cape Adare where he found the hut left by Borchgrevink of the George Newnes Expedition, which wintered there in 1896, this being the first party to winter on the shores of the Antarctic continent. Scott left a record here, as he did on his southward way at Possession Island, Coulman Island, Franklin Island, and Cape Crozier—the easternmost point of Ross Island—prior to heading eastward along the Barrier cliffs. Before doing this the *Discovery* crept slowly through inshore pack, and on the 21st January, less than a month out from New Zealand, she steamed right into McMurdo Sound, and proved it no longer a bay. Scott disproved the existence of the Parry Mountains, and from what he saw in McMurdo Sound was guided eventually to make his winter quarters in the south-west corner of Ross Island.

The expedition landed on the Great Ice Barrier and Scott, brave sailor and fine leader, made a balloon ascent in the inlet he called Balloon Bay. His view from the balloon showed the *sastrugi* or snow waves on the Barrier surface, which he became so familiar with on his many sledging journeys. But at the end of January something occurred of far greater moment than a balloon ascent ; running into a deep bay and approaching the great slabs of solid-looking pack ice which lay ahead of him, he found long, undulating slopes, and swelling mounds, which turned out to be new land ! This he named King Edward's Land after the reigning monarch. Dr. Wilson made a beautiful water-colour showing the purple-blue sea in the foreground,

TERRA NOVA, CAPTIVE IN HEAVY PACK
Photograph taken by Ponting : Scott's Antarctic Expedition, 1910-1913

backed by the Barrier cliffs, most truly and cleverly drawn, then the lone Barrier surface, bounded by the hill tops in white and dark purple shades, beyond which are gold and copper-hued clouds, surmounted by that sad, heavy cloud bank, which tells of approaching winter.

The altitude was calculated as between 2,000 and 3,000 feet for the highest peaks, and the snow-covered ridges and undulations appeared uniformly white, except for a few outcrops of rock, with occasional crevasses. The ice walls that beset this hitherto unvisited country rose to a height of 280 feet. They were all photographed by Skelton and sketched by Wilson, and so Scott's first Antarctic venture records have been enriched by good illustrations.

The winter quarters were established in 78° South, 167° East, in a small bay protected from the northward by a little spit of land called Hut Point on which a magnetic observatory was erected ; Scott spent two winters here. The main sledging expeditions were Scott's southern journey over the Barrier ice—in this, accompanied by Dr. Wilson and Shackleton, Scott

85

reached 82° 17′ South ; Lieutenant Royds made a journey south-eastward over the Barrier ; Lieutenant Barne, south-westward to the entrance of the inlet which now bears his name ; Armitage carried out pioneer journeys to the glaciers which connect with the inland plateau of Victoria Land, and Scott, after the second winter, made a remarkable journey up the Ferrar Glacier and into the heart of the ice-capped plateau and up on to the plateau summit, which he describes as, "this terrible, limitless expanse of snow," and "so fearsomely monotonous." During this sledge journey Scott, Evans, and Lashly covered practically 1,100 miles at an average of 15½ miles a day, and climbed heights which totalled nearly 20,000 feet !

Unfortunately, when the relief expedition in the little whaler, *Morning*, came back with the news that the *Discovery* was held in the grip of the heavily frozen sea and compelled to face her second winter at Hut Point, the Government flew into a panic and despatched a second relief expedition, with two ships, the *Morning* and *Terra Nova*, carrying 32 tons of gun-cotton and orders which amounted to "blast the *Discovery* out or else bring back her crew."

It may be mentioned that thanks to Scott's records, placed as already described, we in the first relief expedition had followed his progress on what I call "a great Antarctic paper-chase." From a second record, left at Cape Crozier, we learnt the *Discovery*'s whereabouts, and bringing back Shackleton, who was suffering from scurvy, and half a dozen others, Captain Colbeck, who commanded both relief expeditions, was able to give the Admiralty a comprehensive account of Scott's work and whereabouts. Colbeck pointed out that the first winter had been unusually severe and the ice conditions abnormal. However, the *Terra Nova* was purchased, and after the second relief voyage had contacted Scott, and the *Discovery* had been set free, the three ships sailed in company for New Zealand and home.

After taking part as a youngster in both relief expeditions, I was appointed second-in-command of Scott's next South Polar venture. Scott's second and last expedition's history is well known to most Britons. As a young lieutenant, I was put in charge of the Dundee whaler *Terra Nova*, and the expedition was fitted out to cover two Antarctic winters, although it was decided not to keep the ship south, but to build huts instead. The main expedition wintered at Cape Evans, some 15 miles north of the *Discovery*'s old winter quarters, and from this point, after several depot-laying trips and other sledge journeys had been made and a great deal of scientific knowledge acquired—geological, hydrographical, zoological, geodetic, and physical—and a special study of ice structure and glaciation made, the sledging season commenced. Winter journeys, notably that by Wilson, Lieutenant Bowers and Cherry-Garrard, added to our Antarctic knowledge ; temperatures as low as 77° below zero were lived through with no other protection but sleeping-bags and light tents ; valuable spring and summer journeys were carried out by the physiographer and geologist and the great nine-hundred-mile journey to the Pole itself was made by Scott, Wilson, Captain Oates, Lieutenant Bowers, and Petty Officer Edgar Evans. Dogs, ponies and motor sledges were used, the ponies dragging the food supplies to the foot of the Great Beardmore Glacier, which Shackleton had discovered and ascended in 1903. Scott was helped by a system of supporting parties which turned back in 81° 15', 83°, 85° and 87½° South, and on the 4th January, 1912, the last supporting party, which had given up one of its number to make more easy the final dash and the long homeward trek, said good-bye to Scott and turned northward. I had charge of this hazardous return. With me were Chief Stoker Lashly and Petty Officer Crean. It was a disappointment to my party that we could not all go to the Pole—a great disappointment, but we had been brought up to treat misfortunes with a smile and successes with a cheer.

We took enough food to get us back to latitude 87° where we had established a depot. We made a short march with Scott's team to see that with their load increased by what we had brought along they could manage without unduly straining. They got along finely for three or four miles, then they halted and said, "Good-bye." We shook hands all round, and we felt very moved as we looked into their eyes, and at their smoke-begrimed, bearded faces.

There were cakes of ice on their beards, weather scars, split lips, and frost-bite marks, but their rugged faces had become very dear to us, and it seems a few weeks, rather than thirty years, since that memorable "Goodbye."

Scott was a Devonshire man; Dr. Wilson, Uncle Bill, as we called him, beloved as he was by us all, came from Cheltenham. Captain Oates, of the Inniskilling Dragoons, was a bright-eyed, sturdy Yorkshireman of the rugged type that miners love and will follow through any danger—he was the last one ever to speak to me in that party. His final remark was cheerful, "I am afraid, Teddy, you won't have much of a 'slope' going back, but old Christopher is waiting to be eaten on the Barrier when you get there." Christopher was his pony. Lieutenant Bowers from Rothesay, whom Scott describes as the "hardiest man that ever undertook a Polar journey," was full of enthusiasm. His only concern was not for himself, but for our short-handed sledge team, which, through loss of his instruments, would have a precarious journey back. And then there was Evans, Seaman Evans, a Herculean Welshman who had been with Scott in every one of his hard sledge journeys in the *Discovery* expedition, and in this one. His great frame, encased in frost rime, made him look like a big, strong bear.

We gave three good cheers for the Southern party as they stepped off, and then turned our sledge, and commenced our lonely march to the base. We frequently looked back until we saw the last of Captain Scott and his four companions, a tiny, black speck on the horizon. Little did we think that we would be the last to see them alive, that our three cheers on that vast, frigid table-land on the summit of the Polar ice-cap would be the last appreciation that they would ever know.

My two companions, those veteran sledgers Crean and Lashly, both died recently and I alone remain of those who accompanied Scott to the heart of the Antarctic Plateau. Never in the history of Polar exploration has Fortune, that fickle mistress, treated two parties so differently. My party, short-handed, without instruments, almost expected to be overtaken, and, working on the ratio of five to three, we used to imagine that Scott would average 18 miles a day on the short distance to the Pole, and anything up to 25 miles coming back light on ski, with a fair wind to help him along, whilst we could only hope to manage 15 miles at best. Actually, it turned out quite differently—whenever our fate depended on good fortune, we got it, if ever men did.

To start with, shortly after leaving Captain Scott, we had a three-day blizzard. The wind was from the south, and we set the floor-cloth of our tent as a sail and drove along like a small craft scurrying before the gale. We covered incredible distances, and although in the driving snow we got somewhat to the eastward of our intended route, that did not matter. Scott's party faced this blizzard, which held them back, sapped their strength, ate into their bones, and must have left them at the end of each day's march exhausted, numbed and in agony. Then the next stage ; when we found ourselves right above the Shackleton Ice-Falls, some miles too far to the eastward of where we should have been. We had taken over three days to march round and avoid these Ice-Falls on the outward route, and it struck me that if we dared take our lives in our hands and toboggan over the Falls, we should save three days' marching time, at least, and of course that amount of provisions. Well, I've run a good many risks in my life, on land, at sea and in the air, but no hazard I have ever lived through compares with that tobogganing over the Ice-Falls. It makes me sweat even now, whenever I think of it. We came through in about twenty minutes, scared, bruised and literally with our hair standing on end. (That wasn't very hard, we hadn't any hair brushes, not even a comb with us.)

Now Scott did not take this risk, he very properly came back by the outward route, not taking the mad flight over the Ice-Falls, but he used up three vital days, and of course, that much food.

But let me tell you what happened when eventually we got down to the Beardmore Glacier, and back to that frozen Sahara, the Great Ice Barrier— we had fine weather, and calm or fair winds for the whole 500 miles back : it was not even unbearably cold. Poor Scott, when he reached the Barrier, found bitter weather conditions, the thermometer standing at 40° to 50° below zero pretty constantly and, instead of the prevailing southerly wind which every sledge party had experienced hitherto on the Barrier, he had dead head-winds reaching gale force almost daily. It is true I developed scurvy when well northward on the Barrier and the heroism of my two

DOG SLEDGE, SHOWING MOUNT EREBUS IN THE BACKGROUND
Photograph taken by Ponting : Scott's Antarctic Expedition, 1910-1913

companions, Crean and Lashly, alone helped me to safety, but we did have fair winds which enabled them to set our tent floor-cloth as a sail and that helped us along as much as a full sledge-team would have done.

Now, let us go back to Scott's team emerging from the blizzard when close to the Pole. Very soon after, the sharp eyes of the little Scotsman, Bowers, detected a black speck on the horizon. It turned out to be a flag flying from a snow cairn and long before they came up to this, Scott's men found dog tracks, ski tracks and sledge tracks, many of them, which they followed to the Polar area. What a disappointment !

We knew nothing of this, but Scott's men now knew that Roald Amundsen, the gallant Norseman, had forestalled them. On January 17th, 1912, Captain Scott reached the South Pole ; he found a tent with a Norwegian flag flying above it and a record left by Captain Amundsen, which told that the Norwegian Expedition had reached the South Pole only a month before. Scott in his diary writes, "What a terrible place." He makes notes of what he finds but never from any member of this valiant Polar sledge-team comes one word of complaint. Scott says that "Amundsen has done his work, and done it well."

And now for that long homeward march of over 900 miles, when everything turned against them ; head-winds, little setbacks, and unlooked-for

89

tragedy. Seaman Evans, the strong man of the party, slipped on some blue ice and hit the back of his head, sustaining severe concussion. The party did all they could to help Evans forward, but his condition caused the gravest anxiety. Reaching the Beardmore Glacier, the party commenced to descend; Wilson's hands and feet were in a bad state of frost-bite and Evans, nearly at the foot of the Glacier, again fell, hit his head very badly and must have injured his brain. Sadly the party fought on, but Evans died on the 17th February, just when they came to the Barrier.

After burying poor Evans, near Desolation Camp where we had killed our starving ponies on the outward march, Scott's bereaved party now pushed forward with a fine perseverance although they must have known, by their gradually shortening marches, that little hope of reaching their winter quarters remained.

Captain Oates had done all he could to tend poor Evans's frost-bitten hands and feet and in doing so there is no doubt that he exposed himself too much and *he* was the next to fail. His condition caused deep concern. He struggled on bravely for nearly three hundred miles more, until, on the 17th March, his birthday, having been helped forward by his companions who did their utmost for him, this very gallant gentleman, realising that the salvation of the party depended on his self-sacrifice, deliberately walked out of the tent during a cruel blizzard and strove through the snows until he dropped and died in his tracks, giving his life to save his three companions, Scott, Wilson, and Bowers, now beset with hardship. Bravely these three pushed on for two or three more days, Scott writing in his diary a hope that they might meet the end in the same fine spirit—and assuredly the end was not far.

Scott's little team pitched their tent for the last time, when only 11 miles from a big food depot, and then they were overwhelmed by a blizzard, which, from their records, we know lasted nine days. With food for two days, and fuel for one hot meal, they faced the end. Scott's last message to the public has now become a saga. With the pencil dropping from his frozen fingers, his ending lines, "For God's sake look after our people," and, "How much better has this all been than lounging in too great comfort at home," are so inspiring and so noble that we can well turn again and again to the story of Captain Scott for our inspiration.

The *Terra Nova* had arrived at Cape Evans from New Zealand on February 4th, 1912, and landed stores for a further winter, as well as mules and additional dogs. I was rescued by Dr. Atkinson on the 20th February, and brought to the edge of the Ice Barrier whence I was carried on a sledge on board the *Terra Nova* and thought to be a dying man.

Scott was not expected back at Hut Point before the 10th or the 15th March, but as day after day passed with no signs of him, Dr. Atkinson, who now took charge, began to fear the worst. It was impossible to keep the *Terra Nova* after the 27th March, new ice was forming and the ship had not been prepared for wintering. She sailed on that day for New Zealand, and though one or two attempts were made to go out and succour Scott the rapidly approaching winter made going impossible, and the dog teams would not face the terrible weather encountered.

A second winter was passed in gloom and sorrow at Cape Evans, for not only had our beloved leader failed to make the base, but Campbell's party had not been picked up and were left marooned in Terra Nova Bay. The story of the six men forming this team is one of the most heroic on record. With four weeks' sledging provisions, they faced eight months of fearful hardship, living in an igloo which they had painfully dug for themselves. After the sun came back, but not until September 30th, with one man almost dying of dysentery, Campbell's party sledged 200 miles across the treacherous sea-ice and piedmont southward until they were able to be sure of firm sea-ice in McMurdo Sound over which they trudged to Cape Evans, arriving all out, but alive.

Much more could be written about Scott's second and last expedition, apart from the spectacular sledge journey and Scott's tragic end—the ascent of Mount Erebus, the scientific journeys into the Western Mountains, and the splendid physical, geological, biological, and hydrographical results obtained not only by those based ashore, but also by that fine company under Lieutenant Pennell in the *Terra Nova* who charted Oates Land and other coast-lines and who took a great number of deep-sea soundings which added to our knowledge of the Ross Sea and the great ocean way that separates New Zealand from the mountainous sub-continent of Victoria Land.

SHACKLETON

ERNEST SHACKLETON was an Irishman, a merchant seaman who was specially chosen for service with Scott whilst in the Union Castle Company, and although he did not complete his service in the *Discovery* expedition through being invalided home, the spirit of Antarctic adventure never left him.

In February 1907 he planned a bold bid to reach the South Pole, together with a good, sound, scientific programme. He purchased one of the best built of the smaller wooden whalers, the *Nimrod*, and sailed from London on the 20th July, 1907. Calling at Cape Town to refuel, he made for Lyttelton, New Zealand, that favourite starting place for modern British Antarctic explorers, and there embarked ten Manchurian ponies, a motor-car, and as much coal as the bunkers and deck space could hold. His Irish imagination caused him to charter the collier *Koonya* to tow him down to the pack ice, thereby extending his steaming radius greatly. The *Nimrod* sailed from New Zealand on New Year's Day 1908, and after a very rough passage through the mountainous seas and the roaring forties, where the wind reached hurricane force and the *Nimrod*'s bulwarks were smashed in and two of the ponies so injured that they had to be shot, the *Nimrod* and the *Koonya* parted company when fairly surrounded by icebergs.

Shackleton, with splendid steaming radius available, proceeded eastward along the Great Ice Barrier, to the position of Balloon Inlet, which had disappeared. In its stead was a wide opening which he christened the Bay of Whales. It was here in January 1911 that the *Fram*, with Amundsen's expedition, was sighted by the *Terra Nova* in Scott's last expedition whilst a landing was being sought for Lieutenant Campbell and a small party of Scott's men. Shackleton tried to extend Scott's discoveries in the vicinity of King Edward VII Land, but was compelled to turn westward after encountering very heavy ice, which caused the *Nimrod* to leak. Much against his will, he was forced to choose Cape Royds for his winter quarters, being more than twenty miles north of where the *Discovery* had been frozen in. His shore party consisted of fifteen scientists and sailors, and included Professor David of Sydney University, Dr. Mawson of Adelaide and R. E. Priestley, who subsequently served as a geologist with Scott.

Shackleton built a medium-sized hut, where he wintered in 1908, and whilst David, Mawson and McKay made a journey to the north-westward, and reached the Magnetic Pole, Shackleton, with Lieutenant Adams, his second-in-command, Dr. Marshall and Frank Wild, made what will always stand out as one of the greatest sledge journeys in history. Four ponies, each dragging a sledge load of over 600 lbs., commenced what has been described as "one of the greatest hunger marches." His party built beacons, cairns of ice to guide them homeward, an example which Scott's men followed two years later. On the 26th November, 1908, Shackleton trod further south than ever man had before, passing Scott's first "farthest South" 82° 17'. And now every new mountain, every new feature of that extensive, high, glaciated land became Shackleton's own discovery. Two great mountains, Markham and Longstaff, which Scott had placed on the map were succeeded by other grand peaks, and as he and his companions trod over virgin barrier ice they grew amazed at their own southward progress. On the 2nd December a great glacier showed up, which led almost due south through the mountains, and when Shackleton camped to have his lunch he made a momentous decision which he communicated to the other three, and that was that they should ascend this glacier which he subsequently named the "Beardmore." Hopes ran high, so high that a small, reddish granite mountain was christened Mount Hope, and from its flat summit the southern group was further reconnoitred. Half-way up the glacier a massive, round-topped mountain was seen. Shackleton afterwards christened it the "Cloud Maker" as its summit was nearly always obscured by low stratus clouds. Unlike Scott, Shackleton managed to get a pony named Socks well on to the glacier itself. This proved to be a mistake, for poor Socks early on disappeared down a yawning chasm, the snow

INTERIOR OF A CREE INDIAN TENT

Coloured aquatint from Sir John Franklin's *Narrative of a Journey to the Shores of the Polar Sea, 1819-1822*

VIEW OF THE ARCTIC SEA FROM THE MOUTH OF THE COPPER MINE RIVER, MIDNIGHT, JULY 1821

Coloured aquatint after Back

From Sir John Franklin's Narrative of a Journey to the Shores of the Polar Sea 1819-1822

bridge of which bore the weight of a man, but not that of a heavy pony. This loss meant a great deal to the men, who had counted on the pony meat to help feed them, as they won further south. The passage up the glacier was a difficult one, but most interesting—fringed as it was by mountains, cliffs, and small glaciers. Fossils were found, and even coal, and a good rough sketch survey made ; a new mountain range, named after Queen Alexandra, was discovered on the western side of the Beardmore ; other ranges followed named the Commonwealth and Dominion Ranges, in honour of their Australian expedition mates. Finally the Inland Plateau which Shackleton describes as "the bleakest and most horrible part of the earth" was gained, and in spite of crevasses and a compulsory reduction in their food allowance, with pretty low temperatures and often bad surfaces, the inimitable, witty, and lovable leader fought on to the 87th° of latitude. A further food reduction left the party weak and the high altitude, more than 10,000 feet up as they were, gave them headaches and great lassitude. But although his party were rapidly weakening, they managed to pull their sledge-load on until it became necessary, due to blizzard and other circumstances, to build a depot and push on, dragging not much more than 70 lbs. per man. Shackleton and his comrades loyally took the risk of leaving that depot of foodstuffs out of sight of landmarks or any leading marks by which it could be located. Then came blizzard weather and a gale followed by frostbite and snow-blindness, and painful cuts on their faces. On the 9th January, Shackleton realised that to go on further meant death to them all, and then, in latitude 88° 23′ South, a little flag presented to him by Queen Alexandra was flown at his furthest South, and the Polar Plateau taken possession of in the name of King Edward VII. They were only 97 geographical miles from the South Pole when they turned and commenced that terrible homeward march. Fortunately their old tracks showed up, and where their fur-clad feet had pressed down into the snow the force of the blizzard had swept the snow away all round and little 9-inch-long shapes appeared, standing cheerfully above the surface like so many blancmange moulds—a chain of these frequently appeared to guide them on their way. This meant a very great deal ; it spared unnecessary observation to be taken by theodolite and worked out with ice-bitten fingers in the meagre shelter of their now sadly worn tent.

The homeward march was a race with death, and, in spite of their small sledging ration, they marched as much as 26 miles in a day, and sometimes ran out of all their provisions, except cocoa and tea, on which they lived until they found their way on to the next depot. January 28th brought them back to the Barrier, and then even their rejoicing ceased, for Wild developed dysentery. This is indeed a bad business. It results often in haemorrhage from the bowels, and the white snow is covered by patches of blood which are alarming to behold. The red-letter day in Shackleton's diary came when they reached a well-marked depot laid by a supporting party, but in spite of this Marshall nearly died, and it was only due to Shackleton's swift and successful decision and his unconquerable optimism that the party reached the old hut left by Scott in *Discovery* days. Shackleton's landing party was picked up by the *Nimrod* which sailed for New Zealand on the 4th March, 1909, and brought back this heroic band to safety.

Shackleton's next efforts were made in the re-named Norwegian whaler which now became the *Endurance*. On this occasion he planned what was known as the "Trans-Antarctic Expedition," and secured the whaler *Aurora* to sail from the New Zealand side whilst he intended to start with dog teams from the Weddell sea. It was planned that the Ross Sea party should take stores for his use to the Beardmore Glacier and meet him at Mount Buckley where he first found coal. Shackleton had seventy dogs, and his plan for the transcontinental sledge journey was as bold as any ever made.

Shackleton left South Georgia in the *Endurance*, entered the pack in 60° South, and penetrated a couple of degrees or so into it. By Christmas Day he had made some 350 miles southing, but such gigantic floes were met with that further progress was held up until the ice loosened and he advanced a further 250 miles. He then came to open water in 69° 47' and, steaming and sailing through dark-green water, sighted an ice barrier and land, which was undoubtedly that discovered by the Scottish explorer, Dr. Bruce, in 1904. Shackleton passed Bruce's farthest South on the 12th January, 1915. New land was named the "Caird Coast" and about this time the biologists made a great haul of specimens. After confirming other explorers', notably Filchner's, discoveries, and shortly after a near approach was made to Vahsel Bay, Shackleton's expectations of landing on January 19th were frustrated by close pack besetting the ship, and failing to work free they prepared to winter in the ice. Nothing daunted, he put his dogs out on the floe and trained them, and his men as well, keeping up their spirits in the Shackletonian way, and preparing a provision-stack lest the *Endurance* should be crushed. Winter was soon upon them, and although the ship was once or twice nearly crushed she withstood the pressure until long after midwinter's day, when more screwing and grinding caused the *Endurance* to lift and list and finally fall back into the water. By mid-October the ice pressure had increased seriously, until the *Endurance* listed nearly 30°. The end was not far off now, and late on October 26th the ship began to leak badly, and was finally crushed and annihilated. Shackleton preserved some extraordinary pictures of the last of the *Endurance*.

His foresight in making "Ocean Camp" on a very thick floe saved his crew. The floe was drifting north and the period of waiting was anxious. The ice was gradually breaking up, and when March arrived a swell was noticed. On the 23rd, Shackleton sighted Joinville Island, and on April 8th, 1916, he saw Elephant Island, and realised that he must make this land as best he might. So on Sunday, the 9th April, embarking the expedition in three boats, he started for what he hoped would be safety. His men behaved

ENDURANCE CRUSHED BY ICE
Shackleton's Antarctic Expedition, 1914-1916

ENDURANCE IN PRESSURE ICE
Shackleton's Antarctic Expedition, 1914-1916

magnificently, singing as they worked at the oars, among heaving and grinding floes. After adventures that fell nothing short of a miracle, a landing was made on Elephant Island by all three boats without losing a single man. The story of the party's hardships and sufferings is a terrible one, and the voyage of the whale boat *James Caird* with Worsley, Crean, McCarty, Vincent and McNish, with Shackleton in command, is the story of the finest boat journey on record. The men's sleeping-bags were soaked in icy salt-water, and watch and watch, three at a time, one steering and the other two baling, they lived through a legend. The ice-beset boat nearly sank with the weight of the frozen sea-water which encased it, and on 6th May the boat nearly met her end. A gigantic wave broke through the white-capped seas, the men found themselves in "a heaving chaos of tortured water ; but somehow the boat lived through it. . . We baled with the energy of men fighting for life . . . and after ten minutes of uncertainty, we felt the boat renew her life beneath us . . ." And so the story goes on until they mercifully reach South Georgia.

How this grand man Shackleton made contact with those modern Vikings, the whaling crews there, would take a great deal of space, but in the whaler, *Southern Sky*, he made his first attempt to relieve the Elephant Island party, failed, then tried again in the Uruguayan steam trawler *Instituto de Pesca* and this time also failed, then a third attempt in the little schooner *Emma* which likewise failed and finally a fourth and successful attempt was made in the Chilean Government steamer *Yelcho*. When the twenty-two men, so finely commanded by Frank Wild, were found all well after four and a half months' separation, the first words they uttered were not of joy at their rescue, but, "Thank God the boss is safe."

Having seen to the safety of the *Endurance* company in the Weddell Sea, Shackleton's immediate anxiety was to make sure of the safe return of the *Aurora*'s crew, which had also suffered disaster, for the ship had broken from her moorings in McMurdo Sound and drifted northward, while making her way back to New Zealand. However, she was repaired and overhauled. The ship again visited McMurdo Sound, embarked those left behind, and on February 9th, 1917, arrived back in New Zealand. The Trans-Antarctic journey was never made, but in spite of all that they went through, only three men were lost in the entire expedition.

Shackleton's last Antarctic enterprise was made in the *Quest*. I saw this ship in Iceland and sadly shook my head—she was no ship for the South Polar ice and in her Shackleton had sailed in 1920. Short of funds, he had been unable to obtain a stout enough ship for the voyage. This little sealer of only 125 tons was too lively for heavy seas and too slow to achieve much. Her engines gave trouble, the hull seemed wrong, and to me she looked like a floating coffin. She leaked badly but nevertheless managed to reach South Georgia and anchor at Grytviken on the 4th January, 1922, in the same place as the ill-fated *Endurance* had done. Before he turned in on the night of the 4th January, 1922, he wrote in his diary :

"At last, we came to anchor in Grytviken . . . A wonderful evening.
In the darkening twilight I saw a lone star hover
Gem-like above the bay."

and that was his last. He died that night, and when talking to the youth of our nation, I always quote those words he was so fond of :—

"Never for me the lowered banner,
Never the endeavour lost . . ."

MAWSON

DOUGLAS MAWSON was a Yorkshireman, born in Bradford, but since he had spent most of his life in Australia, that island continent has every right to claim him even though *he* has every right to count himself as a great British Polar explorer. Mawson differs from the seven *dii majores* of Polar exploration, in that he was a scientist, strong in character, in body and in mind. He typified all that is best in the Australian. He was a born leader.

He joined Shackleton's *Nimrod* expedition in 1907, as physicist, and as such compiled many of the most important scientific reports of that eminently successful expedition. Besides this, as one of Shackleton's surveyors, he made a detailed map of South Victoria Land between McMurdo Sound and Mount Nansen.

With Professor David of Sydney University, and Dr. Mackay, Mawson made an astounding sledge journey (commencing in the southern spring of 1908) over the sea ice, past the Drygalski Ice Tongue and on to Terra Nova Bay from which the party struck away up through the mountains to the inland plateau, and on, guided by their dip needle, until it stood vertical and showed that they had reached the Magnetic Pole, in 72° 25′ S., longitude 155° 16′ E., where they planted the Union Jack, and gave three cheers for the King. In that journey alone, Professor David and Douglas Mawson proved themselves worthy to rank with the foremost Polar explorers of all time. They travelled no less than 1,260 miles in 109 days' marching, with a load which was often greater than 230 lbs. per man. Mawson also accompanied Professor David in the notable climb to the summit of Mount Erebus, whose altitude they estimated from aneroid and hypsometer readings at 13,970 feet—indeed an exploit to be proud of.

Like other Antarctics who returned to their normal professional duties, Mawson soon felt the lure of little voices, that strange call that made John Masefield's seaman long for "a tall ship and a star to steer her by." That same call that makes the Far Eastern navigator's nostrils scent the pungent odours of the China Seas, just as it makes the P. and O. and Orient Line sailors' nostrils quiver for the eucalyptus-laden breeze from the Great Australian Bight, and, in the case of Antarctic venturers, makes them yearn for that curious hiss which they know so well, when the green heart sheathing rubs through the pack ice and tells them that they are once more in the realm of the Great Unknown. I sometimes feel this weird, yet not unattractive call, when things are at their easiest, and life is too full of pleasure. Franklin felt it, Hudson felt it, Crozier knew it too, Scott felt it, and Shackleton never could get right away from it. They all knew those little voices when their last hours of life were ebbing away in the Polar ice, and they felt so unmistakably the bleak wind from a Greater Atmosphere. And so Mawson sailed southward again; this time in command.

The first Australian Antarctic expedition was undertaken soon after Scott organised his last expedition. Mawson planned to work Adélie land and properly connect it with South Victoria Land, and alone of all South Polar explorers he achieved what he had set out for in its entirety. He took Captain John King Davis as his second-in-command, and Master of the seasoned whaler, *Aurora*. He also had with him Frank Wild, that tough little seaman, who even in civilised lands looked like an Elizabethan. He

WHALING STATION, SOUTH GEORGIA
Shackleton's Antarctic Expedition, 1914-1916

reminded me of Drake's men and Frobisher's men, and Chaucer's knights
and squires, as I have always pictured them. It may be mentioned that the
Aurora was so old that she had gone to the relief of the United States
General Greely's expedition in 1884. Mawson took with him in this 600-ton
weakly-powered veteran vessel forty-nine Greenland dogs as his principal
transport. He fitted his ship with wireless, and with this communicated
constantly with Australia via a W.T. station, which he established on Macquarie Island. He left Hobart on the 2nd December, 1911, a year after
Scott had sailed south in the *Terra Nova*, and was soon wallowing in a
Southern Ocean gale. After leaving Macquarie Island he was nearly three
weeks making Antarctica, then the *Aurora* encountered the ice. New land
appeared on January 2nd, and Mawson's men saw an iceberg which they
found to be covered with earth. Two days later a vertical wall of ice was
seen. It was found to be trending southwards and they followed in that
direction. This proved to be a low barrier attached to a new coast. The ice-
cliff rose to a height of 200 feet, and after encountering a typical blizzard
which obscured everything from view, a steep snow-clad promontory, rising
to 2,000 feet, was seen, and then Mawson's great geographical discoveries

commenced, from just within the Antarctic circle to the south of the D'Urville Sea. New bays and capes were charted at the beginning of 1912, and fairly shallow water, largely ice-free, permitted Mawson to set up his main base at Cape Denison in what he christened Commonwealth Bay. He was disappointed with the featureless nature of the new land, and although he gave his own modern name to what he discovered, it was by Mawson that the name of D'Urville Sea was given in honour of the French explorer who had first sighted Adélie Land, further to the westward, in the year 1840. Another base was set up under Frank Wild to the westward. Mawson was extremely fortunate in his choice of Hurley as his camera artist. Hurley and Ponting rank as the two great photographers and cinematographers of modern British Antarctic expeditions, and I shall never forget a day spent in company with these two men of genius, looking through their superb illustrations of the Great White South.

It fell to this distinguished Australian explorer, Mawson, to prove the non-existence of certain Antarctic lands that earlier explorers had placed on the very sketchy maps in the possession of the leading geographical societies of Europe and America, notably Sabrina Land and Côte Clarie. Mawson's maps show quite an archipelago, which includes the Mackellar Islands, the Way Islands, Stillwell, Close and Hodgeman Islets. It is considered that Mawson's men faced generally worse weather conditions than any previous expeditions to the South Polar regions. In Mawson's historic book, *The Home of the Blizzard*, storms are told of in which quite frequently the wind force exceeded one hundred miles an hour, and his huts were only prevented from being blown away because they were so deeply embedded in snow.

Mawson's Cape Denison party consisted of eighteen men, who built two huts, one to live in and the other to be used as a laboratory and workshop. Besides this, two magnetic huts and a transit house were constructed, and an engine and dynamo were installed. This expedition was remarkable for the heavy snowfall which had the advantage of protecting the huts. There is a delightful little harbour at Cape Denison, almost completely land-locked—one of the few pleasant features of the locality. Hurley, the photographer, made some clever photographs showing men leaning against the wind at incredible angles "the head being level with the hips," and although Scott and Shackleton both tell of terrible blizzards, their weather conditions were a great deal more comfortable than those experienced by Mawson. Mawson's sledge journey, with Mertz, a well-known mountaineer and ski-running champion of Switzerland, and Lieutenant Ninnis, is virtually an Antarctic saga. It may be called his Far Eastern journey, and covered 600 miles out and back. Mawson took seventeen dogs and 1,700 lbs. of equipment and supplies. Ascending the continental slope on a south-easterly course to a height of over 2,500 feet, Mawson discovered and helped map two huge glaciers, which he called after Mertz and Ninnis. One of

SIR JAMES CLARKE ROSS 1800-1892
Water colour by an unknown artist
By courtesy of the Royal Geographical Society

LOOKING NORTH IN McMURDO SOUND
Water colour by Dr. E. A. Wilson

his dogs was lost in a crevasse after four had already been killed, and he nearly lost one of his sledges, which hung in a crevasse but was skilfully recovered. The party had fearful weather, but pushed on intending if possible to sight Oates Land, which I had named after I succeeded Captain Scott in command of his last expedition. On December 14th, 1912, Ninnis fell with his sledge through a snow bridge into a yawning chasm, and was lost. What a tragedy—the tent had gone and Mawson and Mertz had nothing but a spare tent cover to protect them against the rigours of that awful climate. With the few dogs remaining and no food for them except old furs and scraps, the bereaved pair commenced a race against death and started homeward for Cape Denison. Coming back to an earlier camping ground where a spare sledge had been left, they made tent poles out of its runners, and with six starving dogs and a meagre supply of sledge rations and kerosene with which to cook dog-flesh and supplement their provisions, they continued towards their base. Mertz was badly frost-bitten, they were cold, and growing rapidly weaker. On January 7th Mertz became delirious, and had several fits. He was obviously dying, and although Mawson did everything possible Mertz passed away soon after midnight, leaving his gallant leader alone on the frozen waste. Mawson's outlook was wellnigh hopeless, and two days later he wrote "There is little chance of my reaching human aid alive." A blizzard held him up next day and another delayed him further. His feet were in shocking condition, but his strong will kept him going. After some awful falls into crevasses, which somehow he managed to get out of, his guardian angel guided him to a mound on which a bag of food had been placed by a search party which left news that the *Aurora* had returned, after the winter.

Had Mawson reached this point six hours earlier, he could have returned to Cape Denison in time to board the *Aurora*. As it was, after being delayed a week by a blizzard, he got back to Cape Denison just in time to see the ship sailing away! However, a small party was remaining at the hut with whom he faced the second winter. This party, which wintered a second time on the bleak coast of Adélie Land, consisted of seven, whose loneliness was enlivened at breakfast-time by wireless news, Mawson being the first British explorer to establish wireless in the Antarctic.

Mawson was fortunate in having Captain J. K. Davis in command of his expeditionary ship, for this well-known Antarctic navigator charted a great deal of new coast-line, sailed over the charted position of earlier explorers' land, found new territory which he named Wilkes Land, so named in honour of the American explorer who voyaged thereabouts in 1840, and on February 1st, 1912, in latitude 65° S. and longitude 116° E. he sounded in 927 fathoms, continuing to the westward. A gigantic ice-tongue was discovered and named "Termination Tongue" since its position lay in that assigned by Wilkes to his Termination Land. It was over a hundred miles out of sight of the nearest land.

On February 12th, Captain Davis made the important discovery of an open sea which now bears his name. New lands were found, and on February 13th, high snow-covered coast-line was observed and subsequently christened "Queen Mary Land." Near here, Wild's party were disembarked and their base established on the Shackleton ice-shelf 17 miles from the mainland. Wild had seven companions with whom he spent a somewhat uneventful winter.

In 1930 Mawson again visited Antarctica and completed his Polar plans by exploring in the vicinity of Enderby Land.

It may be said of Mawson's Expedition that it is credited most justly with having added more geographical and scientific discoveries than any previous Antarctic expedition ; but the work goes on and will go on. Gino Watkins in the North, Rymill and Ryder in the South, are type-specimens of what our British Commonwealth of Nations has to show in the youthful British Polar explorers of to-day. How finely, how worthily, they are upholding the traditions and the heritage handed down to them by those whose Homeric deeds I have done my best to portray.

BRITISH
MOUNTAINEERS

BY

F. S. SMYTHE

THE PIONEERS

NOWADAYS, mountain climbing is considered one of the world's most adventurous sports. It is both a stimulus and a test, a stimulus in that it enables men and women leading sedentary lives in cities, offices and factories to rejuvenate themselves through hard exercise in health-giving sun and air, a test because it brings out qualities of determination, leadership, strength, skill and endurance. Then, it brings its devotees into contact with Nature untamed and unspoiled, Nature at her grandest and most beautiful. It appeals particularly to Englishmen, who throughout the ages have inherited a love of adventure and the pioneering instinct that makes its accomplishment possible.

From the earliest times, mountains have been regarded as mysterious and aloof from the ordinary affairs of plain and city. Our ancestors looked upon them with awe and fear. Gods, devils, dragons, the spirits of the damned dwelt on their inaccessible summits ready to wreak vengeance on the rash intruder. They refused the plough, interposed barriers between peoples ; they were of no commercial value ; they were ugly.

Yet, as man slowly and painfully emancipated himself from his primeval fears and superstitions, a spirit of inquiry gained ascendancy. What was to be found on those terrible summits where the lightning played and the blizzard had its lair ? What did the world look like from icy heights where the clouds paused to repose themselves ? Every age has produced men ahead of their time in thought and deed ; poets, philosophers, scholars, scientists and explorers. So it was in mountaineering. Fearfully and cautiously, then with a greater daring, familiarity and understanding, a few bold spirits began to cross mountain ranges and climb mountains. At first this was usually for the sake of commercial enterprise or for military reasons. The Alpine passes were opened up for both purposes, from the time when Hannibal drove his elephants across them to the time when immense tunnels were driven to link Italy with France and Switzerland. Slowly the spirit of inquiry overcame a repugnance for mountains as useless, ugly and inconvenient excrescences and it began to be realised that they were beautiful also, and that to view them and adventure upon them was an inspiring experience. Religious considerations had something to do with this. Since Moses ascended Mount Sinai to receive the Ten Commandments, down to the present day, most of the world's religions have associated mountains with their mysticism, and this provoked a pantheism which has helped to influence man's feelings for the heights.

Englishmen were not only pioneers in the sport of mountaineering but they took a great part in the opening up of difficult mountainous countries. To them was due the crossing and exploration of the Rockies, settlements in the mountainous areas of New Zealand, the exploration of the Himalayas and many other regions. As with the sea and, more recently, the air, the mountains were in their blood. It is true that the spirit of adventure, and it must be added a zest for commerce, were greater in the first place than a liking for mountains ; Dr. Johnson's opinion of the Scottish Highlands was that "this uniformity of barrenness can afford very little amusement to the traveller." In Goldsmith's view, hills "interrupt every prospect." Two typical views were those of John Evelyn, the diarist, for whom the Simplon Pass consisted of "horrid and fearful craggs and tracts" ; and of Bishop Berkeley who, on the Mont Cenis Pass, was "put out of humour by the most horrible precipices," and considered that "every object that here presents itself is excessively miserable." It was left to poets such as Byron, Wordsworth and Shelley to perceive beauty in mountains, and to a few mountain-lovers such as Bourrit, Conrad Gesner, Simler and an enterprising Catholic priest, Father Placidus à Spescha, to want to climb mountains for their own sake as well as merely to view them.

In the eighteenth century, when the grand tour of Europe was becoming popular as an itinerary to be undertaken by every young man of wealth, erudition, and fashion, Chamonix was visited by an active young Englishman named Robert Windham together with his tutor, Dr. Pococke, and sundry of his friends. They engaged some guides and porters and scaled the steep pine forests to the Montanvert. Not content with this they ventured upon the Mer de Glace and were thus in all probability the first Englishmen to tread an Alpine glacier.

Forty-five years later, in 1786, Mont Blanc was scaled by Dr. Paccard and a chamois hunter Jacques Balmat, largely as a result of the enthusiasm

VIEW OF MONT FURKA WITH THE RHÔNE GLACIER
Water colour by William Pars, c.1770

THE LÜTSCHINEN ISSUING FROM THE LOWER GRINDELWALD GLACIER

Coloured aquatint by C. M. Descourtis after G. Wolf

of that great scientist De Saussure who, as early as 1760, considered that the mountain ought to be climbed, and subsequently offered a reward to anyone who could find a way to the summit. De Saussure himself scaled the mountain the following year, and was followed about a week later by Colonel Mark Beaufoy of the Tower Hamlets Militia. This last was the first great British ascent in the Alps and it was followed next year by that of Mr. Woodley : he was accompanied by Bourrit and a Dutchman named Camper, but was the sole member of the party to reach the summit.

After that, the ascent of Mont Blanc became something of a fashionable adventure, whilst ascents began to be made elsewhere in the Alps. Such ascents were largely exploratory and the majority of them were made for scientific reasons, as the time had not yet arrived when it was considered justifiable to climb mountains save in the cause of science. There were of course exceptions. The two summits of the Gross Glockner, the highest mountain in Austria, were scaled in 1799 and 1800 respectively by an Austrian party animated primarily by enthusiasm for the mountain, whilst there were numerous other ascents of an exploratory rather than scientific nature. On the whole, however, the opening up of the easier snow summits of the Alps had a scientific background and is associated with names such as Agassiz, Desor, De Saussure and Professor Forbes. The last named was a Scotsman, and although his interests were primarily scientific and he specialised in the study of glaciers, he was undoubtedly a mountaineer with a genuine love of mountains. He made various ascents including those of the Jungfrau and Riffelhorn, both of which mountains, however, had already been climbed. Of the latter peak an interesting story remains to be told. It was generally assumed to have been first climbed in 1841 by a party of English students. Thirty-three years later, some American tourists on the summit were engaged in the fascinating pastime of dislodging boulders and hurling them down the precipice on to the glacier below when they came upon a javelin or spear head. It would seem, therefore, that even if mountains were regarded with abhorrence throughout the Middle Ages there were times when primitive man ventured upon their summits.

After Forbes came John Ball, an indefatigable traveller and mountaineer who did much to popularise the Alps by compiling an Alpine guide-book ; he was Colonial Under-Secretary in Lord Palmerston's Administration. Another Englishman who drew public attention to the Alps, but in another way, was Albert Smith. He was a prototype of the young hiker, camper and mountaineer of to-day who, with limited means, spends a short but infinitely precious holiday in the hills. Thus far mountaineering had been, and was to be for many years, the almost exclusive preserve of eclectics, of Government officials, University dons and professional men generally, who with ample time and money at their disposal could afford long holidays in the Alps and the expense of guides. In 1838, Smith, then twenty-two years old, arrived at Chamonix with twelve pounds in his pocket. Instantly he fell under the spell of the mountains and was so anxious to make the ascent of Mont Blanc that he offered to go as porter for anyone who would take him. He failed in his ambition, but returned to the attack in 1851 with some Oxford undergraduates who were delighted to climb with him when they learned that he was "Mr. Smith of London, the well-known comic author." This time he succeeded, but the ascent provoked much undesirable publicity. In the course of an article, the *Daily News* wrote, "De Saussure's observations and reflections on Mont Blanc live in his poetical philosophy ; those of Mr. Albert Smith will be most appropriately recorded in a tissue of indifferent puns and stale fast witticisms, with an incessant straining after smartness. The aimless scramble of the four pedestrians to the top of Mont Blanc . . . will not go far to redeem the somewhat equivocal reputation of the herd of English tourists in Switzerland for a mindless and rather vulgar redundance of animal spirits."

But Albert Smith remained unabashed. He was by nature a born showman, and such are impervious to criticism and abuse. He wrote an interesting and entertaining book about Mont Blanc and, constructing a model of the mountain, set out to describe it and his experiences to all and sundry. His *Mont Blanc in a Box* show was a popular success and, however much it may have been scorned by the eclectics, undoubtedly did much to bring the beauty and interest of the Alps to the public attention.

"Per Nives Sempiternas Rupesque Tremendas"
Engraving from *Peaks, Passes and Glaciers*,
Volume I, edited by John Ball, 1859

THE GOLDEN AGE

IT is not improbable that Albert Smith's popular Alpine entertainment had something to do with the development of the sport of mountaineering, as distinct from the scientific-cum-exploration and dare-devil adventure attitude that prevailed from 1786 almost to the middle of the nineteenth century. Edward Whymper, who was later to write the most dramatic of all chapters in the history of the sport, recorded in his diary that he witnessed it as a youth, and so too must many others of the pioneers. Albert Smith's enthusiasm was too great and his showmanship too expert not to leave a mark.

Precisely how or why mountaineering took on a new lease of life as a pure sport is not easy to say. It is generally assumed that Mr. Justice Wills's ascent of the Wetterhorn in 1854 ushered it in in this guise. Dates, however, are apt to be misleading, and while this ascent undoubtedly helped to set a new fashion, its importance has been over-estimated. Furthermore, this ascent, still assumed by many to have been the first of that mountain, was actually only the fourth. It did, however, mark the beginning of an epoch, for the ensuing ten years saw the conquest of practically all the great peaks of the Alps. These conquests were almost all of them made by Englishmen and their guides, and it was they who developed the craft, the technique and the skill necessary to overcome peaks far more difficult than any hitherto assailed ; they who by persuasion and example raised from rude Alpine peasantry a *corps d'élite* of guides, and improved the former rough-and-ready implements of mountaineering to suit the new and more exacting conditions of mountain craft. In a word, Englishmen were responsible for the great sport of mountaineering.

I have written of this sport that it was a new fashion. So it was, in a limited sense, but never had the followers of any fashion, not even those who sought notoriety by descending Niagara in barrels, to endure such obloquy as the dons, schoolmasters and parsons who set out to scale the untrodden peaks of the Alps. The revolution, for revolution it was, must be examined against the tendencies of the age. It was an age of peace but never of stagnation, an age in which the arts and sciences flourished apace, an age which had the potentialities for setting in motion something far better than the wheels of a materialism, which for the past half-century have raised dust clouds to choke and obscure the spiritual vision of man. It was as though some vision had been dimly discerned : the vision of the mountains ; and, lo, they were beautiful ; and more than being beautiful, they inspired a contest of a new nature, a friendly contest that had in it no jarring element, no bloodlust, that exercised every muscle, that lit every corner of the mind with beauty, that made for enduring friendships. All these things the pioneers perceived in mountain climbing and much else besides. They were content to have discovered something that was not merely new, a phase, a fashion, but something enduring like the snowy heights that would provide enjoyment and inspiration for generations unborn. Mountains were no longer ugly and terrifying. An aspect of Nature had been discovered, or re-discovered, it matters not which ; the adventurous instinct of Englishmen had found a new outlet, something to off-set the steady days of peace and prosperity. The ascent of the Wetterhorn signposted a way already visible.

In his book, *Wanderings Among the High Alps*, Wills gives a dramatic account of the ascent :

"Suddenly, a startling cry of surprise and triumph rang through the air. A great block of ice bounded from the top of the parapet, and before it had well lighted on the glacier, Lauener exclaimed, 'Ich schaue den blauen himmel !' (I see blue sky). A thrill of astonishment and delight ran through our frames. Our enterprise had succeeded ! We were almost upon the actual summit. That wave above us, frozen, as it seemed, in the act of falling over ! Lauener's blows flew with redoubled energy. In a few minutes a practicable breach was made, through which he disappeared. . . . As I took the last step, Balmat disappeared from my sight ; my left shoulder grazed against the angle of the icy embrasure, while, on the right, the glacier fell abruptly away beneath me, towards an unknown and awful abyss ; a hand from an invisible person grasped mine ; I stepped across, and had passed the ridge of the Wetterhorn !"

Such accounts did much to instil enthusiasm in the minds of adventurous young Englishmen.

The great snow peaks were the first to be ascended, for they were the easiest to climb, and the art of rock climbing was not developed until the advent of the English. Thus the several peaks of Monte Rosa fell over a period of thirty-eight years. Dr. Parrot, a Russian, who made the first ascent of Ararat, scaled the Parrot Spitze (14,643 feet) in 1817, but it was not until 1855 that the highest and rockiest point of the mountain (15,217 feet) was ascended by five Englishmen, the brothers G. and C. Smyth, the Rev. Charles Hudson, Birkbeck and Stephenson.

While Albert Smith was busy lecturing and, incidentally, amassing a fortune of thirty thousand pounds, a growing band of young Englishmen were engaged in tackling the more difficult among the great Alpine peaks. Apart from those already mentioned, were E. S. Kennedy, T. W. Hinchliff, William and B. St. J. Mathews, F. Vaughan Hawkins, William Longman,

PROFESSOR J. D. FORBES AND E. S. KENNEDY
Engravings by H. G. Willink and Edward Whymper

the Rev. J. Llewellyn Davies, the Rev. J. F. Hardy and several others. Many of them were accustomed to meet at one or other of the Alpine centres such as Zermatt, Grindelwald and Chamonix, and on their return home liked to discuss their experiences and make new plans for the future. It was in this way that the first of all mountaineering clubs, the Alpine Club, came to be formed in 1854. The first President was Kennedy, and there certainly was never a more active or enterprising club, for it was between 1854 and 1865 that its members climbed the great majority of the more difficult peaks of the Alps. At first the members met in Hinchliff's rooms but the club presently acquired premises of its own, together with an indefatigable editor in John Ball, who collected the narratives of members into the first of a series of books known to climbers the world over as *Peaks, Passes, and Glaciers*. A little later, a club publication, *The Alpine Journal*, was regularly produced, by means of which knowledge of mountains and mountaineering, together with kindred arts and sciences, was disseminated.

In Britain, at least, the surest method of arousing enthusiasm in a new sport is the formation of an enterprising club. It was not long before the Alpine Club attracted members—men such as Professor John Tyndall, a noted scientist of the Victorian era ; Sir Leslie Stephen, the foremost literary critic of his time, and many others, including a young wood-engraver named Edward Whymper. It is also interesting to note that Albert Smith was an original member, and this in a club in which professional qualifications, as well as purely mountaineering qualifications, were by no means overlooked.

For many years mountaineering, as already indicated, appealed for the most part to the leisured and professional classes. Every season little coteries of climbers were to be found at Zermatt, Grindelwald and other centres.

Guides were employed, not because the climbers were necessarily incompetent to climb without them, but because the rigid Victorian standards of "gentlemanliness" demanded that the hard manual labour of load-carrying and step-cutting should be undertaken by professionals. At the same time, there were many guides who were something more than carriers and pointers-out of paths, men who readily learned to recognise practicable routes and who, by virtue of lifelong residence among mountains, grew to be expert craftsmen in the art of mountaineering. The rough, uncouth peasant soon became expert in the new technique, and trust, confidence and affection were established between him and his employer. Nowadays, when guiding as a business is rapidly becoming extinct, it is customary for some to sneer at the pioneers and to attribute their successes to the work of their guides. Such, however, was by no means the case. More often than not, the amateur was responsible, not only for the attempt on a new peak, but for the discovery of the route, and the guide's work was limited to step-cutting and leading up rocks.

The tourist who nowadays engages guides to climb the Matterhorn is shepherded up and down that mountain. The guide, who knows every foot of the way, is virtually master of the situation. In the Golden Age of mountaineering the amateur was ultimately responsible for all vital decisions.

Yet it was not to be supposed that the adventurous and independent spirit responsible for the development of this new sport of mountaineering should always be content to seek professional help. Many mountaineers are agreed that the most enterprising and brilliant climber of his time was the Rev. Charles Hudson who, as already noted, was associated with the Smyth brothers in the first ascent of the highest point of Monte Rosa. In 1853, at the age of twenty-five, he made, in defiance of all orthodox procedure, repeated attempts in the month of March to climb the Aiguille du Goûter of Mont Blanc, finally ascending alone almost to the summit and reconnoitring a new route up Mont Blanc. Two years later, he made guideless ascents of the Klein Matterhorn and the Breithorn, then, returning to the Chamonix district with his friends Ainslie, Kennedy and the Smyths, made the first guideless ascent of Mont Blanc, and at the same time opened up a new route to the summit from St. Gervais. During the next ten years he made a number of other first-rate ascents, including the first ascent of Mont Blanc over the Bosses du Dromédaire, the route now followed in preference to the Ancien Passage, the first complete passage of the Mönchjoch in the Bernese Oberland and the second ascent of the Aiguille Verte by a new route. Not only was he a self-reliant and skilful climber, but an expert route-finder into the bargain, with the eye for mountain topography of a born mountaineer. Thus, unlike Edward Whymper, who by the end of 1864 had made seven attempts to climb the Matterhorn, he was quick to seize upon the east face of that mountain as the most practicable route to the

MR. ALBERT SMITH'S 'ASCENT OF MONT BLANC'
The Egyptian Hall, Piccadilly, December, 1852

summit. His association with Whymper in the ultimate conquest of the peak, and his tragic death during the descent, will be told in the next chapter. In the public eye, Whymper more than anyone was the conqueror of the Matterhorn, but the fact is that Hudson's share in that conquest was in some respects greater than Whymper's; had he lived, he would have gone down to mountaineering posterity as the mountaineer *par excellence* of the Golden Age.

To mention all the British climbers of the 'fifties and 'sixties would be to catalogue a long list of names, but there are certain figures which cannot be omitted even from this brief account. Foremost among scientist-mountaineers was Professor Tyndall. As with Professor Forbes, science came first, but science was also a convenient peg on which to hang a love of mountain adventure, and his first ascent of the Zermatt Weisshorn and attempts on the Matterhorn were sporting ascents in which science, however much the mutations of the air, the structure of the glaciers and rocks, and the "atmospheric thrust" may have occupied his attention, was relegated to a relatively unimportant place. Then there was Professor Bonney, another scientist, who made many pioneer ascents, and crossed innumerable passes particularly in the then little-known French Alps; John Ball, who, as already mentioned, contributed much to a topographical knowledge of the Alps, in

117

particular the Eastern Alps and Dolomites, and the "irrepressible" F. F. Tuckett whose expeditions occupy no less than fifteen pages in the Alpine Club register ; indeed this great mountaineer and traveller really deserves a book to himself. Then there were the Walker brothers, the Birkbecks, the Rev. H. B. George, F. C. Grove, E. S. Kennedy who made a number of fine guideless expeditions, the three Mathews brothers, A. W. Moore, A. M. W. Adams Reilly who made many fine ascents in the course of his surveys, and numerous others.

After *Scrambles Amongst the Alps*, by Edward Whymper, a book which was later to attract universal attention and inspire countless young men to climb mountains, the most attractive volume dealing with ascents in the Golden Age is *The Playground of Europe*, by Sir Leslie Stephen. This "fleetest of foot of the Alpine Brotherhood" brought a critical and discerning eye to the problems of mountaineering and to read his accounts of the first crossings of the Jungfraujoch and Eigerjoch is to capture something of the spirit of the age. He climbed mountains solely for fun and relaxation and, as a result, his writings make better reading than the dry academic accounts of those who sought to conceal their love of mountains and mountain climbing beneath the vestments of science. Indeed he amused himself at the expense of Professor Tyndall when he wrote, apropos of the first ascent of the Zinal Rothorn, ". . . the temperature was approximately (I had no thermometer) 212° (Fahrenheit) below freezing-point. As for ozone, if any existed in the atmosphere, it was a greater fool than I take it for."

Like all the pioneers, and indeed like most Englishmen of action, Stephen was mortally afraid of allowing his pen to stray into a sentimental morass. It was one thing to love mountains and to discover inspiration upon them but quite another to endeavour to define or interpret that love. Like a love letter read in a law court, it became vulgar, even immoral, when exposed to the public eye. From the beginnings of mountaineering it has been left to the poets who, alas, with one or two exceptions were all non-mountaineers, to attempt to reveal the beauty of high places. This is not to say that mountaineering has not produced good literature. That it appealed to men of academic distinction ensured that it should receive its due. A good criterion of the worth of any sport is the literature it produces and, measured against the quality of its narratives, mountaineering is easily first of all sports. The story was good and it was well told, but like the best champagne it was very dry. Its limitations were imposed by the sheer inability of ordinary men to translate into intelligible language the immemorial call of the hills. And so we must be content to discern the Golden Age through books such as *Peaks, Passes and Glaciers*, of which a later mountaineer wrote that it was "so inspiring a gospel of adventure and full, free life, that the call summoned to the hills an army of seekers after the promised gold." In this way was the mystic call of Nature, so long the preserve of a few writers and poets, manifested through a new sport to ordinary men.

By courtesy of the Trustees of the British Museum

TWO STAGES IN THE ASCENT OF MONT BLANC
Colour prints by George Baxter, 1804-1867

VIEW OF BREIT-LAUWINEN

Coloured aquatint by C. M. Descourtis after G. Wolf

THE FIGHT FOR THE MATTERHORN

ONE summer's day in 1860, a youth aged twenty tramped up the stony mule-track along the St. Nicholas Thal to Zermatt. His name was Edward Whymper and he was apprenticed to his father's business of wood-block engraving. Already he had shown considerable artistic talent and William Longman, of the well-known publishing house of that name, had commissioned him to visit the Alps and make a series of sketches for a forthcoming publication.

A mile from Zermatt he turned a corner and the soaring peak of the Matterhorn came suddenly into view. Strangely enough this youth, aflame as he already was with the zest for mountain climbing, was not impressed. In his diary he wrote, "Saw of course the Matterhorn repeatedly ; what precious stuff Ruskin has written about this, as well as about other things. When one has a fair view of the mountain as I had, it may be compared to a sugar-loaf set up on a table ; the sugar-loaf should have its head knocked on one side. Grand it is, but beautiful I think it is not."

At Zermatt he was warmly welcomed as a recruit for mountaineering by the climbers assembled there, Leslie Stephen, Walker, Hinchliff and others, and the last named offered to coach him on the Riffelberg, an offer that was gratefully accepted. On this, his first Alpine season, he attempted no high or difficult ascents but he did a prodigious amount of walking and crossed several passes of moderate altitude, on one of which he was deserted by his guide, a circumstance which prejudiced him against guides : he had yet to learn that the skilled Alpine guide was of an altogether different calibre to the peasant who escorted tourists over easy passes.

The following year he returned to the Alps and, accompanied by R. J. S. Macdonald and a Frenchman, Jean Reynaud, made the first English ascent of Mont Pelvoux in Dauphiny ; a climb which gained for him entry into the Alpine Club the same year. Having thus whetted his taste for mountain adventure he began to look for more ambitious projects. The two finest peaks then unclimbed were the Weisshorn and the Matterhorn and, after an unsuccessful attempt to climb Monte Viso and a visit to the Mont Cenis tunnel in the construction of which he was keenly interested, he made for Breuil on the Italian side of the Matterhorn. He arrived there a few days after Professor Tyndall had made an unsuccessful attempt on the mountain, having already succeeded with his guide J. J. Bennen in climbing the Weisshorn. Whymper accordingly decided to lay siege to the Matterhorn and, undeterred by its local reputation for inaccessibility, sought out and engaged a guide. The latter proved little more efficient than his guide of the previous summer and, when the first real difficulty was encountered at 12,650 feet, declined to go on. This reverse had no other effect on the tough young Englishman than to make him more than ever determined to climb the mountain, which he believed to be accessible over the broken Italian ridge, and in 1863 he returned to the attack accompanied by Macdonald and two Zermatt guides. The weather was bad and an icy storm enveloped them above the Col du Lion. It was Whymper's first experience of a hurricane in the High Alps. He wrote, "We clutched our hardest when we saw stones as big as a man's fist blow away horizontally into space. We dared not attempt to stand upright, and remained stationary on all fours, glued, as it were, to the rocks." It was too much for the faint-hearted guides and they refused to return for another attempt.

Whymper was undaunted. This second reverse merely brought out his granite qualities. He was more than ever determined to succeed. Thus far he had had bad luck with guides, but a new figure now came on the scene. Jean-Antoine Carrel, the "Old Soldier" of Breuil, believed like Whymper that the Matterhorn could be climbed. Furthermore, he was determined to make the first ascent for the honour of Breuil and of Italy. He and his brother had already attempted it and, as a result, he considered the mountain as "a kind of preserve." He now condescended to allow Whymper to engage him as his guide.

This time the party advanced beyond their previous highest point, to a height of 12,992 feet at the foot of a huge rock pinnacle in the ridge known as the Great Tower, some 240 feet beneath the point attained by the Carrels the previous year. But once again bad weather supervened and enforced a precipitate retreat.

Macdonald then had to return to England. Whymper, left to his own devices, sought to engage Carrel but the latter could not, or would not, accompany him. So he went alone. It was a risky business, but to climb the Matterhorn had now become an obsession. His boldness and skill were rewarded when he reached a height of 13,400 feet, only 1,400 feet from the summit, but on the descent he narrowly escaped total disaster. He had

PROFESSOR TYNDALL
Drawing by George Richmond, 1864

passed the difficulties when, on rounding a corner, he slipped and fell nearly 200 feet down a steep gully. He managed to stop himself on the brink of a precipice and scramble up to a safe place before fainting away from loss of blood.

Most men would have been content to let well alone. Not so Whymper. A few days later, having recovered from his wounds, he set out for the fifth time, accompanied by the Carrels and Luc Meynet, a little hunchback who had already acted as porter, but again a sudden storm enforced retreat after a height of 13,150 feet had been reached.

123

Once again the haughty Carrel refused to accompany him, so he set out on a sixth attempt accompanied only by the hunchback. He reached a point a little above his previous highest but the steepness of the rocks and the weakness of the party made retreat obligatory. He arrived back at Breuil only to find that Professor Tyndall had arrived with his guides for another attempt on the mountain. At first Tyndall invited Whymper to join his party, but a little later rescinded the invitation, apparently on the advice of his guide Bennen who probably regarded Whymper as an irresponsible young hot-head, a circumstance that led to a bitter dissension between Tyndall and Whymper. Thus Whymper had the mortification of seeing the party start off without him, but had the somewhat vicarious satisfaction of pouring coals of fire on Tyndall's head by loaning him his tent which had been left on the mountain. Long and earnestly and tormented, as he writes, "with envy and all uncharitableness," he watched the mountain next day. At one time there was a report of "men on the summit," but in the evening he saw the party returning. "There was no spring in their steps—they, too, were defeated."

Between his attempts on the Matterhorn, Whymper made many other fine ascents including the Ecrins and various cols in Dauphiny, ascents in the range of Mont Blanc with Adams Reilly, the first passage of the very difficult Col Dolent which ranks to-day as one of the stiffest ice climbs in the Alps, the first ascent of the Aiguille Verte and various ascents in the Zermatt district. During most of these climbs he was accompanied by Michel Croz of Chamonix and it was from him, and also from Christian Almer of Grindelwald, that he learned the worth of a great guide. For both these men were great ; Croz was a man of verve, fire and titanic energy ; Almer tempered dash with caution, a man of superlatively good judgment. It was an admirable combination. The pity of it is that the Matterhorn was not assaulted earlier by this formidable trio.

The drama of the Matterhorn had in it all the elements of a Greek tragedy. Frustration, disappointment, mischance, all contributed to the final denouement. In 1864, Whymper had to hurry back to England just after he had arrived at Zermatt with Adams Reilly, having traversed the difficult and dangerous Moming pass, when everything was set for an attempt on the Matterhorn. Whether or not this would have been made by the east face is not certain but, had this route been attempted by this strong and competent party, there is little doubt that success would have been gained.

The 1865 season was a good one. Whymper was now beginning to realise that the east face of the Matterhorn was easier than it looked. Yet Croz and Almer were against it. In the end it was agreed to attempt one further possibility before investigating it. This was a great gully leading to a point high on the Furggen ridge of the mountain. It was an absurd route and showers of falling stones sent the party back in hasty retreat. The guides

ZERMATT
Water colour by John Ruskin

were discouraged ; they believed the Matterhorn to be impossible ; but Whymper was still undaunted, and proposed that instead of descending to Breuil they should straight away attempt the east face. It was necessary to cross the Furggjoch in order to reach the Hörnli at the foot of the face, but the pass proved more difficult than usual. As they stood there undecided, snow began to fall and in response to the entreaties of his guides Whymper was forced to return to Breuil.

After this, he climbed on the range of Mont Blanc and in the course of eighteen days ascended more than 100,000 feet of mountain-sides, many of them previously untrodden, a *tour de force* which stands unique in the annals of mountaineering.

But the Matterhorn was ever a lodestone and soon he returned to it. Unfortunately, Croz was unable to accompany him, having arranged the previous winter (on not hearing from Whymper until it was too late) to climb with Birkbeck, whilst Almer, when he heard of yet another proposed attempt, declared emphatically, "Anything but the Matterhorn, dear sir ! Anything but the Matterhorn." Thus Whymper reluctantly dismissed him at Breuil together with his other guide, Biener, who was even more emphatic

J   125

in his detestation of the mountain, and sought to engage Carrel. The latter was against leaving his beloved Italian ridge and attempting the Swiss side and it was eventually agreed that, in the event of failure on the east face, the Italian ridge should be again attacked.

On the evening of July 8th, when Whymper had completed his preparations for the east face, a messenger arrived at Breuil to say that an Englishman was lying seriously ill at Valtournanche. It was a call Whymper was unable to refuse, and he at once hastened down the valley. On the way he met an Italian with his baggage, accompanied by the two Carrels. Whymper told J. A. Carrel to remain at Breuil, and reminded him of his promise to accompany him over the Théodule Pass the same night. Carrel replied by saying that he had been engaged by a "family of distinction" and was not free to work for Whymper after the 11th.

Having walked down to Châtillon to procure medicine for the sick man, Whymper returned to Breuil on the 10th. The weather was bad next day and he was forced to remain idle. On the morning of the 11th he learned to his consternation that a large party of mountaineers, including Carrel, had set off for the Matterhorn. The "family of distinction" had been none other than Signor Giordano, a geologist and mountaineer, who was acting on behalf of Signor Sella, another Italian mountaineer. Whymper was furious ; he had been "tricked and bamboozled." But all was not yet lost. If he could only get to Zermatt over the Théodule Pass he might be able to engage guides and still make his attempt on the east face. But how ? There were no guides or mules available to accompany him. At this point Lord Francis Douglas arrived with his guide, young Peter Taugwalder. He had already made a fine ascent of the Ober Gabelhorn by a new route and on the strength of this Whymper suggested that they should join forces in an attack on the east face. Douglas agreed, and the combined party hastily crossed the Théodule to Zermatt where they engaged old Peter Taugwalder, the father of their present guide ; and then there arrived at Zermatt the Rev. Charles Hudson, together with his protégé, D. R. Hadow, a youth of nineteen, and Michel Croz who had been engaged by Hudson when Birkbeck had fallen ill. They, too, were intent on attempting the Matterhorn and, as it seemed to Whymper undesirable that there should be two parties on the same route at the same time, he suggested an amalgamation. Hudson agreed, and in response to Whymper's inquiry as to the capabilities of Hadow, replied that he, Hadow, had done Mont Blanc in less time than most men. This was true, but anyone sound in wind and limb can climb Mont Blanc, whereas a rock peak like the Matterhorn is an entirely different proposition. Hadow was totally unfitted to be in the party, and his inclusion was the prime cause of the disaster that followed. A secondary, but by no means unimportant cause was the large size of the party. The blame for the catastrophe that followed must be apportioned equally between Whymper and Hudson.

The party left Zermatt on July 13th, and proceeded over the Hörnli to

THE SUMMIT OF THE MATTERHORN
Engraving by Edward Whymper from the *Ascent of the Matterhorn*, 1880

the foot of the east face. They bivouacked at a height of 11,000 feet and, after a comfortable night, commenced the ascent. To his astonishment, Whymper found the rocks much easier than he had anticipated. Indeed the face was a fraud, and places that had appeared utterly impracticable when viewed from the Riffel were so easy that no rope was necessary for the greater part of the way. Making rapid progress they reached the point where a vertical cliff bars further progress over the face. To avoid this they bore to the right over a shoulder on to the upper part of the north face. Here the climbing was considerably more difficult for the rocks were slabby. (Fixed ropes now assist the climber over this section.) Hadow needed continual assistance, but all went well and at length the slope eased off. Here Whymper, who had been in a fever of impatience throughout the ascent, in case he were forestalled by Carrel and his party, dashed

127

ahead with Croz to the summit. The snow was untrodden. But there was another and equally high summit. Together with Croz he hastened there. Suddenly he saw the Italians, mere specks far down their ridge. They were retreating ; their attempt had failed. With shouts of triumph Whymper and Croz prized away boulders with their ice-axes and sent them hurtling down the precipice.

Whymper had won, but his triumph was shortlived. For an hour the party remained on the summit basking in the sun and enjoying the marvellous panorama. Then they tied on the rope ready for the descent. Here a fatal mistake occurred. There were three ropes. Two were strong and one weak. It was intended to fix the weak one to the rocks in order to facilitate the descent of the difficult section. Instead, although there was more than enough strong rope for the whole party, the weak rope was used between Lord Francis Douglas and old Peter Taugwalder. This was subsequently to lead to much acrimonious controversy and scandalous assertion. Even Whymper went so far as to suggest that the substitution was effected by old Peter out of self-interest, and the poor old man was virtually hounded out of his native village and forced to reside abroad. Yet the responsibility, if any, was not his but Whymper's and Hudson's, while Croz, as leading guide, should have overseen the roping. It is better to regard the whole affair as an oversight, carelessness arising out of the natural elation of success and the desire to be down and off the mountain as quickly as possible. In any event, there were now two weak links in the chain, Hadow and the rope. The combination proved fatal.

The party were on the slabs. They were going slowly, one by one, and moving with the utmost circumspection. It was particularly trying work for Hadow, and Croz, who was first man down (as most experienced guide he should have been last), was taking hold of his feet and placing them on the small holds. Croz was moving down a step himself, and had laid aside his ice-axe the better to assist Hadow, when suddenly the latter slipped. Croz was caught quite unprepared. Hadow's feet struck him in the small of the back and knocked him from his holds. The two men fell. Hudson who was next on the rope was unable to resist the shock and was pulled from his steps and Lord Francis Douglas was similarly dragged down. The remaining three, the Taugwalders and Whymper, when they heard Croz's startled exclamation braced themselves as well as they could. Old Peter was moderately well placed and hugged a rock with his arms. The strain came. They held, but the weak rope between Lord Francis Douglas and old Peter Taugwalder snapped in mid air. The four falling climbers were beyond aid. For a few seconds Whymper and his companions endured the terrible spectacle of seeing them sliding down the slabs, spreading out their arms in vain endeavours to save themselves. Then they disappeared and fell down the great precipices of the north face on to the Matterhorn glacier four thousand feet beneath.

The descent of the three survivors was a nightmare. The Taugwalders were utterly unnerved, and momently Whymper expected another accident. At length, however, they reached the shoulder and began the descent of the easier east face. Here they were benighted but after a wretched bivouac were able to reach Zermatt next day.

In this way ended the most momentous and dramatic chapter in mountaineering history. The repercussions were many. The Press united in denouncing mountaineering as an absurd, foolish and unjustifiable sport, and so general was the condemnation that Queen Victoria was moved to inquire whether it could not be stopped by law. In the opinion of one great Alpine historian, Captain J. P. Farrar, the accident held back the tide of mountaineering for half a generation of man. Be this as it may, the check was only temporary. Whymper never again undertook great pioneer climbs in the Alps, even if he did in the Andes, and it is doubtful whether he ever really recovered from the disaster and the disagreeable publicity that followed upon it. Yet mountaineering had come to stay and British climbers were to take part in many another great pioneer climb both in the Alps and elsewhere.

"Croz ! Croz ! Come Here !"
Engraving by Edward Whymper from *Scrambles Amongst the Alps*, 1871

THE GROWTH OF MOUNTAINEERING

UNDOUBTEDLY the Matterhorn disaster had grave effects on British mountaineering, yet, if during the years immediately following 1865 there were few recruits to the sport, the Alpine Club continued its activities undismayed by public criticism and ridicule ; in doing so it acted in the best traditions of British sport. In the years following upon it there were numerous ascents : Mont Collon, one of the Pennine giants, was climbed by G. E. Foster in 1867 and the highest point of the Grandes Jorasses on the range of Mont Blanc fell to Horace Walker in 1868, Whymper having already climbed the secondary summit in 1865.

The 'seventies saw not only a marked revival of mountaineering but the advent of one of the most indefatigable British climbers that has ever trodden a mountain. This was the Rev. W. A. B. Coolidge, who in the company of Miss Brevoort made many ascents, particularly in the wild Dauphiny region. Coolidge was animated not only by a love of mountaineering but was interested in its history, and became its leading historian as well as a writer of guide-books remarkable for the exactness and accuracy of their information. There can have been few more dogmatic and forceful clerics. It is said that he quarrelled with practically every member of the Alpine Club, and his quarrels more than once resulted in his resignation from the Club, for mountaineers take themselves, their sport, their opinions, and their veracity very seriously. His most famous quarrel was with Edward Whymper, whose account of a jump during the first traverse of the Ecrins in 1864 he questioned in the course of his obituary notice of Christian Almer, and the Alpine firmament vibrated to the thunder of the doughty and self-opinionated contestants. Coolidge's greatest ascent was that of the Meije in Dauphiny, one of the finest and most difficult peaks in the Alps. Others of his Dauphiny ascents included the Grande Ruine, the Pic Coolidge, Les Bans, and the southern Aiguille d'Arves. Coolidge survived well into the age of modern mountaineering and was well known as the "Lion of Grindelwald," at which place he resided for many years.

If the technique of snow and ice craft was scarcely capable of advancement, except in the study of snow and glacier conditions, rock climbing offered promise of ever increasing skill and daring. The greatest rock climb made during the Golden Age was undoubtedly that of Carrel's party, who succeeded in reaching the summit of the Matterhorn via the Italian ridge, and a most sensational traverse across the west face of the mountain by what is now known as Carrel's Gallerie, but it was not until the 'seventies that this specialised form of mountain craft took on a new lease of life. Among its exponents were Dr. Güssfeldt, who was without question the greatest Continental mountaineer of the day, de Castelnau and Duhamel, not to mention Coolidge who by his ascent of the Meije may almost be said to have inaugurated it.

THE GRANDES JORASSES AND THE DOIRE TORRENT, VAL FERRET
Engraving by Edward Whymper from *Scrambles Amongst the Alps*, 1871

An even more specialised form of rock climbing developed with the ascents of the granite slabs, cracks and chimneys of the Chamonix Aiguilles (needles) and the rough vertical precipices of the Dolomites. Some who read this will have visited Chamonix and ascended to the Montanvert. They will remember the clustered Gothic-like spires of the Aiguilles grouped before the serene snow dome of Mont Blanc, and in particular the terrific peak of the Dru. To the unitiated this last looks hopelessly impracticable, but its highest point was reached by Messrs. C. T. Dent and Hartley as long ago as 1878, an ascent that stimulated the equally difficult ascent of the second peak in 1879 by a Chamonix guide named Charlet. Thus was the fashion set for a new and even more exacting form of climbing.

131

The 'eighties and 'nineties might almost be described as the Silver Age of British mountaineering. They saw the ascent of the highest point of the tooth-like Aiguille du Géant by W. W. Graham, who was later to make some great pioneer ascents in the Himalayas to heights up to 24,000 feet, and the ascent of the Aiguille Blanche de Péteret, one of the buttressing peaks of Mont Blanc, perhaps the most formidable mountain in the Alps, by Sir H. S. King. But prince among rock climbers, and the prototype of the modern rock climber and mountaineer, was A. F. Mummery. It has been said that he was blackballed for the Alpine Club because of his guide-less climbing, and that when he sought election a second time Coolidge, who was not so conservative as some of his elderly confrères, quietly slipped some of the "no's" from the ballot box into the "aye's." Be this as it may, Mummery's example, and not least his fresh and joyous style of writing as exemplified in his classic *My Climbs in the Alps and Caucasus*, exercised a profound influence on mountaineering. If the old boiling-point thermometer and geological notebook excuse for mountain climbing still prevailed in certain quarters, Mummery killed it stone-dead. He climbed simply and solely for the fun of the thing. The thinnest, most elegant, most difficult of the Chamonix pinnacles were grist to his mill, and to his doughty guides Alexander Burgener and Venetz. The Aiguile des Grands Charmoz fell in 1880, and the following year saw him poised on the top block of the now world-famous Grépon, after the hardest rock climb that had ever been accomplished up cracks and slabs that even to-day scarcely constitute "an easy day for a lady" contrary to Mummery's own optimistic speculations, though ladies nowadays do far harder climbs than that. Mummery was not one ever meekly to follow behind guides, and in the company of his friends Professor Norman Collie, Geoffrey Hastings and W. C. Slingsby, who earned for himself a great name as the pioneer of Norwegian mountaineer-ing, he made the first ascent of the Dent du Requin, another formidable needle on the range of Mont Blanc. He was, however, no mere rock gymnast as his attempt on the north ice wall of the Aiguille du Plan and the first crossing of the fearsome Col du Lion between the Matterhorn and the Tête du Lion testifies, for these are ice climbs of extreme severity, whilst the first ascent of the Matterhorn by the Zmutt ridge was first and foremost a great mountaineering achievement. It is a curious circumstance that of the early explorers of this last-mentioned route nearly all of them died violent deaths within a few years. Among them was Burgener, one of the strongest and finest guides the Alps have known, who was killed by an avalanche near the Bergli hut in the Bernese Oberland. It is probable that Mummery died in the same way. In 1895 he visited the Himalayas, accom-panied by Professor Collie and the late Brigadier-General the Hon. C. G. Bruce, to attempt the ascent of the 26,660-foot peak of Nanga Parbat. After one determined attempt he set out with two Gurkha orderlies to cross a high glacier pass and if possible make another. He was never seen again,

By courtesy of the Trustees of the British Museum

THE GLACIER DES BOSSONS, CHAMONIX
Water colour by John ('Warwick') Smith, 1786

THE MER DE GLACE OR GLACIER DES BOIS

THE PASS OF LLANBERIS, WALES
Engraving from John Ball's *Peaks, Passes and Glaciers*, 1859

and it is presumed that the party was overwhelmed by an ice avalanche. Perhaps the fairies believed to dwell there took him to themselves. The name Mummery still pervades mountaineering. Long after many famous names are forgotten simple natives will point upwards to the shining snows of Nanga Parbat and say, "There Mummery Sahib lies." Who could wish for a better epitaph or a grander resting place?

Nanga Parbat has since been attempted by a German-American expedition and three German expeditions. Two met with disaster from storm and avalanche, and it would seem that it had little use for Hitler and the swastika. The mountain became a sort of preserve for Germans and it is well, therefore, to remember Mummery and his Gurkhas. When Mr. Eric Shipton and I proposed making an attempt I received indignant letters from Germany. It was, according to my correspondents, unsporting of us to try ; the mountain was Germany's. British mountaineers do not look on mountaineering in this way. If they have been the only ones to attempt Mount Everest it was because the Tibetan Government categorically refused permission for any but a British expedition. Perhaps with their Oriental insight and love of peace, as well as veneration for their holy mountains, they realised what an infiltration of Nazi gospellers would mean.

The growth of mountaineering has ever been animated by the desire to explore, the longing to tread where no human foot has trodden before. In its beginnings the quest was for new peaks, but when the peaks were climbed the pioneering instinct devolved into a search for new routes, a search that has perforce developed of recent years into attempts to master the all but impossible. Side by side with the later developments of Alpine mountaineering the technique of rock climbing, and even of snow and ice work on a limited scale, was developed on the British hills. This was all to the good.

It prepared men and women for the more difficult and complicated art of Alpine climbing. They learned self-reliance on the hills in all manner of weather, they gained an eye for mountain country and learned above all to climb rocks of extreme difficulty safely and confidently. There is no space here for the story of British rock climbing ; it is a history in itself. It is associated with many great names such as Mr. W. P. Haskett Smith, J. M. Archer Thompson, the Abraham brothers and Owen Glyn Jones who was killed on the Dent Blanche in 1899. To-day, climbing in Wales, the Lake District and Scotland, where Alpine conditions are to be found in late winter and spring, especially on the north face of Ben Nevis, and where climbs as fine and long as some of those on the Chamonix Aiguilles may be enjoyed on the gabbro of the Coolins in Skye, is a fine art, so much so that the rubber-shoes expert, accustomed to spend hours in negotiating a cliff of super severity, finds himself at a disadvantage when called upon to climb a great Alpine peak where speed over ground of moderate difficulty is the first essential. Then the British rocks afford those of limited means or too short a holiday for the Alps with the keenest form of concentrated enjoyment. Literature, as already indicated, has had much to do with the popularising of mountaineering. Several books have already been mentioned. There were many others, whilst in recent years a steady stream has developed into a spate.

If the Alps are now the "Playground of Europe" the Dominions still afford scope for the same pioneering instinct that distinguished the Golden Age of Alpine climbing. The great peaks of the Rockies, such as Mount Robson and Mount Assiniboine, the complicated ridges of the Selkirks, and the wild tangle of peaks of the Coast Range of British Columbia, have yielded up their secrets to Canadian, American and British mountaineers. In New Zealand, Mount Cook was first of all climbed and then traversed by a route that ranks in difficulty and interest with any of the greater climbs on the south side of Mont Blanc, and the New Zealand Alpine Club, like the Canadian Alpine Club, has been indefatigable in opening up one of the wildest and loveliest regions of the world. Yet, it is perhaps in the Himalayas that British mountaineering has attracted most attention of recent years ; this will be dealt with in the next chapter. The Golden Age of climbing and exploration will last longer here than in the Alps. It will not be ten years ; it may well extend over ten generations.

Finally, British mountaineers have introduced their sport to many other lands, to the Andes of South America where the names of Conway, Whymper and Fitzgerald will ever be remembered ; to Japan, where it has a huge following thanks to the enthusiasm of the late Rev. Walter Weston ; to the Caucasus of which men such as Freshfield, Mummery and Donkin were the pioneers ; to Norway where the late William Cecil Slingsby is recognised as the Father of Norwegian mountaineering ; and to many other odd corners of the earth.

A CAMP IN THE HIMALAYAS
Lithograph after a drawing by Capt. Sir E. P. Campbell, Bt.

THE HIMALAYAS: MOUNT EVEREST

AFTER the Alps, the story of Himalayan climbing is the most interesting and in many respects the most dramatic in the history of mountaineering. When it is remembered how enormously mountaineering skill and technique has advanced of recent years and how, thanks to science and invention, equipment has improved, it must be a source of wonder to many that out of the fifty or sixty summits in the Himalayas exceeding 25,000 feet only two, Nanda Devi and Kamet, have so far been reached, whilst Mount Everest, Kangchenjunga, K.2, and Nanga Parbat remain inviolate despite the best endeavours of the pick of British, American, German, Austrian and French mountaineers. Yet to anyone who has climbed amidst these two thousand miles of mountains with their innumerable summits exceeding 20,000 feet, it is not difficult to understand. Many of the lesser peaks have been ascended, some of them fifty and more years ago, but above 25,000 feet new factors come into operation. Roughly, there are three main difficulties in high Himalayan climbing ; the difficulty of the mountain, and the Himalayas being geologically young are steeper than the more weathered Alps, the altitude, and the weather.

The first difficulty is purely technical, but it interacts with the second. A place that to surmount in the Alps merely requires a simple arm-pull may well prove impossible at 26,000 feet because of the lack of energy-giving oxygen. Men have reached 28,000 feet without any artificial aid. Therefore it is known that every summit bar, possibly, Everest, is physiologically accessible, and it is probable that Everest also can be reached. To a large extent the body adapts itself to the lack of oxygen at high altitudes, which adaptation is gained by the climber who climbs slowly, stage by stage. At the same time, above 21,000 to 23,000 feet a deterioration of physique takes place, leading to a rapid loss of weight and appetite, to sleeplessness and a reduction of physical and nervous stamina ; so that in the words of Mr. Eric Shipton a mountaineer high on Everest is like "a sick man climbing in a dream." The third difficulty, the weather, is the greatest difficulty of all, and in almost every case of failure on a great Himalayan peak, storm and blizzard, or an unusually early onset of the monsoon, has been primarily responsible.

High Himalayan mountaineering is therefore a most complex problem in which many different factors have to dovetail into one another like a jig-saw puzzle before success can be achieved.

As in the case of Alpine mountaineering the early visitors to the Himalayas were mostly travellers, geographers and scientists. In this connection names such as Godwin-Austen, the discoverer of K.2, the Schlagintweit brothers, Sir Joseph Hooker and Sir Francis Younghusband will be remembered.

Then came the explorer-mountaineer, Lord Conway, the Duke of the Abruzzi, the Bullock Workmans, General Bruce, W. W. Graham (who was, however, more of a mountaineer than anything else), Dr. E. Neve, Dr. A. M. Kellas, Dr. T. G. Longstaff, whose ascent of Trisul, 23,406 feet, in 1907, remained the highest for more than twenty years, D. W. Freshfield, and C. F. Meade. It was not until after the Great War that mountaineers began to devote their energies specifically to the ascent of one or other of the great peaks.

Climbing Everest or any other of the highest peaks of the Himalayas is a very different affair from climbing a peak in the Alps. The latter takes no longer than two or, at the most, three days ; the former may take several months, and is akin to a rush for the Pole in its concentrated hardships, difficulties, dangers and discomforts. Its motif is achievement, rather than pleasure, though there is always pleasure in achievement. To enjoy Himalayan mountaineering aesthetically one should keep below the 25,000-foot level and tackle peaks of moderate altitude where the fight is against the mountain rather than against your own incapacities in the thin, cold air at greater altitudes.

Everest stands on the frontiers of Nepal and Tibet, both countries normally closed to Europeans, and it was not until 1920 that the Dalai Lama, the ruler of Tibet, gave permission for British climbers to visit Mount Everest. The expedition that went next year was primarily a reconnaissance,

JUMNOTREE, THE SOURCE OF THE RIVER JUMNA
Drawn by J. B. Fraser and engraved by R. Havell & Son

and its principal climber, George Leigh-Mallory, discovered what appeared to be a possible route up the mountain, and reached a height of 23,000 feet on the North Col, which lies between Everest and the neighbouring North Peak. Yet it would be foolish to limit an Everest party merely to climbers

139

THE MOUNT EVEREST EXPEDITION, 1938
Camp 6, showing the East Rongbuk Glacier

when so much valuable scientific work can be accomplished, and succeeding expeditions, with the exception of the 1938 expedition, tackled Everest with the knowledge that, even though they failed to climb the mountain, they would bring back valuable physiological, geological, topographical, botanical, zoological and ethnological data, in this way justifying the expenses of the expedition.

In 1922 Capt. G. I. Finch and Major Bruce reached a height of over 27,000 feet aided by oxygen apparatus, whilst another party, consisting of Mallory, Dr. T. H. Somervell and General E. F. Norton, got to nearly 27,000 feet without using oxygen apparatus. A little later the monsoon broke and the warmer airs and snowfalls which it brought rendered the slopes of the North Col so dangerous that when an attempt was made to re-open Camp Four an avalanche occurred and seven of the native porters were swept over an ice cliff and killed.

In 1924 a third expedition made a determined attempt to reach the summit. Terrible weather and temperatures more than 20° below zero Fahrenheit were experienced, and this, combined with the lack of oxygen, which is as much the fuel of the human body as petrol is of a motor car, drove the party down to the base camp. They returned, and eventually Norton and Somervell established a camp at 26,800 feet and from it made

THE MOUNT EVEREST EXPEDITION, 1938
Camp 6, showing the slabs and the North-East Ridge

an attempt on the summit. At 28,000 feet Somervell was unable to continue because of a frostbitten and congested throat due to rapid breathing in the intensely cold dry air. Norton struggled on alone for another hundred feet before exhaustion compelled him to retreat also. Had it not been for the terrible hammering they had already endured from the weather on the East Rongbuk glacier and the North Col it is probable that they would have succeeded.

A few days later Mallory and the youthful Andrew Irvine set out to make another attempt, this time using oxygen apparatus. N. E. Odell, who was splendidly acclimatised and should by virtue of his greater mountaineering experience have accompanied Mallory in place of the comparatively inexperienced Irvine, followed the party a day behind them to collect geological specimens. On the day they left the highest camp to make their attempt on the summit he saw them "going strong" along the broken crest of the northeast ridge. It was only a fragmentary glimpse between swirling mists and it was the last ever seen of them, for they failed to return. In Mallory, Everest lost its most formidable opponent and mountaineering one of its most brilliant figures. Of him Norton wrote, "It was the spirit of the man that made him the great mountaineer he was : a fire burnt in him and caused his willing spirit to rise superior to the weakness of the flesh." He was indeed "a knight 'sans peur et sans reproche' amongst mountaineers."

Not until 1933 was there another Everest expedition. This experienced terrible weather and was repeatedly driven back from the slopes of the North Col by blizzards ; then by even worse weather from Camp Five at 25,700 feet, where some of the porters were badly frostbitten. If the porters had thrown in their hand they could hardly have been blamed, but the Sherpas from the Sola Khombu valley in Nepal and the Bhotias from Tibet are much more than porters. They are adventurers ; they are astoundingly tough ; they are natural mountaineers capable of withstanding cold and hardship ; they are cheerful, brave, and intensely loyal. When the final chapter of Everest comes to be written their names and accomplishments deserve to be inscribed in letters of gold. But the porters were not only willing but anxious to return to the attack. "We will pitch a camp higher than any camp has been pitched before. Then it is up to the sahibs to finish the job." Such was their spirit. They did.

Camp Six was pitched at 27,400 feet, and from it two attempts were launched on the summit, firstly by P. Wyn Harris and Lawrence Wager, and secondly by Eric Shipton and myself. Both failed at 28,100 feet, the height reached by Norton in 1924. Once again the weather supervened and by covering the smooth outward-shelving slabs in powdery snow rendered the ascent impossible. During the course of their attempt Wyn Harris and Wager discovered an ice-axe which can only have belonged to either Mallory or Irvine. It is thought that one of them slipped. The other put down his axe the better to hold the rope in both hands and check the fall of

WEDGE PEAK
One of the peaks of the Kangchenjunga group

his sliding companion. He failed to do so and the ice-axe was left there, sole testimony of the disaster.

Since 1933 there have been two more attempts and one reconnaissance, but cruel luck dogged the footsteps of the climbers, for exceptionally early monsoons prevented them from getting as high as the 1924 or 1933 expeditions. The 1938 expedition struggled up to over 27,000 feet but found it impossible to tread the roof-like slabs leading towards the final pyramid owing to quantities of soft and unstable new snow.

That Everest can be climbed there is no doubt, and probably without the aid of oxygen apparatus which although ideal in theory has been found difficult to adapt practically to the steep and difficult work near the summit, owing to its weight, clumsiness and the limited amount of gas that can be carried by the climber. Turning to other aspects of Himalayan mountaineering, the small British expedition that I organised in 1931 was successful in climbing the first of the twenty-five-thousanders, Kamet, 25,443 feet. In 1936 another British expedition went one better by climbing Nanda Devi, 25,660 feet, the highest peak in British-administered territory, whilst it is interesting to note that a Polish expedition succeeded in climbing the lower but very difficult east peak of the same mountain in 1939. Meanwhile the Germans were busy in attempts on Kangchenjunga and Nanga Parbat. Those on Kangchenjunga were marked by exceptional skill under the leadership of Paul Bauer and were carried out with great energy and determination in the face of extreme technical difficulty. The same cannot be said of Nanga Parbat. It is obligatory on Himalayan climbers to safeguard their lines of communication so that in the event of bad weather the party can retreat to well-stocked camps. This the Germans failed to do and, instead of getting the two fittest climbers to the highest camp well supported from lower camps, as is the usual procedure on Everest, a large group of them collected there together with their porters. Then the weather broke. The tents, evidently of poor fabric, failed to withstand the tearing force of the wind, and they were forced to retreat in the storm. The retreat developed into one of the greatest catastrophes in mountaineering, and the great majority of the party died of cold, hunger and exposure. An even worse disaster occurred in 1937 when a party pitched a camp within range of ice avalanches and were overwhelmed in the night, sixteen Germans and porters perishing.

The foregoing sketches but briefly some of the major features of Himalayan mountaineering. Much other less spectacular but very good work has been done, and it cannot be too emphatically stated that the Himalayas afford the mountaineer of modest means with a splendid field for exploration and climbing together with one or other of the branches of science. There are innumerable peaks round about 20,000 feet of a difficulty sufficient to test the most skilful of Alpine-trained experts, and it is on such peaks that the sport of mountain climbing is best discovered in the Himalayas.

144

A PERSONAL ADVENTURE

I am now going to tell you about a personal experience which happened to me in Switzerland—in the Bernese Oberland. One day in July, 1925, a friend, Mr. J. H. B. Bell, and I left Grindelwald and walked up to the Strahlegg hut, one of the refuges built for climbers. We intended to climb the Schreckhorn, the most formidable peak in the district. Incidentally, Schreckhorn means Terror Peak; it is an appropriate name as I have good cause to remember. After a couple of nights at the hut we climbed the mountain over its difficult south-west ridge. The weather was perfect, so much so that we went on to traverse the neighbouring peak of the Lauteraarhorn. It was a longish day and took us nineteen hours. The Schreckhorn certainly failed to live up to its reputation then, and I remember with something more than ordinary pleasure our long scrambles over its rough firm rocks.

After that, Bell and I planned another climb, but in reconnoitring it Bell damaged his foot and we were unable to start off for it. Meanwhile, two other climbers, Messrs. A. Harrison and C. M. K. Douglas, had arrived at the Strahlegg hut intending to climb the Schreckhorn, and it occurred to me that they would enjoy the ascent over the south-west ridge, the route Bell and I had taken, much better than the ordinary easier route. So I asked them if they would care to join forces. They were agreeable ; thus for a second time I found myself setting off to climb the Schreckhorn.

Dawn was just breaking as we walked over the little Schreck glacier towards the mountain. It was a very queer dawn, one of the most extraordinary I have ever seen in the mountains. The sky overhead was clear but in the south great banks of oily clouds were piled up in heaven ; but they were a long way off and seemed powerless to harm us. What was queer about that dawn was its colour. The earth and the atmosphere were pervaded with a green tinge and when the sun rose it poured not its usual red glow on the mountain tops, but the same unearthly green, a green the

145

colour of the light emitted by an X-ray tube. None of us had seen anything like it before and we didn't know what to make of it. However, the sky around remained clear and we saw no particular reason for abandoning the climb and returning to the hut. So we carried on, and presently the green colour vanished in the full flood of the risen sun and everything seemed to promise fair weather and an enjoyable scramble.

In order to reach the crest of the south-west ridge we had to climb a wide gully about twelve hundred feet high. It was not an easy job getting into the gully because the foot of it was defended by a *bergschrund*, which is simply a large crevasse separating the foot of a mountainside from the glacier at the base of it. Fortunately at one place there was a tongue of snow bridging the rift and we were able to crawl gingerly across one by one, each of us held by his two companions on the rope. Above the *bergschrund* was a steep ice slope. Up this we cut steps with our ice-axes and presently found ourselves well in the gully. Here the going was easier up slabby rocks and patches of well-frozen snow and we made rapid progress. At the same time it was not a place to take liberties with and I dare say would have seemed a horrible place to anyone who wasn't a mountaineer.

At seven o'clock we emerged from the gully on to the rocky crest of the south-west ridge, and had only to clamber along it to reach the summit, which was now full in view, another twelve hundred feet or so above us.

But before going on we stopped for a bite of breakfast. As we ate we had a good look at the weather. It was much the same as before. The sky overhead was clear and the sun was shining brightly whilst in the south the same oily masses of cloud were poised over the distant Rhône valley and the ranges of the Pennine Alps. There seemed no immediate prospect of it breaking, and even if it did we told ourselves that we would be over the summit and down the mountain by the ordinary way without trouble. So once more we decided to carry on. The south-west ridge of the Schreckhorn is very steep and sharp but it is also very firm, and made of a rough, reddish-coloured schistose. It was a sheer delight to climb. Here and there were difficult bits, vertical walls, over which we had to move one at a time, but for the most part we could climb all together. So engrossed were we with the climbing that we never gave another thought as to the weather, and in warm sunlight scrambled up and up towards the sharp summit of the mountain which every minute loomed nearer and nearer.

We were about five hundred feet from the top when, of a sudden, we heard a long-drawn peal of thunder. We paused and looked round. A few minutes before the north-west sky had been clear, but now it was choked by a great wall of inky black cloud. It was an extraordinary formation, clear-cut and level like the crest of an ocean roller, and it extended across the whole width of the sky in that direction. It did not take us more than a few moments to realise that this cloud was moving towards us and moving with amazing rapidity. Every second the thunder boomed louder and louder until its peals were merged into a continuous din. It was exactly as though some devastating artillery barrage was creeping in our direction.

Between us and the approaching storm stood the peak of the Eiger and we saw the clouds engulf it and vicious tongues of lightning stab and flicker all over it. There was no time to retreat ; we must find what shelter we could. In any event it was essential to get off the knife-like crest of the ridge on which we stood as it would soon be a target for the lightning.

It is often difficult or impossible to descend from the crest of an Alpine ridge, but luck was with us. Twenty feet lower was a ledge partially sheltered by an overhanging bulge of rock above. We were able to climb down to it and there we sat in a row with our legs dangling over the precipice. As it seemed to us that the steel heads of our ice-axes might attract the lightning we left the axes lying on a patch of snow near the crest of the ridge.

We had not long to wait for the storm. We heard the furious bombardment of the elements as they expended some of their fury on the Eiger. Then the sun suddenly disappeared behind a whirling smother of mist and the storm was upon us. The Schreckhorn is a sharp isolated peak and it received the full blast of the electrical energy locked up in the thunderclouds. There was a sudden blinding flash of mauve fire and a simultaneous explosion, not the crackle and roll one usually associates with a thunderstorm, but a sharp violent explosion like a bomb. Then came another flash and another and another. Then the heavens opened to release a deluge of hailstones, a curtain so dense that in a matter of seconds the mountain was white with racing cascades. Through the hail the lightning burst in blue flames and the mountain seemed to shake and shudder to the explosions of thunder. How near it was striking I cannot say, but it cannot have been more than a few yards distant because the thunder seemed simultaneous with the lightning. Suddenly there was a flame that seemed to scorch our very eyebrows and fill the air with darting streams of blue fire. There was a crack like a colossal whip, then a crash, and a mass of rock split off from the crest of the ridge by the lightning hurtled past us and plunged down the precipice. For a moment we wondered whether we were still alive, but we had little time to wonder about that or anything else for the flames and explosions were deafening and stunning in their frequency and force. I do remember, however, that in one brief lull Harrison remarked imperturbably, "Well, I came though the whole war in the Suicide Club (which as you may remember was the name given to the Machine Gun Corps) and was several times the only officer left alive, so we ought to get through this all right."

Meanwhile the hail had changed to snow and this fell so fast that the rocks were soon covered two or three inches deep. Things began to look pretty unpleasant, but just when we were wondering how we were going to get down again the storm suddenly eased off, the thunder and lightning ceased as though by magic, and the sun peered out. We clambered back to the ridge where to our relief we found our ice-axes uninjured; more than once we had wondered whether they would have been destroyed by the lightning. The question now was whether to go on or go back. If we went on we should have to climb five hundred feet over snow-covered rocks but should get an easier route down. If we went back by the way we had come the going would certainly be difficult with so much new snow on the rocks. On the other hand, supposing another storm developed, to be caught on or near the top of the Schreckhorn was not to be thought of for a moment. We decided to retreat by the way we had come. It was a providential decision. Had we not made it I should not have lived to tell the story.

The slushy snow concealing the handholds and footholds made the climbing difficult and our descent correspondingly slow. We were not far from the point where we had to leave the ridge and descend the twelve-hundred-foot gully when again we heard the ominous and horrid booming of thunder. We made every effort to get off the crest of the ridge into the gully but quick as we were the storm was quicker still. As we reached the head of the gully and turned away from the ridge into it the storm was upon us like a tiger, an even worse storm than the first if that were possible, a hurricane of wind, hail and snow and appalling nerve-shattering lightning. The topmost part of the gully consisted of smooth rock slabs and now that these were covered in snow climbing was none too easy. Harrison and Douglas were below moving cautiously step by step whilst I was above them in the responsible post of last man down. I was a few feet below the crest of the ridge and was feeling a bit more confident now that I was not on that lightning-blasted crest. But something, Providence again if you like, made me decide to halt and put the rope round a projecting rock until my friends were in a safer position. I had only just done this when I received a tremendous blow on the head, just as though I had been sandbagged. At the same moment I have a dim recollection of blinding blue fire and a terrific concussion. For a second or two there was blackout, then I woke up to find myself off my holds and hanging on the rope. Had I not placed the rope round the projecting rock I must have fallen and pulled Harrison and Douglas with me to destruction. Amid the general inferno of wind, blizzard, and crashing thunder they were unaware of what had happened and were still moving down. I shouted to them, "I've been struck," and they paused. Then I made my way slowly and painfully down to them. I was trembling all over and it was only with the greatest difficulty that I could control my limbs.

Providence had not finished its intervention in our favour. We had to halt a few minutes to give me time to recover. A little later, a fall of rock, doubtless dislodged by lightning from higher up the mountain, fell into the gully a short distance beneath us and swept it from end to end. Had it not been for the delay due to my being struck by lightning we must have been right in its path and been wiped off the slate.

THE SCHRECKHORN FROM THE GRINDELWALD GLACIER
Sketch by E. T. Coleman from *Peaks. Passes and Glaciers*
Volume II, edited by E. S. Kennedy, 1862

But our troubles were by no means at an end ; indeed the worst was to come. The storm developed to a pitch of ferocity such as I have never experienced before or since in the Alps. The wind reached a hurricane. Worse still, the temperature fell and the slush and water that had melted during the brief interval of fine weather between the storms froze on the rocks in sheets of ice. It was a case of hacking away with our ice-axes and of groping with our hands for the holds. Our progress got slower and slower. Frequently we were unable to move at all, and for minutes at a time had to cling on as best we could while the blizzard raged at us, beating us with snow until our clothing and faces were sheeted with ice and we could barely see out of our eyes. I shall never forget the sound of the wind. The lightning was still striking the ridge to one side of the gully ; we could see its streams of fire, yet the wind rivalled the crash of the thunder. Sometimes its approaching gusts made a noise like an express train in a tunnel; sometimes they tore up the gully with a terrible, tearing, rending sound, sometimes they burst upon us with a roar like thunder. So thick was the writhing, wind-tortured snow that frequently we could not see one another, and one man would step down on the head of another, whilst the rope became so encased in ice as to be almost unmanageable.

It could not go on. In four hours we had descended only about 700 feet, little more than half the gully. The wind and the cold were doing their work.

Our hands had lost feeling, our bodies were getting colder and colder. The fight could not go on much longer. Presently there would be collapse, a slip and—finish.

It was then that Providence came to our aid for the fourth time that day. The snow-clouds swept aside, the wind dropped. It was a miracle. Somebody said, "What about some chocolate ?" It had been impossible to eat before. Now it was possible ; that chocolate put life-giving warmth and energy into our bodies. The dead feeling left them and we were able to go on moving even if very slowly. The storm returned but not with the same force as before. We could keep on going. It took six hours to descend that twelve-hundred-foot gully but we did it at last. Our steps in the ice slope below had been blotted out by the blizzard, but we were able to cut a new staircase. We could not find the snow bridge over the crevasse but we found a place we could jump. So at last we reached the glacier, and our difficulties were over. There we shook hands ; we had not expected to get down ; it was a gesture of thankfulness. For my part I could not wish for two more stout-hearted companions than Harrison and Douglas.

We paused to gaze up at the snow-wreathed crags of the Schreckhorn and to listen to the wild orchestra of the storm still raging among them. Then, very tired, we trudged down to the longed-for warmth and shelter of the Strahlegg hut.

THE VALLEY OF THE JUMNA SHOWING THE TWO GRAND PEAKS OF BUNDER PUNCH
Drawn by J. B. Fraser, engraved by R. Havell & Son, from Fraser's *Himalayas*, 1820

BEN NEVIS

Water colour by William Turner of Oxford

MODERN MOUNTAINEERING

BY the end of the last century all the major peaks of the Alps had been climbed, many of them by several routes, and mountaineering in Europe was sharpening its skill in a search for more and more difficult routes. During the present century the search has become greatly intensified, so that it is now possible to say that climbing has reached the limit of human power and skill and that to overstep it merely entails the employment of extraneous aids. The most significant development has been the increase in guideless climbing. Here again it is interesting to note British mountaineers took the principal pioneering part. Some of the climbs of Hudson and Kennedy have already been mentioned. Then there was Girdlestone who wrote *The High Alps Without Guides*, the first volume on guideless climbing, which was however greeted with disapproval by his contemporaries of the Alpine Club who had come to regard the guide as a *sine qua non* of respectable mountaineering. But with the passing of the eclectic age and the popularising of mountaineering, guideless climbing became an inevitable and logical development of the sport, because not only did it make mountaineering possible for the would-be climber with limited funds but it catered for the independent and adventurous instinct of young men. The old days when the guide was no more certain than his employer that a peak could be climbed had passed ; routes were well known and the guides who climbed them did so almost to a time-table. To-day the craft of guiding is a rapidly dying business put out of action by its own superlative efficiency. The fact is that it is far, far better fun to climb without guides, and if guiding is to persist its principal functions can only be training those who want to learn the mountain craft and conducting tourists up fashionable peaks such as the Matterhorn and Mont Blanc. Failing such employment it is safe to say that guiding will be virtually extinct before another generation has passed.

The first fourteen years of the twentieth century were good years for British mountaineering. They saw such mountaineers as Messrs. Raeburn and Ling, Hope and Kirkpatrick, H. O. Jones, Captain Percy Farrar who represented all that was best in British mountaineering, Mr. R. L. G. Irving who incurred the censure of the Alpine Club by taking his pupils up mountains without guides, but whose justification was the production of George Mallory and several other fine mountaineers who added greatly to the credit of the sport. Then there was Mr. G. Winthrop Young (the present President of the Alpine Club), the doyen of modern British mountaineering, and the greatest of its poets, who by precept and example exercised a profound influence upon it.

Yet thus far, that is up to 1914, mountain craft progressed gracefully and rhythmically, reflecting as it were the settled and slowly progressive policies of the age. The Great War divided mountaineering into two distinct streams. It is indeed interesting, in view of the recent conflict, to examine briefly the development of the sport in this light.

The well-being of any great sport depends on the traditions of good sportsmanship established by generations of good sportsmen. Mountaineering is no exception. It has had its rivalries and jealousies, what sport has not ? but until the past twenty years it has been singularly free from any taint of nationalism. Mountaineers of all nations were concerned to climb for the fun of climbing, and even the fight for the Matterhorn hinged on personal rivalry and ambition, and Whymper's imputation that Carrel was anxious to climb the mountain for the honour of his native valley and of Italy was probably more of a dramatic touch than anything else. Of late years the cheap and sensational Press has made much of the Everest expeditions from a national standpoint, but the climbers themselves would be the first to refute a charge of nationalism ; they have tried to climb Everest simply because they wanted to climb it and for no other reason. After the last war, however, a different spirit began to manifest itself on the Continent. Germany had been beaten, and the Germans are a proud people ; it was necessary above all things that they should rehabilitate themselves in the eyes of the world. They must be not only good sportsmen but the *best* sportsmen, better than the sportsmen of any other nation. This infection, founded as it was on a sense of grievance and inferiority, manifested itself in every international sports gathering in which Germans took part ; it was particularly marked at the Olympic Games, it impinged with brutal force on the fair sport of ski-ing ; with the advent of Hitlerism it spread to mountaineering. I became first cognisant of it during the International Kangchenjunga Expedition of 1930 when every member was issued with a flag which he was expected to keep flying over his tent. It was the ambition of the Germans to plant their flags on the top of each mountain. The emblem issued to me was a Union Jack with the stripes the wrong way round, made in Germany. Running short of pocket handkerchiefs on one occasion I used it as a substitute to the horror of my German companions. Possibly, indeed, the alleged decay of democracy dates from this. It was this flag-waving inferiority complex, for it was nothing else, that led the Germans into their desperate assaults on jealously "preserved" mountains and into equally desperate assaults in the Alps on mountain-sides that no sane mountaineer with any responsibilities would have embarked upon. It led also to the new, and, in the opinion of British climbers, undesirable technique of scaling otherwise impossible rock faces by means of pitons (iron spikes). One may admire the courage of the performers but scarcely the spirit animating the performance. As in other field sports the merit of mountain climbing lies in the simple and direct contact of the sportsman with the terrain. It lies also in knowing where to draw the line. An ice-axe, nailed boots and crampons may be accounted necessary implements in the craft of mountaineering, but to hammer a way up precipices by means of scores of

IN THE GARHWAL HIMALAYAS, 1937
Camp at 20,000 feet on the Mana Peak

spikes and nails is outside the customs and traditions of the sport. The fisherman is not only concerned with the number of fish he catches; if he were he would employ dynamite. The Germans of the Third Reich preferred dynamite. Except in the increase of guideless climbing and the use of rubber shoes on the extremely difficult routes now undertaken on the British crags there is essentially no difference in the spirit in which climbs are now made by British mountaineers than that existing seventy-five years ago. It may be expedient to climb Mount Everest with oxygen apparatus, but speaking personally I would prefer to fail on that mountain without oxygen rather than to climb it with oxygen, for to my mind the whole charm of mountaineering lies in the employment of skill and energy with the minimum of artificial aid. It is the climbing, not the getting up that matters most in mountaineering.

It is to be hoped that from now on the sportsmen of the world will realise that it is the sport alone that counts and that future international contests will help to promote the best, not bring out the worst in men, for it is only thus that the sportsman can truthfully say, "it was worth while."

BRITISH SEAMEN

BY

DAVID MATHEW

1588

THE Spanish Armada marked the first real threat of the invasion of England by a great army and a naval force since the Norman Conquest. The Royal Navy had not hitherto been called upon to meet a serious challenge. It seems right to begin therefore with the game of bowls—Sir Francis Drake on the Hoe at Plymouth above that unchanging harbour with the steep fields sinking into Cawsand Bay and southwards beyond the Sound the swell breaking on the Eddystone. The detail of that game and Drake's reply is traditional and not improbable ; it dates back to 1624, the story of Captain Fleming of the *Golden Hind* reporting that the Spaniards were off the Lizard. "There is time for that and to beat the Spaniards after."

The commanders of the Fleet were composed, to put it roughly, of privateersmen, who had but little conception of a royal navy, and of military officers, for the most part courtiers, who were ready to defend the Queen's Highness whether on land or on sea. It is not too much to say that the future of the Navy was born from the strategic insight of Francis Drake. He was in many ways the perfect Elizabethan of tradition, short with a ruddy beard, utterly self-confident, quick to suspect enmity, a man of the boldest courses and courageous phrasing. He had a quick pictorial imagination. "The wind commands me away. Our ship is under sail." And then come his sayings on the King of Spain. "He is allied with mighty Princes and Dukes in the Straits." "Prepare in England strongly, and most by sea. Stop him now and stop him ever."

Now about forty-eight, Drake was at the height of his powers. In the previous year he had destroyed the Spanish ships in Cadiz harbour, thus developing the conception of seeking out and destroying the main naval forces of the enemy. Seven years earlier he had completed the voyage of circumnavigation which had brought him so much fame. It was back in 1567 that he had sailed with his cousin Hawkins on the ill-fated expedition to San Juan de Ulloa. Since then he had racked the Spanish Main ; the capture of the silver caravan by Nombre de Dios ; the burning of Portobello ; the haul at Venta Cruz ; the ravaging of Cartagena.

His announcements were like the call of the trumpeters before his cabin in the *Golden Hind*. "Divers huge ships loaden, burnt 32, sank a great argosy." Drake had a proved ascendancy over the men who sailed with him. He was never slow to quote the text-books of the art of war. "If Hannibal had followed his victories he had never been taken by Scipio." There was a contrast between his clear courageous judgment and that preened Elizabethan phrasing. Drake was, perhaps, most at home with the wealthy, tight-fisted, tough shipowning families like the Hawkinses of Plymouth and the Fenners of Chichester. Sir John Hawkins, who had been Treasurer and Comptroller of the Navy, was with him now as his rear-admiral, as were Thomas Fenner and Martin Frobisher the navigator, "a man very valiant but harsh and violent." Over against them there stood the Lord High Admiral.

Charles, Lord Howard of Effingham was a great officer of state who in this crisis commanded the Queen's forces on the sea. His character does not emerge with any clearness. It seems that he was shrewd and proud with a vein of humour. For his station he was not rich and he kept a weather eye upon his fortune. He was brave and malleable. Lord Howard's letters from the fleet have a synthetic ring. Even when they are written in his own hand one can feel the sailors speaking, that readiness "to voyage to the Rio de la Plata," the use of Drake's own metaphor. A practical sense led the Lord Admiral to be swift to accept advice. In command of several of the naval ships he had placed his landsmen relatives, Thomas Howard, Sheffield, Southwell. His son-in-law Dick Leveson, aged seventeen, was in his flagship the *Ark Royal*. These young courtiers pressed forward, ready to defend their country and gather in the pickings and earn the Queen's good favour. They need not be remembered, for this was the seamen's battle.

Thomas Fenner has left a paper which indicates how well the great force based on Plymouth guarded that hundred miles of sea. "It was thought meet," he wrote, "the 5th of July to bear out into the sea, until Ushant bare of us E.S.E., and Scilly N.W. by N., some 15 leagues of either, with pinnaces placed between the body of the fleet and Ushant, as also Scilly,

SIR FRANCIS DRAKE, b.1540(?) - d.1596
Contemporary plate possibly by J. Hondius

thereby none to enter the Sleeve but that we must have sight of them."
In these words there rings a confidence which has seldom proved more
amply justified.

The English fleet was impressive, some forty ships, whether furnished
by the Queen or by the merchants, fit to lie in the battle squadrons ; faster
than the Spaniards, with finer lines and more weatherly. They were not the
small ships of legend. The fleet flagship the *Ark Royal*, Frobisher's *Triumph*,
Hawkins's *Victory* were all vessels of over eight hundred tons, each carrying
a mixed armament of forty guns and a crew of over four hundred men. The
Spaniards, viewing the conflict from the angle of land war, burdened by their
victualling ships and transports, had to face a naval force already formidable.

159

To the English adventurers, with their dash and their eye for loot and their coarse vivacity, there must have appeared something improbable and statuesque about the Armada's captain-general, Medina Sidonia. There was a hieratic quality about the scene at the council of war held, on reaching the Channel entrance, in the stern cabin of the *San Martin*. The Spanish admirals sat with their rich sober velvet and their chased sword-hilts, and considered the rules of the military art as the ships lay in those dancing seas to southward of the Lizard. A fresh breeze was blowing from the Scillies, and the morning sun had caught the painted sails.

They longed for the soldiers to fire off their harquebuses and for the gentlemen to use their steel in conflict. It was a dream ill thought out and not revived in naval warfare. The English conquered through their conception of the rôle of gunnery, through their fire power and their speed. After their victories in the Channel, they drove that cumbrous ill-led hostile fleet out into the North Sea and away from those pavilions by Ostend where the Prince of Parma waited with his army.

The threat of invasion vanished and did not recur till Napoleon's days. The last stages of the war with Spain were anti-climax. In 1591 the *Revenge*, which had worn Drake's flag in the Armada battles and was now commanded by Sir Richard Grenville, was attacked by overwhelming Spanish forces off Flores. With this action the quality of imperishable defiance entered into the history of sea warfare. But Grenville, like his cousin Walter Raleigh and the latter's half-brother Sir Humphrey Gilbert, gave only a portion of his thought to naval matters. These men were high political adventurers, colonisers and navigators. Gilbert's 'Discourse of a Discoverie for a New Passage to Cataia' haunted them. Frobisher had passed Greenland and reached Frobisher Bay in an attempt to find the way to China. They were far removed from Howard of Effingham but linked with Drake as he sat at his cabin table, while his ship moved through the ice-calm waters of the South Pacific, drawing new charts of the Americas and painting them with their proper colours, a mixture of heraldry, hydrography and bestiary.

In 1595 Drake set out on his last journey to the Spanish Main, now better guarded and much less rewarding. Fever had wasted Nombre de Dios and the golden days were fading. With Drake, sent on purpose to control him, was Sir John Hawkins, who had been for a long time a dockyard admiral. He had been responsible for much construction, for the "most royal and perfect estate" of the Queen's ships, for the introduction of the use of the bowline and the practice of striking topmasts. Hawkins was a stern man, wary, harsh, passably honest, and beset by enemies. He sympathised, as Drake could not sympathise, with the Queen's agony at the possible loss of the capital which she had invested in her seamen's enterprise.

They failed at San Juan de Puerto Rico, and Hawkins died at sea off the Virgin Islands. "Which will you have," we find Drake exclaiming, "the great city of Honduras or the streets paved with gold by Lake Nicaragua?"

CHARLES, LORD HOWARD OF EFFINGHAM, LATER EARL OF NOTTINGHAM
Lord High Admiral 1585-1618
Contemporary engraving probably by Thomas Cockson

The fever from the coast played on the ships and the Admiral sickened.
Two of his last sentences, spoken to Captain Maynard, have come down to
us. "I know no more of the Indies than you do. I never thought a place so
changed, as it were from a delicious and pleasant arbour into a vast and
desert wilderness." In the early morning of 28th January, 1596, Sir Francis
Drake died abreast of Porto Bello.

It is always difficult to be positive, but it seems that with Drake's death
there went the fleets which through an active lifetime he had created and
commanded. Through the Queen's reign the pull of sea adventure had been
powerful in the West Country. Grenville was a Cornishman, and many of
the other leaders came from Devon. A list compiled in 1582 gives four

thousand seamen from Cornwall and Devon out of a total of eleven thousand five hundred in the ports of the whole country. From all the fishing villages of western England and from the small harbour towns and the farming lands young men had gone to man the Elizabethan ships.

With Hawkins, Drake and Grenville lost on service and Frobisher also dead the previous year, Sir Walter Raleigh alone remained. Though much less of a naval figure, for he was in essence a Renaissance magnifico, Raleigh set the lines of later doctrine. The attack on Cadiz in 1596 was planned upon Drake's practice. West Indian waters were to remain for over two hundred years a centre of English naval warfare. Nelson described the seas in which Drake died as "the station of honour."

1639

ALMOST forty years of peace separated the Spanish wars from the sea fight in the Downs during which Tromp destroyed Oquendo's vessels and ushered in the great decades of Dutch naval power. In England the conception of the Royal Navy had advanced and the work of the fleet was becoming regular, however casual and unprofessional the manning.

The custom of striking topsails in recognition of the King of England's sovereignty in all home waters was well established. It went with the quiet chase for pirates in the summer season. The military expedition to relieve the Huguenots in the Isle of Rhé had been the only preparation for more serious warfare.

King Charles I himself had a concern for the great ships which would preserve his regality in the Narrow Seas. The quality of the amateur, so characteristic of the Van Dyck age, was reflected in the naval service. Volunteers of rank and fashion would crowd the quarterdecks on each summer voyage. The way of life at the admiral's table was a prolongation of the movement of Whitehall. "I pray," wrote one of these volunteers to his London factor, "send hither Sir John Suckling's play."

Besides, in the King's attitude there was blended a precise interest in mechanical contrivance with a serious appreciation of both line and splendour. Surely this was not lost upon that courtier who built the *Sovereign of the Seas*. This masterpiece of Phineas Pett came at the climax of the reign ; laid down in 1635 and finished two years later. She was very different from the ten little *Lion's Whelps*, small three-masted square-rigged ships of about 185 tons, carrying some twelve guns each and useful against lesser pirates. The *Sovereign of the Seas* was in contrast with the old crank vessels which had carried the King's flag since the early years of King James's reign. She had three tiers of ordnance and ten persons could stand upright in her great lanthorn. The lines 'Upon the Great Ship' hit off one aspect of the impression created by this warship most exactly :

THE FOUR DAYS' FIGHT, 1ST-4TH JUNE, 1666
Engraving by J. Ottens

> I meane the ship so lately built,
> Without, within soe richly gilt ;
> O never man saw rapier hilt
> > Soe shine.

The manning of these ships was already the concern of individual captains who, with their subordinates, were already shaping into a corps of sea officers. This was an interlude between the periods of hard fighting. Naval vessels now conveyed ambassadors and other persons of distinction overseas.

There was competition for the honour of this service. It was much to the advantage of a sea officer to secure the influence of powerful patrons. Sitting in his stern cabin, with the gold-leaf about the doorway and the caryatides on the quarter gallery, the prudent commander would scan the Court. Relationships were formed by mutual service. There was no security of employment and, of course, no pension. Each captain kept an eye upon a post ashore.

The letters of Lord Conway, a volunteer in the *Triumph* in the summer cruises of 1636 and 1637, give a clear impression of the fleet under Lord

RICHARD DEANE, GENERAL-AT-SEA, b.1610 - d.1653
Oil painting by Robert Walker

Northumberland coming slowly to the Downs, the ships beating up against the wind, and on the beach the waiting loyal crowds. The whole scene breathed the preservation of the King's regality ; it was far from the world of Robert Blake.

Nevertheless, the Navy which would in later years be the instrument in the hands of that great General-at-Sea was in a state of relative efficiency. The hoys with ordnance were stopped at Gillingham and unladen. The moulded timber was brought down on carts into the dockyard before the onset of the miry season. The officials of the Trinity House surveyed the hulls of Captain Pett's and Mr. Goddard's ships, and gave their opinion on the contriving of the ports for the gun-carriage. (Into this set routine was thrown a contractor's comment that he would as soon build a ship in hell as in Deptford Dockyard). A great boom swung across the Medway below Upnor, composed of masts and iron and cordage and the hulls of ships and pinnaces.

It was in 1649 that Robert Blake, heavy as a meteor and as unexpected, began his eight years of supreme command at sea. He was a landsman, in person short and compact, Somerset by origin, a merchant by profession, a military leader by instinct and experience. Resolution he possessed and a

GENERAL AND RARE MEMORIALS
pertayning to the Perfect Arte of
NAVIGATION:
Annexed to the PARADOXAL Cumpas, in Playne:
now first published: 24. yeres, after the first
Inuention thereof.

FRONTISPIECE TO JOHN DOE'S *GENERAL AND RARE MEMORIALS*, 1577
By courtesy of the Curators of the Bodleian Library

THE CAPTURE OF GIBRALTAR, 1704
Coloured engraving by Johann August after Paul Decker

dynamic energy. He had been annealed in the fighting for the Parliament. This was the year in which King Charles was killed. Blake was a convinced Republican, insular and self-reliant with the Old Testament phrases on his lips. "Died Abner as a fool dieth." Not many of his letters have survived. We obtain few glimpses of him. Aubrey has a note, from hearsay only, of Blake's time as an undergraduate at Wadham College. "He was an early riser and studyed well, but also tooke his robust pleasures of fishing, fowling, etc. He would steale swannes." From this dim background one fact stands out. It seems that his high tradition must have sprung from his sober, incessant, purposeful offensive spirit. Recognition was not withheld from him. "He did," wrote Aubrey his political opponent, "the greatest actions at sea that ever were done."

He had Cromwell's confidence and with him were other officers like Richard Deane and George Monck who belonged to the same tradition of strong military leadership. Their characters were very fitted for the hammer-and-tongs fighting of the coming wars. Among the younger commanders was Edward Montagu, who was to be Pepys's patron.

These wars with Holland lasted on an average some two years each ; they were exclusively naval and concerned with trade. In the first stage in particular the fleets operated to guard or to attack great merchant convoys. In this respect they foreshadowed the naval struggle through the eighteenth century. There was an absence of strategic design and no tactics inspired by imagination. In these engagements the squadron flagships acted as the centre of a fighting nucleus. The conception of the line of battle was only developing during these conflicts. It was to lead to the idea of the classing of the more powerful types of vessel as 'ships of the line,' the forerunners of the battleships. The significance of the weather gauge, which enabled a sailing ship to outmanœuvre her opponent, was well appreciated. Blake's cruises in the Mediterranean laid the foundation of English naval power within the Straits. The capture of Jamaica by Penn and Venables was a combined operation aimed at the seizure of territory and not merely at the ravaging of towns and shipping. The picture of the classic age of navies under sail was now being built up.

The battle of the Kentish Knock, the disappointing action off Dungeness and the battles off Portland and the Gabbard were stages in Blake's command at sea. Later there came his destruction of ships in harbour in which he (or his navigators) showed most expert seamanship, the burning of the Tunisian pirate ships at Porta Farina, and then Santa Cruz de Tenerife, the final victory. Blake came in, anticipating Nelson's attack on the same harbour, with a sea breeze and a flowing tide, intending to destroy the ships before the ebb-tide would take him out. This was in April 1657, and that winter he had blockaded the Spanish coast, for the Commonwealth had declared war on Spain. That August, worn by scorbutic fever, Robert Blake died in his flagship the *George* at the entrance to Plymouth Sound.

THESE Dutch wars fought in the Channel seem to be governed by Raleigh's dictum. "And I know it to be true that a fleet of ships may be seen at sunset and after it at the Lizard, and yet by next morning they may recover Portland." Grindingly in the three days' fight and in the four days' battle they fought their way along. Each of the three wars had a series of fleet actions unplanned and rigorous. When possible they manœuvred in a line ahead of small squadrons with the wind abeam. The red, white and blue squadrons, which till after Trafalgar were to give their titles to the flag officers of each colour, date from this time. The effect of a mere temporary command of the sea proved to be slight. The English had their victories and the Dutch sailed up the Medway taking the *Royal Charles*, burning the *Royal Oak* and the *Loyal London*. As the ships' names suggest, this was the Restoration Navy with Charles II upon the throne. Montagu had brought him back and been made Earl of Sandwich.

The courtiers went out to join the fleet, and in the first sea fight of the war of 1665 Falmouth and two more of the King's friends were killed on shipboard.

The end of Montagu, now Sandwich, is typical of that time. We see him in Pepys's Diary and on Lely's canvas ; the distinguished easy carriage, the extravagance and sensitiveness, the lovely singing voice, the thick moustache, the high arched eyebrows and that wide patrician forehead. He was grown heavy and the gout pressed on him. The days were past when he had smoothed the way for the King's liaisons. Now he was neglected and opposed to that attack upon the Smyrna Fleet which opened the third Dutch War. He is shown walking gently in Lord Burlington's garden leaning upon the shoulders of Charles Harbord and Clem Cotterell and complaining that though he was Vice-Admiral of England he knew nothing of the plans for the campaign of the coming summer. "This only I know that I will die and these two boys will die with me."

His flagship the *Royal James* was attacked in Southwold Bay and engaged by the *Groot Hollandia* and other heavy warships. "Brave Montagu," we read, "being all in fire and smoke that nothing but his flag was to be seen from seven till about one, was fired by a pitiful fire-ship." Towards 2.0 p.m. the *Royal James* "flew into the air." Sandwich was last seen on his quarterdeck with his sword at his side and his sweeping black-plumed hat in his hand. The George and the star of the Garter were on his breast. He carried a jewelled watch and wore a seaman-like ring containing a small compass. In his pocket were his rings and his great blue sapphire. Essentially it is the end of a Cavalier.

As a contrast we have the scene recalled by Pepys of the wounded seaman put ashore at Harwich after the four days' battle who brought to London the news of the engagement "his face black as the chimney and

EDWARD MONTAGU, EARL OF SANDWICH, b.1625 - d.1672
Admiral of the Blue and General-at-Sea
Oil painting by Sir Peter Lely

covered with dirt, pitch and tar and powder, and muffled with dirty clouts
and his right eye stopped with oakum."

The West Country entries of the Elizabethan navy had now given place
to a wider area of recruitment. The transfer of men from the merchant ships
to the Royal Navy was increasingly common, and when a fleet was fitted
out for the wars or for the Mediterranean or Tangier, stout men could be
found to go on such a venture. Discipline was still rudimentary and women
were not driven from the ships until the real voyage began. Coming down
the London river they were sometimes allowed on board as far as Deal or
Dover. A description of the commissioning of the *Assistance* shows the
young women of the town singing 'loth to depart' in punch and brandy.

Often as the beer turned sour on the commissions, it was fresh in peace-time on the English coast. The officers' mess, a conception now developing, already flowed with ale and jugs of claret.

East Anglia was at this time a main recruiting-ground for officers. Sir Christopher Myngs, "a very stout man and a man of great parts and could have been a most useful man at such a pinch of time as this," who died of wounds after the four days' battle, was a Norfolk man as were Sir John Narborough, the leading admiral of the last years of Charles II's reign, and Clowdisley Shovell who married Narborough's widow. Thus early do we find the naval contribution from Nelson's county. Some of these flag officers had, like Benbow, entered through the merchant service, but none of them can be claimed as "tarpaulins." They came from substantial families, the sons of tanners, weavers or yeomen farmers, the stock which gave the officers to Cromwell's Ironsides. Illiteracy was the great barrier to the promotion of the prime seaman.

Improvements in ship design throughout this century were not remarkable. After the Restoration English warships were built upon French models which had storage space for six months' provisions and carried their lower tier of guns four and a half feet above the water-line. Even so, during this period and far into the eighteenth century, the lower-deck gun-ports had to be closed in rough weather. Another limiting factor in regard to the naval actions of this time was the very small training arcs of the guns of the larger vessels.

Viewed from another angle these last years of Charles II were the heyday of the buccaneers. Sir Henry Morgan's sack of Porto Bello took place in 1680. Among the survivors of the pirate squadrons was William Dampier the hydrographer whose name ushers in a later age. Titus Oates made a voyage as a naval chaplain and Captain Kidd's connection with the Navy seems far away, but Dampier suggests the modern world. He discovered Dampier's Land in West Australia and the Dampier Passage between New Britain and New Guinea. He was pilot of the ship which rescued Alexander Selkirk, the prototype of 'Robinson Crusoe,' who had been marooned on Juan Fernandez island. In 1689 there was founded the Board of Admiralty.

1704

THE capture of Gibraltar in this year, a relatively trivial enterprise conceived in a casual way by Admiral Rooke, marks a stage in naval history. Henceforward Britain was to hold the western gateway to the Mediterranean, the fortress and the anchorage. This was to prove a factor of great significance in every war. The leading admirals of King William's reign were both alive and both ashore, Arthur Herbert, Earl of Torrington, who had commanded the fleet which brought the Prince of Orange to Torbay, and Edward Russell, Earl of Orford, the victor of Barfleur and La

The Bombarding of Dieppe by Their Majesties' Bombships, 1694
Contemporary engraving

BATTLE OF SOLEBAY, 28TH MAY, 1672
Oil painting by P. Monamy

Hogue. They came of great political families and were both officers of standing who gave themselves to politics and received from that same quarter their high commands, their peerages, their unemployment.

Since the Revolution of 1688 no further gentleman of rank had taken charge of naval vessels as an experience between bouts at Court. By this time, with the War of the Spanish Succession under way, the Navy had developed in respect to its cadre of officers that fully professional character which was to mark the high eighteenth century. On the side of organisation much was due to James II and the officials whom he supported during his tenure of the post of Lord High Admiral. The bomb vessels, so characteristic a feature of the early Georgian Navy, date from his reign.

The term first-rate was now in use to describe the principal naval ships. There were nine of these vessels in the Service and they each carried a very large complement. The *Britannia* when in full commission had a crew of over seven hundred men. The second-rates and the third-rates, the predecessors of Nelson's seventy-fours, made up with the largest ships a battle fleet of eighty vessels. The ships of this period were heavy and without the fine lines of the eighteenth century. They were very similar to the *Sovereign of the Seas*. Contemporary engravings show the long sheer of their decks and the high stern cabin, the wall sides and the thick wooden gun-port lids. The ships with their great bowsprits, their sprit sails and sprit topmasts always appear to ride down by the head.

SIR CLOWDISLEY SHOVELL, ADMIRAL OF THE FLEET, b.1650 - d.1707
Oil painting by Michael Dahl

Signals were made not by combinations of flags but by changing their positions, according to a system introduced by Admiral Russell in 1691. Observations were taken by the aid of Davis's quadrant and an improved astrolabe. The ratings of ordinary and able seamen were already established. The Admiralty fixed the prices at which clothing could be supplied by a contractor or slop seller. While there was as yet no seamen's uniform, the slops available included grey jackets lined with red cotton and garnished with eighteen brass buttons, kersey waistcoats of Welsh red, red shag breeches with leather pockets and white tin buttons, grey woollen stockings and round-toed brass-buckled shoes.

Naval organisation was efficient and most clear. There was a plethora of courts martial. The Admiralty had become that great factor in the British fighting services which it was henceforth to remain. Samuel Pepys had died in retirement in the previous year. Josiah Burchett, formerly Mr. Pepys's clerk, had entered on his long tenure, which lasted from 1695 till 1742, as Secretary of the Admiralty. Questions of the captains' lists and promotions of flag officers and the claims to post rank already aroused acute concern. The vocabulary had settled, and the entries in Rooke's and Martin's Journals could belong to any subsequent period in the days of sail. An extract dealing with Admiral Rooke's return to London will make this evident :

"Monday, Nov. 16, 1702. Blowing, dirty weather, wind round the compass." The naval life had reached that norm which was to prove so glorious. In fact the whole of this run of years must be regarded as a prelude to greater things.

In themselves they were disappointing with the memory of convoys slipped away and of disastrous storms. There was Admiral Benbow's death in 1702 at Port Royal of wounds received in the action at Santa Marta. Captains Kirkby and Wade were shot for disobeying him. There was Rooke's victory at Vigo and his indecisive battle at Malaga. "It was," wrote Captain Martin of this action, "hot work and hot weather, and they had a long summer's day before them."

There was the weary search for prizes whose capture would have meant so much to the new captains without private means. "It was then hazy," noted Captain Martin recording his movements in the *Grafton*, "and concluding they had tacked in the night, he tacked to the northward, steering N. in order to join them, the wind at E. by N., Cape Spartel bearing E. by N., twenty-two leagues, Cadiz N.E., thirty leagues, Cape St. Mary's N.N.E., thirty-three leagues ; at night he saw Cape St. Mary's bearing N. by E. four leagues." Added together this suggests a drear fatigue.

Amid much unrewarded cruising there were from time to time the great disasters. In 1694 Sir Francis Wheler perished in the *Sussex* off Malaga, and thirteen years later Sir Clowdisley Shovell was drowned when the *Association* struck the Bishop and Clerks outside the Scillies. Both flagships went down with all their ships' companies. Again, in the great storm of 27th November, 1703, fifteen hundred seamen died when the vessels in which they served were wrecked upon the Goodwins. These heavy losses

THE ACTION OFF LAGOS, 18TH AUGUST, 1759
Coloured engraving published by Macgowan & Davis, 1781

Glorious Victory over the French

BRITISH TARS *or the* TRIUMPHANT.

REPRESENTATION OF THE ENGAGEMENT on the 18th of JUNE, 1793,

Between His MAJESTY's Ship *LA NYMPHE*, of 32 Guns, 250 Men,

CAPTAIN EDWARD PELLEW,

And the FRENCH NATIONAL FRIGATE *LA CLEOPATRA*, of 40 Guns, 320 Men,

CAPTAIN JEAN MULLON.

By courtesy of the Parker Gallery, London

ENGAGEMENT BETWEEN THE *NYMPH* AND THE *CLEOPATRA*, 18TH JUNE, 1793
Coloured engraving published by William Lane

were partly the result of the long wars which lasted, with only five years' interval, from 1689 until the Peace of Utrecht in 1713. All warships were kept in full commission. It was the necessities of the service which caused them to beat up past Ushant in the winter weather.

It was at this period that the influence of politics, conceived along the lines of Whig and Tory, first began to affect the lives of senior officers. The new world was more serious but not the less political. Rooke held that Portsmouth seat which has so seldom assisted the careers of English admirals. He was superseded because he was out of sympathy with Godolphin's ministry. Admiral Leake, who had relieved the siege of Londonderry as a young captain, was dismissed with Harley's fall. The outlook on politics which carried most weight with the authorities was that of the decided, robust and silent Whig.

1740

THE outbreak of the War of the Austrian Succession found the Navy already marked by a strong corporate tradition, but as far as its leadership was concerned unimaginative and set and rigid. In 1731 the King's Regulations and Admiralty Instructions were first issued. The forfeited Derwentwater estates were set apart to assist the support of Greenwich Hospital which was now completed. Sir James Thornhill had decorated the Painted Hall.

Changes had come about in the long peace. The reflecting quadrant had been introduced. Seamen had been long familiar with wooden lighthouses upon the coast, but Rudyard's wooden structure was now set up on the Eddystone and the first moored lightships, those at the Nore Sand and at Dudgeon Shoal, had been towed into place. Through these years the first and second rates were laid up every winter. As late as 1745 Admiral Vernon drew attention to the risk involved in keeping three-deckers at sea during the winter months.

The political ties lay heavy on the upper reaches of the Navy List which contained only ten flag officers, the Admiral of the Fleet and the Admirals, Vice-Admirals and Rear-Admirals of the Red, White and Blue squadrons. The principal naval figure through the time of peace had been the elder Byng, the victor of Cape Passaro, a swift and careful adherent of the Prince of Orange and of the House of Hanover. Naturally the rare Tory flag officer like Admiral Vernon was very apt to receive hard measure. The successful admirals were old and close and Whig, like Sir Charles Wager.

Two conceptions which were to be important in service life begin to figure in journals and diaries, the idea of prize money, which can be traced at work in Queen Anne's reign, and the emergence of the naval family. Haddock and Wager and many other officers came from the Thames

Estuary, their fathers being masters or gunners in naval ships or victualling agents in Deptford or Chatham. The Hardys and the Rowleys and their cousins the Martins were now established in the inner core of traditional naval stocks with 'interest' at the Admiralty.

The battles of this time were never fought to a finish. There was none of Nelson's determination to destroy the enemy. The maintenance of the line of battle, that formation of ships sailing in line ahead, had become a fetish. There seems little doubt that the indecisive actions characteristic of the first half of the eighteenth century were due to the practice of engaging on roughly parallel courses preserving the line of battle with strict care. St. Vincent was to describe these "half-begotten battles." "I have often told you," he wrote to his friend Jackson in a famous sentence, "that two fleets of equal force can never produce decisive events unless they are equally determined to fight it out, or the commander-in-chief of one of them bitches it so as to misconduct his line."

The position was complicated by the character of the chess-board admirals, their diplomatic functions (for they often acted as ambassadors) and their haughty carriage. The central charge in the court martial after Mathew's action off Toulon turned upon a contradiction in the admiral's orders, for he made the signal to engage the enemy without having cancelled the signal for the maintenance of the line of battle. "His pride," wrote Charnock of Admiral Mathew, "was that of a man who entertained a proper sense of his own dignity and command, most feelingly alive to every slight insult." It is recorded that when the vice-admiral visited the commander-in-chief on board his flagship the *Namur* before the battle of Toulon, "Admiral Mathew did not on this occasion treat Mr. Lestock with the respect due to his rank; for on the vice-admiral asking him if he had any particular orders and instructions for him, he said 'No,' observed that it was a cold night and desired him to go aboard his own ship again." Surely this needs no comment.

In all the documents relating to the case of Admiral Byng, who was sentenced to death for gross negligence in his failure to relieve Minorca, one is always conscious of the degree to which the tactical doctrine then in vogue deadened all independent action. Borough had attacked Drake for failing to hold a council of war and Byng sheltered himself behind one. These were the dark hours before the dawn of high personal initiative.

The author of 'Biographia Navalis' describes Byng as a great observer of forms and of ancient rules of discipline, "austere, rigid almost to a degree of undue oppression, and proud even beyond comparison." A difficult period of naval history was closed on that March afternoon in 1757 when with a gale blowing down into Spithead from W.N.W. the unfortunate admiral was shot on the quarterdeck of the *Monarque*.

Two events stand out in these years which from a naval point of view were on the whole so unsatisfactory, Vernon's attack on Porto Bello which

CAPTAIN LORD GEORGE GRAHAM IN HIS CABIN
Oil painting by William Hogarth, 1697-1764

caused the inn sign of *Vernon's Head* to spring up across the country, and Anson's voyage of circumnavigation which was a major exploit. In 1744 the *Victory*, flagship of Admiral Balchen, disappeared on her way up the Channel in a gale and is considered to have been lost upon the Caskets. In 1743 the *Cumberland* returned from a two years' commission in the West Indies and her surgeon Tobias Smollett went ashore to settle down to write 'Roderick Random.'

1759

THE Seven Years' War brought in 1759 Boscawen's and Hawke's victories at Lagos and Quiberon. A new naval generation was growing up and a direct link unites these seamen with those who served in Nelson's fleets. The idea of a close blockade of the French coast dates from this time. It was a policy initiated by Admiral Hawke, later disliked by Howe and later still favoured by Collingwood and Nelson. The attack on Conflans' fleet among the shoals of Quiberon Bay in southern Brittany was the first instance of the *decisive* battle of which the end of the century was to see such fine examples. The opposing fleet was not destroyed ; it was not another Nile ; but the enemy's action was wholly paralysed. It was the year of Wolfe's death on the Heights of Abraham.

In character Lord Hawke himself was one of the finest of the English admirals, singularly selfless, generous to his subordinates, very careful of his men, gifted with judgment and great fire. He was a silent holder of the Portsmouth seat and he moved untouched by Pitt's dislike. There is a reassuring quality in the white hair, a little uncared-for, and in that blunt and determined face. He was, indeed, the father of the great Navy. The future commanders were close about him. At Quiberon, Howe was captain in the *Magnanime*, Keppel in the *Torbay*, Bridport in the *Minerva*. Rodney was a rear-admiral supporting in the Channel. During this war Thomas Paine, the author of the 'Rights of Man,' served as a seaman in the *King of Prussia*.

With Hawke there went Boscawen who died in 1761 before peace came, a flag officer whose qualities never received full opportunity. He stands with Anson, who so cared for the diet of his ships' companies, as an administrator determined to improve the conditions of the Service. He had been marked for life by his experience as a boy while serving in the West Indian flagship during those months when three successive admirals and four thousand men had died of virulent fever caught when lying off the Bastimentos. He introduced Sutton's ventilating apparatus, an arrangement of windmills and air pumps, on board the *Namur* when sailing in her to the East Indies. Incidentally he was one of the first to make real use of Trincomalee, then still in Dutch hands, as a naval base.

Mrs. Boscawen was a fashionable, devoted, lettered 'blue-stocking,' a phenomenon among the wives of admirals. Boscawen was not without his troubles. "I'm told," wrote his wife, "he [Vice-Admiral Knowles] has been shut up with Lord A. [the first Lord] continually since he came home. And now, I suppose, this working brain is to relieve you." Gout, tension and apoplexy chased one another up the Georgian flag list.

A final quotation from Boscawen will give an impression of life on shipboard. "All the officers," wrote 'Old Dreadnought,' "swing in hanging cots, and were stowed with convenience. After I left the ship [the *Torbay*] Captain Keppel permitted canvas cabins to be built. I never permit, nor have for many years, nor ever will, in any ship that I go to sea in, standing cabins." He was determined always to be ready to clear for action.

A great change at this period was brought about by the development of the fast-sailing frigate. The name had been familiar since the sixteenth century and had been in constant use in the last three French Wars ; but it was only in 1748 that the twenty-eight gun frigates carrying all their fire-power on a single tier were introduced into the Royal Navy. The seventy-fours, reinforced by the sixty-fours, had now become the standard type of

THE HON. EDWARD BOSCAWEN, b.1711 - d.1761
Admiral of the Blue
Oil painting by Sir Joshua Reynolds

British battleship. The new system was to endure unchanged until after the close of the Napoleonic Wars. The ships had a long life on active service; Nelson's *Victory* was launched in 1765. Meanwhile the fifty and sixty gun ships were modified or abandoned. They were at once too light for the line of battle and too slow for normal cruising duties. The forty-four and forty gun ships were cramped two-deckers and their place was taken by the new

N

181

frigates. In 1757 the first thirty-six gun frigates *Pallas* and *Brilliant* were built under the superintendence of Sir Thomas Slade.

This new construction went side by side with certain changes in naval life and with a new type of engagement. There was an increase in the number of those single-ship actions which were to prove so marked a feature of the later wars. As far back as 1709 Captain Mathew in the *Chester* had taken the *Gloire* in the Soundings, but the duels in the Seven Years' War more frequently took place between ships of the line, as in the case of the capture of the *Courageux* 74 by the *Bellona*, a predecessor of Talbot's classic battleship action in which the *Rivoli* struck to the *Victorious*. There was, however, an early instance of a true frigate action in the engagement in which the *Bellone* was taken by the *Vestal* commanded by Captain Hood.

The first impression gained of naval life in the reign of George III is the fact that discipline was more taut and punishment much more severe than in the previous century. The flogging for various offences was invested with more ceremony and was itself much heavier than in the warships of the Restoration. Leave was much harder to obtain. The work of the press-gang was at its height, and the practice of giving bounties to secure seamen on a ship's commissioning was now established. Side by side with these changes there went an increase of deserters, particularly marked on the colonial stations.

At the same time these years saw the appearance of the humane captain. Admiral Howe when in command of the *Magnanime* had granted leave of absence to his ship's company watch by watch. Howe, "as undaunted as a rock and as silent," to quote Horace Walpole's phrase, had something of the hold over his men that Nelson was to achieve by his personal ascendancy. He used "to go below after an action, and talk to every wounded man, sitting by the side of their cradles, and constantly ordering his live-stock and wines to be applied to their use at the discretion of the surgeon, and at all times for the sick on board."

Shortly after this period the health of seamen was improved by the hygienic rules adopted by Captain Cook on his voyages and by the lime juice and lemons introduced by Gilbert Blane to check the ravages of the scurvy. Meanwhile although the general standard of life improved, a new strain told upon the crews of certain ships. It was the smaller ships, the sloops and frigates, which were usually by far the happiest but also provided the cases of the greatest misery. A captain far from home and not sailing in company might prove a strong oppressor. There were special circumstances in the celebrated mutiny of the *Bounty* under Lieutenant Bligh ; but other later cases were, perhaps, due to the rapid promotion during war-time of young captains of marked initiative and ungovernable temper. The mutiny of the *Hermione*, when under the command of Captain Pigot, and the actions which led Captain Hamilton to be 'broken' in the *Medusa* in part resulted from this cause.

JOHN JERVIS, EARL OF ST. VINCENT, b.1735 - d.1823
Admiral of the Fleet
Mezzotint by J. R. Smith after G. Stuart

Commander J. A. Gardiner's 'Recollections' give a clear picture of the
Navy in the years before the Revolution ; the life of all those generous
officers, so free from ambition, so far removed from 'interest' at the Admiralty, so hot in their few resentments, so fortunate in their immense
capacity for liquor. It is in the light of this appreciation that one can understand such episodes as the courts martial in the *Phaeton* in 1788. The great
Navy was at its height, oaken and pickled.

After each section of his autobiography Commander Gardiner gives a
list of the officers who served with him in each commission. The following

entries relating to his shipmates in the *Brunswick* and the *Edgar* need no comment.

"Smithson Waller. Purser.

A very generous fellow, but kept it up too much ; since dead.

John Key. Second Lieutenant.

Dead. Cocoa Jack was no man's enemy but his own.

Tom Edwards. Midshipman (in the *Edgar*).

Dead. A lieutenant, a good fellow and played the flute delightfully."
One is conscious that the Navy was a uniting bond and there is always the impression of an ineradicable efficiency.

The war with the American Colonies, and subsequently with France and Spain, was from the naval point of view a curtain-raiser to the greater conflicts. Its single-ship actions have, however, never been surpassed. The engagement between the *Quebec* (Captain Farmer) and the *Surveillante* off Ushant was, perhaps, the stiffest and most stubbornly contested encounter in the history of the Navy under sail. The French fleet was certainly never more powerful and effective than during these years. The practice of copper-sheathing the ships' bottoms became universal during this war and the carronade, so called from the Carron ironworks in Scotland, which was deadly at short range, was introduced. Both of these changes increased the effectiveness of frigate work and the thirty-eight gun frigates of the Nelson era were now in service with the launching of the *Minerva* in 1780. In action victory went to the ship with the greatest weight of metal.

This war also saw the last of the old type of ultra-political flag officers, symbolised by Keppel, that close manipulator of the inner circle of Rockingham Whigs. His conduct of the indecisive action off Ushant was of less importance than the disastrous dispute with his second-in-command Admiral Palliser, to which this led. Many senior admirals of this period including Anson, Hawke, Howe, Keppel, and St. Vincent became First Lord of the Admiralty ; but the practice of sending a junior Lord of the Admiralty to sea in a subordinate command, as in the case of Sir Hugh Palliser, had no redeeming feature.

Rodney, who won the battle of the Saints' Passage in 1782 on the occasion of the breaking of de Grasse's line, exemplified the passing tradition. He was a fine and in some ways a brilliant officer, immersed in politics and the life of society, ridden with gout, extravagant, easy in his morals, and with a bland remote courtesy which could infuriate. "It is their misfortune," he wrote of his brother officers, "to know little of the world and to live in seaport towns."

By contrast his second-in-command Sir Samuel Hood was in a sense the creator of the finest type of the naval officer of the great wars. Freed from all concern for prize money, his life was bounded by the Service and his mind was concentrated solely on the decisive defeat of the enemy at sea. He was severe and rose by merit. He came from the core of England,

THE QUARTER DECK OF THE *DEAL CASTLE*
'Captain J. Cumming in a voyage from the West Indies in the year 1775'
Water colour by Thomas Hearne

the son of a Somersetshire rectory ; a background similar to Nelson's
without the latter's initial influence. Both men shared that high devotion
to the person of the sovereign which had come to exorcise political attach-
ments. Few letters reveal character more completely than those which
Hood wrote to his friend Jackson as he cruised off Altavela or Cape Antonio
or the Dry Tortugas. Two sentences may be quoted. "The *Torbay* and the
Prince William arrived on the 13th, a noble acquisition, and makes my heart
bound with joy." And again, "I will seek and give battle to the Count de
Grasse, be his numbers what they may."

No officer, except St. Vincent, left a deeper impress on the life of the
Royal Navy. Second-in-command at the Saints' Passage, he was, except for
a certain period in 1781, only in supreme command at sea in war for eighteen months in the Mediterranean. Lord Hood survived past Waterloo. He
was Nelson's exemplar. "Oh miserable Board of Admiralty !" wrote Captain

SURPRISE : Cutting out *HERMIONE,* 1799
Engraving by Whitcombe after Edy

Nelson when his commander-in-chief was recalled in 1795, "they have forced the first officer in our Service away from his command." It is a noble epitaph.

In 1782, a few months before the Peace of Versailles, there occurred the loss of the *Royal George,* flagship of Admiral Kempenfelt, which capsized in Spithead. In the same year 'Vinegar' Parker, the father of Nelson's superior officer at Copenhagen, was lost when his flagship the *Cato* disappeared off the coast of South America. In the new large Navy there was now entrenched a fresh type of high naval family. Parkers, Hothams, Graveses, Gambiers, Harveys, Malcolms and Kings crowded the flag officers' and captains' list at the end of the century.

The captains to whom boys were recommended often took an interest in them when they came on board as volunteers. Thus when James Saumarez joined the *Winchelsea,* aged thirteen, Captain Goodall gave him "constant access to his cabin, allowed him to write there and make extracts from the best authors in his possession." The 'Sailing Directions' had been compiled and a modern code of signals had been devised. The coastal lights were rising one by one. Smeaton's stone lighthouse, with its twenty-four candles, had been built on the Eddystone. The Needles and St. Catherine's lighthouses were completed in 1780 ; the Longships was begun some ten years later.

A point of striking significance is the great size of the Navy. In 1783 there were one hundred and five ships of the line and one hundred and

THE BATTLE OF THE NILE, 1798
Coloured aquatint by Sutherland after Whitcombe

thirty-two frigates in commission. Eleven years later, even after the interval of peace, there were ninety-five ships of the line commissioned and the personnel amounted to eighty-five thousand men. By 1812 the number of seamen had reached one hundred and forty-five thousand, the maximum for the Napoleonic Wars, and, though the number of battleships was relatively constant, there were four hundred and eighty-two smaller vessels on active service. Upon these fleets which were to win Howe's victory of the Glorious First of June, fought off Brest in 1794, Duncan's victory off Camperdown and Jervis's victory off Cape St. Vincent there was to come the impact of the personality of the great naval administrator and the experience of mutiny. The history of the mutinies and the career of Admiral Sir John Jervis, later Earl of St. Vincent, are inseparably connected.

The mutinies of 1797, which were sporadic throughout the fleet and concentrated into the orderly refusal of duty at Spithead and the violent disturbance, fomented by Richard Parker, at the Nore, took place (as do most revolutionary movements ashore) when the living conditions were somewhat on the up grade. Action was planned in the different forecastles during ship visiting.

Howe was brought down as a mediator and the Admiralty, holding a Board at the Fountain Inn at Portsmouth, granted the seamen's demands in regard to the bad quality and short allowance of the victuals, the treatment of sick seamen and the prohibition from going ashore when the ships were in port.

187

In regard to the Nore Mutiny it is not easy to determine the degree of political influence involved. The French Revolution affected certain of the men's leaders and there were in the fleet some United Irishmen from Belfast. Other demands, in addition to those already mentioned, included a more equitable distribution of prize money, the payment of arrears of wages due to the ship's company to within six months of the date of sailing, and the granting of two months' wages in advance to impressed men who received no bounty to enable them to have satisfactory dealings with the slop seller about their outfits. There were also one or two demands which could not have been put forward seriously. Most of the active mutineers at the Nore were quota-men, volunteers brought in by the civil authority. There was variation between ship and ship, the situation in general being better in the frigates. Even at the worst times the popularity of certain officers and the confidence which they inspired was manifest. By the end of the year all mutiny was over and nowhere was it checked more rapidly and effectively than in Admiral Jervis's fleet.

It was the character of Jervis, the disciplinarian, which left such enduring imprint on the Navy. His abrupt phrasing, with sometimes a foretaste of Fisher's biblical vigour, still bites into the memory. "There are," he wrote to the captain of the *Hamadryad*, "men enough to be got at Gibraltar, and you and your officers would be much better employed in picking them up than laying upon your backs and roaring like bull calves." "The discipline and subordination of the Navy," he wrote at the time of the mutinies, "was shook to the foundation by the Grenville Act which transferred the command of the fleet from the officers to whores, landlords, crimps, and lastly to United Irishmen." Another phrase lights up his cheerful attitude towards the Admiralty "who, God knows, are very unfit to advise in any measure beyond the selection of men for Greenwich Hospital." He was, above all, a restorer of discipline and a reformer of abuses. His term of office as First Lord of the Admiralty from 1801 till 1804 was the stormiest on record. St. Vincent was an enemy, an only partially successful enemy, to all easy and respectable and time-honoured corruption. He cared very much for the health and life of seamen. A certain rigidity in the nineteenth century quarterdeck is attributable to him. He was a strategist rather than a tactician. "If I was Minister of Great Britain," he wrote, "I would rather give up Gibraltar and Minorca than Malta." In 1800 this sea fortress had just passed into British hands. St. Vincent had a sense, before his time, of the Eastern Mediterranean.

There was a side of his stern quick personality that was inspiring. "Should we not be grateful to him," wrote Collingwood after the battle of St. Vincent, "who had such confidence in his fleet that he thought no force too great for them ?" And then there is Nelson's dictum. "Of all the fleets I ever saw, I never saw one in point of officers and men equal to Sir John Jervis's who is a commander able to lead them to glory."

H.M.S. *VICTORY* LEAVING SPITHEAD, 1791
Oil painting by Robert Dodd

1805

THE phrase "able to lead them to glory" is under one aspect the key to Nelson's life. The outline of his career is so familiar and his personality was in some respects so complex and elusive that it is, perhaps, best to attempt a swift impression. Horatio Nelson's promotion was rapid ; he was a captain at twenty ; his uncle Maurice Suckling was comptroller of the Navy. From an early age he moved in the midst of high naval affairs in war-time. His dash and that blade-like fragility made an appeal to the wives of the admirals on his station, to Lady Parker and Lady Hughes. His first portrait, that by John Francis Rigaud, was painted in 1781 when he was twenty-three ; Nelson was never an obscure young officer.

He had through life a profound devotion to the Crown and his nervous flaming energy was concentrated on his country's victory at sea. He hated atheists and republicans. It does not seem that he would have made a great peace-time admiral. In fact, except for the *Boreas*, he never held a command in peace. Assuredly he was born for war.

Nelson's singularly candid nature gave and exacted praise. "My zeal for His Majesty's service," he wrote to Lord Howe, "is as great as I once flattered myself your Lordship thought it." Another sentence is complementary. "It is much better (for an officer) to serve an ungrateful country than to give up his own fame." His care for his men was unsurpassed, as also his eye for likely officers. He was loyal to the core to his subordinates. "If Parliament," he wrote from the *Agamemnon* off Toulon. "does not grant something to this fleet, our Jacks will grumble ; for here there is no prize money to soften their hardships: all we get is Honour and Salt beef." The seamen worshipped him ; he knit his captains to him by his conferences in the *Captain* and the *Vanguard* and the *Victory* ; he riled his old superiors. It was not in his nature to assuage jealousy.

As to his fighting doctrine one sentence is famous. "Now had we taken ten sail," he declared in reference to Hotham's indecisive action, "and had allowed the eleventh to escape, when it had been possible to have got it, I could never have called it well done." It was in the evening of 1st August, 1798, that Sir Horatio Nelson, then a rear-admiral, found the French fleet from Toulon at anchor in Aboukir Bay. In a sense all fighting under sail led up to this victory which carried within it the seeds of Trafalgar. It was the sure touch, the speed and the manœuvre, coming up on both sides of the anchored fleet, which proved so devastating and made the Nile so memorable a triumph. Apart from his last day, it is on this summer and autumn of Nelson's life that the attention of the world is fixed, the Nile, the weeks at Naples, and Emma, Lady Hamilton.

His last seven years were those of his love for Emma Hamilton. In this he showed a passionate lit simplicity, an innocence of the world, a high-tensioned perception of offence and gratitude. In all naval matters he displayed a fine professional patience and that immense self-spending energy. Nelson was a judge of men's aptitudes but not of their perplexities. His troubles with his superiors Lord Keith and Sir Hyde Parker were to come from his high one-track imagination. It was this quality which leaves its impress on those sentences that are so well remembered. "The order of sailing is to be the order of battle. . . . No captain can do very wrong if he places his ship alongside that of an enemy."

Copenhagen was on all counts of minor importance. Lord Nelson's great place rests upon the Nile and the long vigil and the last battle with all its prelude. The only quotation in his letters, a memory from 'Henry V,' will fit in here. "But if it be a sin to covet glory."

The year of Trafalgar brought the crown of Nelson's victories. In Whitehall, the Lords of the Admiralty had sat at their fine oak tables with the charts spread out before them. Reports came in which dealt with the camps beyond Boulogne and despatches from the frigate captains who watched for signs of movement in Ganteaume's squadron anchored at Rochefort. Naval vessels would be detached to meet the Indian convoys in the latitude of Gibraltar. Exceptionally they might be in company as far to the south as St. Helena.

These big East Indiamen were sometimes larger than a first-class frigate. High on their sides, which were painted white and black, were the gun ports for the eighteen-pounders with which they could repel the lonely corsairs sailing out from Pondicherry or from Port Louis in the Isle de France. At the Admiralty Sir Charles Middleton held on his course, phleg-

HORATIO, VISCOUNT NELSON, VICE-ADMIRAL OF THE WHITE, b.1758 - d.1805
Facsimile of a crayon drawing by H. Edridge

matic and adroit. Below the level of a personal consideration the clerks in Whitehall in the dusty rooms would drive their quills with steadfast penmanship.

Away with Nelson's fleet there was displayed the same unhurried resolution. "I am at the time," wrote Captain Fremantle in the *Neptune* off Cadiz, "living entirely in my upper cabin, the lower one painting, but what is the use of large apartments and neat without society." It is the atmosphere of the game of bowls.

The old English commanders, with their oaken competence and that self-reliance which was at once so stern and petrified, could not abide the men of the Revolution, nor their atheistical and bloody principles. There was something monstrous in those officers who had been disloyal to their lawful sovereign. It was a stolid reflection of Nelson's distaste for Caracciolo.

Jacobin doctrines did not consort with the wrought snuff-boxes and the demi-johns within the cupboard and the jewelled swords of honour of the Hanoverian Admiralty. The whole country in that agricultural England, so rich and heavy, breathed a stertorous self-confidence. The ships going as light as swallows moved out into the Sound with the sunlight on their canvas. Work went forward in the plough-lands above the Channel with very little thought of Boulogne and Brest.

In the main battle squadrons the routine was accompanied by a pomp and circumstance which ushered in the great achievement. "We have on board," wrote a young officer in the *Defiance*, "Admiral Graves who came in his ten-oared barge, and as soon as he put his foot on shipboard the drums and fifes began to play, and the Marines and all presented arms. We have a fine sight which is the Grand Channel Fleet." Each letter from this period is alive with that confident and adventurous spirit which the high victories, and especially Cape St. Vincent and the Nile, had bred throughout the Navy.

Nelson had commanded the Mediterranean Fleet since the renewal of the war with France after the breakdown of the Peace of Amiens. His great spirit, which he had the power to communicate in large measure, was allied even in his lifetime to an unequalled legend. No British fleet was ever more expectant, and justly expectant, of victory than that which moved from its blockading station to meet Villeneuve's French and Spanish squadrons as they cleared Cadiz on 21st October, 1805. The proposed form of the famous signal is most characteristic of the Admiral, "Nelson confides that every man will do his duty." The actual battle demonstrated most clearly what he himself had called "the Nelson touch." Nelson struck on the quarterdeck of the *Victory* by a bullet from the top of the *Redoubtable* is itself the apotheosis of all sea fighting under sail, combat which never altogether lost the quality of the duel.

The tedium of the period after Trafalgar was relieved by single-ship actions often brilliantly fought. The least competent admirals Calder and Orde were now retired, but Strachan still survived afloat to command at Walcheren. Cornwallis controlled the Channel, and the Mediterranean was left to Collingwood's north-country patience. The pattern of operations, like Duckworth's passage of the Dardanelles, became almost meaningless with Nelson dead. Captain Hoste at Lissa won a small but perfect victory. The *Ajax* was burned to the water's edge as the *Scipion* and *Queen Charlotte* had been burned before her. Three ships and many men were thus lost by fire in the Mediterranean, a record grim and discouraging. In March, 1810, Lord Collingwood died at sea in the *Ville de Paris* the first evening out from Port Mahon on the homeward voyage from his long vigil.

'THE GLORIOUS FIRST OF JUNE' — LORD HOWE'S VICTORY, 1794

Coloured aquatint by Sutherland after Whitcombe

By courtesy of the Parker Gallery, London

THE BATTLE OF COPENHAGEN, 2ND APRIL, 1801

Contemporary Danish engraving

By contrast these years witnessed that wonderful career as a post-captain of Lord Cochrane, afterwards Dundonald. He was promoted in 1801 and dismissed the Service in 1814. He showed in the *Impérieuse* and his other ships that restless daring which was allied to a resource which was unexampled, and to the finest judgment in naval matters. He was wonderfully receptive and inventive as is shown by the 'secret war plan' ; intolerant of peculation ; harassing to his superiors. It was his misfortune that he could speak his thoughts from his place in Parliament.

Cochrane had his share, while in the *Pallas*, in those frigate actions which will always be remembered, names which are inseparable from the frigate conception ; the *Phoenix* and *Didon* ; *Terpsichore* and *Sémillante* ; *Amethyst* and *Thétis*. These showed the English captains and their crews in all their endurance and skill and in their swift light-handed gallantry. They had much to contend against since their vessels were seldom as fast as their opponents and the English frigates were built without gun-ports on the quarters.

These actions took place across the world and the *Guerrière* struck to the *Blanche* by the Faroe Islands. This small ship work was a special element in the Service. Already the officers and men were welded together in a fashion unknown in St. Vincent's flagship. Where there was good gunnery practice and a seasoned complement victory might be predictable. In the brief American War of 1812 it was factors such as these which led Captain Broke's *Shannon* to take the *Chesapeake* and caused the *Macedonian* to strike to Captain Decatur's *United States*.

In certain respects these years, since Nelson first entered the Mediterranean as a commodore, were the most wonderful in the history of the Royal Navy. They closed with Napoleon's defeat at Waterloo. It was indeed the end of an epoch when the *Northumberland* stood south for St. Helena dipping into the long Atlantic swell through the September weather.

1830

THESE were the peaceful days of the last great period of sail. The three-deckers came slowly from the dockyards, and the oak woods of the southern counties could still supply much of the timber that was needed for the British warships. The line-of-battle ships were loftier between decks and the captains' cabins were wide and roomy. The Bible was rather more in evidence, for the Evangelical tide was at the flood. The fleet was fine and formidable and slow. Even under full canvas the principal vessels would rarely make more than eight knots. The brasswork winked and shone and upon three decks there stood the tiers of cast-iron smoothbore guns. Great speed was not consistent with such a weight of armament.

The frigates remained lovely vessels now come with much experience to their last perfection. At Chatham there was lying on the stocks the twenty-six gun frigate *Conway* laid down in 1828 and launched and commissioned four years later. The whole work was leisurely, fruit of a peace-time Admiralty and an astringent Treasury. The *Conway* is chosen as a typical Seppings vessel because thirty years later she was to become the first of a line of ships whose name with that of the *Worcester* is celebrated in the training of officers for the sea.

The 'twenties and the 'thirties were the great days of the East Indies' station while the Indiamen still sailed to Diamond Harbour and the dockyard at Bombay could construct a battleship, the *Asia*, and thus indicate the respective merits of Indian teak and English oak. The Pacific was principally a field for Admiralty survey, and naval ships on their accustomed duties would rarely pass beyond Malacca Straits. The repression of the African Arab slave trade was by now a duty for minor naval vessels. No Asiatic nation possessed a serious fleet and Europe lay in a deep and, for once, an easy peace. The frigates came into Rio harbour and the River Plate. They touched at Cape Town and moved across the Indian Seas. Very perfectly they carried the suggestion that the sea power of Britain was beyond challenge and indeed inevitable. The King's ship would move like a bird into the wide seaways of the eastern harbours, coming in with her spread of canvas and her beautiful bows. To the population of those coasts the English officers seemed rigid and unfathomable as they stood in the heat in that striking uniform with the white waistcoats and white kerseymere knee-breeches. Leave on which the ship's company would prove their humanity was seldom granted in the East Indies squadron. It was a high and final manifestation of one form of peace-time sea power.

Back at home it was a different picture. The last of the Lord High Admirals of England, the Duke of Clarence, who had been deprived of that great post by Wellington in 1828, succeeded to the Crown. Some fifty years earlier he had served in the West Indies ; but successive Ministries had taken care that he had never worn his flag at sea. William IV, with his white hair and that square Hanoverian face, had a love for ceremonial and a Brunswick garrulity. He retained his interest in naval uniform and in an unbuttoned hospitality, loyal to his friendships and his simple grudges. This was the era of the Trafalgar captains who, headed by the new King's friend, Admiral Hargood, had now come into their own. The First Naval Lord was Nelson's Hardy. Collingwood's flag captain Rotherham commanded Greenwich Hospital. The flag officers on the active list recall a roll of the fortunate and experienced officers who had managed to command Lord Nelson's seventy-fours in his last battle ; Laforey of the *Spartiate* ; Bayntun of the *Leviathan* ; Durham of the *Defiance* ; Morris of the *Colossus* ; Berry of the *Agamemnon* ; King of the *Achille* ; Israel Pellew of the *Conqueror* ; Harvey of the *Téméraire*. It was a season of old man's glory. The commander-in-chief at Plymouth was Northesk, who had been rear-admiral at Trafalgar. Maitland, who had received Napoleon in the *Bellerophon*, was only just

QUEEN VICTORIA'S REVIEW OF THE FLEET AT SPITHEAD, 1853
Sepia drawing by J. W. Carmichael

attaining to flag rank. The post-captains' list was crowded with senior officers who had held commands for years in the long wars.

At the naval ports the three-deckers were laid up in ordinary. Out of ninety-five capital ships only seventeen were on active service. And what were seventeen among so many ? It was a haphazard system watered by a cordial generous nepotism and shot at times by enmity. It was never too late to return from half pay at one's country seat, but poor eccentric Sidney Smith pleaded in vain from Paris for Portsmouth or the Nore. The great eighteenth century naval families were fading out, but the quarterdecks of flagships were still crowded with their friendship and alliance. The King led the way with this disordered generosity and Lord Adolphus Fitzclarence received command of the royal yacht at twenty-eight. Inland near Salisbury at Stanlynch, renamed Trafalgar, lived Earl Nelson, Horatio's brother, who half a century earlier had been chaplain in the *Boreas*. He had settled far away because he was not prepared to entertain the admirals.

The gulf between the officers and the seamen, which would soon narrow, was at its widest. Impressment was now over and the seaport towns provided the bulk of the peace-time recruitment. The fishing villages would send their quota, but principally those between the Wash and Bristol. To some extent the southern counties drained into the dockyard centres from Plymouth and Chatham. Boys joined young and their friends were unpolitical. They became skilled seamen, very smart, without book-learning.

They had their full share of the national pride, then very buoyant. Often the children of seamen, they were bred to the life and their opportunities for alternative employment were in the 'thirties meagre and unattractive.

These were the last days of the Portsmouth of the long French wars, the dockyard with its tar and cordage and its stack of ordnance. Beyond the wall there rose the masts and yards of a first-rate ship which had warped along-side the stone jetty. The fast stage-coaches stood beside the accustomed naval hostelries. Around the shores of England the new coastguard stations drowsed in the mild sunshine. The half-pay officers and their families would dominate the lesser watering-places. Telescopes would be set up before each new and inexpensive marine residence. The light fell on the cream stucco of Captain Marryat's house.

1855

THE Crimean War, with its rather ineffective operations against Kinburn and Odessa and Admiral Napier's fruitless Baltic voyage, only served to throw into relief the superannuated officers and the undecided ship designing of the Mid-Victorian Navy. The more recent actions, Exmouth's bombardment of Algiers in 1816 and Codrington's victory over the Turks at Navarino in 1827, provided no precedents for the effect of shell fire on wooden ships which was tested in the Crimean War when Nachimoff destroyed the Turkish frigates sheltering at Sinope. Dundonald, restored to the Navy List since 1832, survived into this age of new experiments.

From a naval point of view paddle-wheel ships were not a serious proposition. The great wooden screw-ships of the line, like the *Agamemnon*, were now passing. Iron had come in and its use for ships' hulls had met with some disfavour for the ill-fated *Birkenhead* had been remodelled as a transport. Armour was now in prospect. Before this war was over the Russians had laid mines off Cronstadt and the French had built their armoured floating batteries.

In the same year Captain Moorsom introduced the beard and this became popular, accompanied at a later stage by the full side-whisker. It was the last period of the old punishments. The recruitment of seamen was becoming difficult and the introduction of the system of continuous service in 1853 was intended to remedy this shortage. The Naval Coast Volunteers, a not very successful experiment, were embodied at this time. In 1859 the Naval Reserve Act brought about the creation of the R.N.R. Admiral Lord Hardwicke, who held for a few months the office of Postmaster-General, unsuccessfully opposed the extension of the R.N.R. to officers. He had also voted in the House of Lords in favour of the retention of the press-gang. The way from the lower deck to the wardroom was probably more difficult

H.M.S. *WARRIOR :* THE FIRST BRITISH IRONCLAD
Engraving by Dutton

at this time than during any other phase of naval history. One detail will throw light on another aspect of the seamen's life. In 1853 Sir Fleetwood Pellew provoked a mutiny in the *Winchester* through his refusal of leave to the ship's company, a refusal which was in part occasioned by the character of the liquor sold in the grog shops of Hong Kong.

In this connection the daily allowance of half a pint of rum per man, served at dinner-time to the tune of 'Nancy Dawson,' had been reduced since 1823 to a quarter of a pint, and this was further lessened by the abolition of supper grog. During the 'thirties, tea and cocoa, later so universal, were introduced into the Navy. From 1839 seamen obtained the right to purchase tobacco at a shilling a pound.

Admiralty administration had been overhauled. The First Lords were, since Sir James Graham's time, inevitably civilians. A form of recognition was now given to the engineering branch and the status of paymasters and medical personnel was regularised. The great body of officers on half pay which had existed for a century and a half was gradually liquidated as a definite retired list and pensions system came into being.

This was the period of Sir William Fanshawe Martin's command in the Mediterranean. "He was," wrote Admiral Bridge, "the greatest flag officer since the Napoleonic Wars and an abler man than Lord St. Vincent." Sir James Hope, whose motto according to Lord Fisher was "Favouritism is the secret of efficiency," and Sir Harry Keppel built up the China station and suppressed the Chinese pirates.

There was a concentrated attention on evolutions under sail. The use of the term fifth-rate and sixth-rate to describe such vessels as the training ship *Atalanta* persisted until 1880. It is worth noting that in 1867 the *Minotaur* (Captain Goodenough) was present at the opening of the new North German dockyard then first named Wilhelmshaven. It was the birth of the Prussian Navy.

1882

THIS was the year of the bombardment of Alexandria and of the signal "Well done *Condor*" made to Lord Charles Beresford on the close engagement of Fort Marabout by his small gunboat. It was a slumberous period whose peaceful character is only emphasised by the interest aroused by the inconclusive duel between Admiral Horsey's flagship the *Shah* and the Peruvian insurgent monitor *Huascar*. Out in Alexandria Bay there lay the new battleship *Inflexible* (Captain Fisher) cleared for action with top-gallant-masts struck and upper yards sent down. This vessel had 81-ton muzzle-loading Armstrong guns in two turrets arranged *en échelon*. She carried on her flying deck the new type of second-class torpedo boat, had Nordenfeldt quickfirers, watertight compartments and two submerged torpedo tubes. Her rectangular fire-tube boilers and horizontal engine gave a speed of thirteen knots.

It was in such ships that the senior flag officers of the war of 1914-18 first went to sea. Lord French of Ypres had been a midshipman a few years earlier, as had Sir Evelyn Wood before him. All through this era the position of seamen was improving and, in these last days of sail drill, smart upper yardmen were especially prized. Gunner Israel Hardy had received the V.C. for his work in the bombardment of Alexandria. In 1889 by a splendid feat of seamanship Captain Kane brought the *Calliope* out of Samoa Roads when the ships of other navies were stranded by a hurricane.

When the *Inflexible* paid off from her first commission, Captain Fisher was appointed to reorganise the gunnery school in the *Excellent* at Portsmouth. Rather earlier Commander A. K. Wilson had been placed in charge of the torpedo course in the *Vernon*. The names of these two officers were to be of crucial significance in the development of the modern navy.

These were the days of the high nineteenth century naval families, the Seymours, Milnes, Fremantles and Hornbys, and the ascendancy of late-Victorian admirals like Sir George Tryon who was lost in the *Victoria*. Sir Erasmus Ommaney and Lord Clanwilliam and Lord Walter Kerr were in their different fashions characteristic figures of these years of peace.

BATTLE FLEET AT SEA
Oil painting by N. Sotheby Pitcher

Sir Cyprian Bridge marked this newer generation by his study of foreign languages and his close investigation of each German naval programme. At this time Vice-Admiral Colomb wrote his lucid treatises on naval warfare.

From now onwards the features of the modern navy stand out more clearly. The monkey-jacket was introduced in 1890 and the present salute in the same year. Protected cruisers were built and the use of fast liners as auxiliary merchant cruisers in time of war became a settled policy. The military top on the mainmast and high ventilator cowls both mark this period. By 1901 warships were painted grey instead of the prevalent black hull and yellow upperworks. Destroyers were by then a vital element in naval warfare and had attained to that silhouette which has changed relatively little in half a century. Minelayers were already introduced and the first submarine came into service in 1904.

The high speed of the protected cruisers, like the *Powerful* which landed the naval brigade that assisted in the defence of Ladysmith, and the general speed of the battle fleet which had now reached eighteen knots, resulted in a very heavy coal consumption. Governing considerations in the disposition of the various squadrons were the fleet anchorages, dry dock facilities and coaling stations.

Good lines began to reappear. The first ironclads, like the old *Warrior* of 1861, had had something of the merit of the wooden steam frigates, but the raft and box battery conception derived from the *Monitor* and culminating in the *Devastation* had ushered in the ugliest period of British naval architecture. Now the light cruisers of the *Adventure* class restored the sense of line and swiftness.

The period of rival building programmes had been reached. The German Navy Law was passed in 1898. The British Fleet was powerful and well-designed and homogeneous, qualities possessed in the wars against Napoleon but in part lost in the 'sixties and 'seventies. Sir Percy Scott had created the modern naval gunnery. Fire control came in during 1905 ; guns could now be loaded in any position and at any elevation ; electric gear replaced hydraulic. Perhaps undue attention was paid to the offensive power of the destroyer. The searchlights swept the harbour entrances.

1910

THE years of peace saw the heyday of the Mediterranean fleet and the China station. The last two decades before 1914 were unmarred by disasters. There were no such losses as the capsizing of the *Captain* and the sinking of the *Victoria*. The stranding of the *Montagu* and of the *Bedford* involved no fatal casualties, and in the China squadron there were summed up all those pleasures, both for the officers and the ship's company, of life in peace-time on a distant station ; the expeditions away from the ship ; the sport ; the weather ; the boat sailing. The situation of the vessels based on Hong Kong was governed by the presence of the potential enemy, von Spee's squadron, and of the new ally, Japan. The China squadron was born of the treaty port conceptions. It was designed to deal with the ships of other European navies in Far Eastern waters. The life was delightful and the scene did not endure.

Malta is at the core of the naval system of the Mediterranean. Generations of Maltese worked in the dockyard and went to sea, principally as messmen. The ships lay in the Grand Harbour at Valetta with the awnings out over the quarter-deck, the funnel markings showing dully in the dancing light, the captain's stern gallery in shadow and the brasswork hot and shining in the August sun. There was the polo and the pulling and sailing and the fleet races. France was now a friend and we policed the road to India.

At home and in high quarters it was a very different picture in these years when the Agadir crisis had come to herald the outbreak of the first German War. A series of dynamic personalities was established in the

By courtesy of the Trustees of the Fitzwilliam Museum

H.M.S. *VICTORY* FIRING A ROYAL SALUTE IN PORTSMOUTH HARBOUR ON THE QUEEN'S BIRTHDAY, 1830

Oil painting by C. J. M. Whichelo

DESTROYER ESCORT IN ATTACK,
Oil painting by Richard Eurich

Admiralty and its purlieus. Churchill had just entered upon the first of his two memorable periods of office. Sir Arthur Wilson was relinquishing his post as First Sea Lord. Fisher with an inexhaustible vitality conjured and rode his own wild tempests. He had done so much. The policy of concentrating upon capital ships carrying an armament of not less than ten 12-inch guns, then known from their prototype as 'Dreadnoughts,' was well established. Turbines had superseded reciprocating engines; water-tube boilers were universal; wireless telegraphy had been installed; the use of seaplanes was in course of exploration.

The calibre of the main armament was all the time pushed up, 12-inch, 13.5-inch, 15-inch. New battle cruisers were pressed forward. The *Queen Elizabeth* was laid down as an oil-burning ship. The fleet organisation was overhauled. Sir John Fisher with his passionate and unleashed energy and that driving wasteful efficiency was never afraid of the spectacular. The German menace was certainly seen very vividly. In the age group below Wilson and Fisher the two outstanding flag officers were Prince Louis of Battenberg and Sir George Callaghan. Upon this situation the war broke.

The first German conflict resembled the Napoleonic Wars and the war of 1939 since in each instance convoy work and the blockade and ultimate defeat of hostile Continent-based fleets were objectives of prime importance. In all three cases there was an initial and abiding shortage of vessels for escort purposes, frigates, light cruisers or destroyers. In Napoleon's time and in the War of 1914-18 there were large opposed forces comprising many battleships. In 1914 the strain fell principally upon the anti-submarine personnel, the destroyers and the Q ships. The small ship fighting was renewed in such exploits as those of Gordon Campbell and of Evans of the *Broke*. There was the early submarine work in the Baltic and in the Sea of Marmora associated with the names of Horton and Dunbar-Nasmith.

In the actions at sea during these years the opposing forces were seldom equal. It was inevitable that the *Emden* should succumb to the *Sydney* and that Cradock should be lost at Coronel. The fighting had a ding-dong quality, for Coronel was the prelude to von Spee's destruction in Sturdee's careful victory at the Falkland Islands. There was monotony in the watch and ward of the main fleet which culminated in the Jutland battle, one of the most interesting encounters in naval history. In the War of 1914-18 the R.N.R. came into its own, and the R.N.V.R. began to take that heavy share which was to become still more crucial in the recent conflict.

Few flag officers have been more carefully selected for their post than Sir John Jellicoe. He had a character very firm and loaded with a sense of responsibility, a balancing clear mind, a mastery of detail, a touch perhaps of Collingwood. He was in the line of succession of those just admirals who have cared deeply for the men whom they commanded. Sir David Beatty will always be remembered for his great spirit. His was a driving force close-coupled with the power to delegate. His reputation can never be as high as if he had held supreme command in a fleet action. The spirit of the French Wars was reflected in Tyrwhitt's and Goodenough's light cruiser squadrons. There was something of the character of a cutting-out expedition or of one of Cochrane's enterprises in Roger Keyes' work at Zeebrugge.

Yet there was not the strain to which air attack subjects the seaman, and there was nothing comparable to the destroyer or submarine work in the Mediterranean in the recent War or to the passing through of the Murmansk and Malta convoys. The dullness was more unrelieved; the life at Scapa, the rain coming up from over the Atlantic, the seas running in the Flow. An impression of immense power was conveyed by the great ships going southwards past the gate and turning eastward through the Pentland Firth; for example the *Tiger* in her first rig with the light paintwork, the smoke streaming from the massive funnels and that long empty quarter-deck with the grey seas racing by.

The warships of that era were certainly among the most satisfying yet constructed, when once the designers placed the turrets on the centre line and got away from the crowded upper decks of the early 'Dreadnoughts' and battle cruisers. Unforgettable among the battle cruisers was the *Hood*, which was surely the most beautiful ship with the most lovely lines that ever sailed in a modern navy. Like the best frigates she attained perfection in her own medium.

In the second German War the struggle was in some aspects much more dangerous and certainly more filled with strained excitement, but it was not more unremitting. There is surely no calling so rooted in the English mind and character as the Royal Navy which now includes a vast mass and cross-section of the manhood of the United Kingdom. Easy and gallant they defend the freedom of the seas and the shores of England.

BRITISH SOLDIERS

BY

S. H. F. JOHNSTON

THE NEW MODEL

THE once familiar red coat of the British soldier was seen for the first time in Windsor Great Park during the April of 1645. The New Model Army, formed by Ordinance of Parliament for a more efficient prosecution of the war against Charles I, was being mustered and exercised in its drill. The infantry of this new force were "Redcoats all," as a contemporary newspaper puts it, regiment being distinguished from regiment by facings of the colonel's colour; the breeches were of "grey or other good colour." The New Model Army was to beat the King at Naseby and the Scots at Dunbar and Worcester; it was to pacify Ireland and for a time govern the newly formed Commonwealth of England; six thousand men from it were to carry its reputation to the Continent and help defeat the Spaniards at the battle of the Dunes; some of its units were to pass, at the Restoration of Charles II, into the new royal standing army.

Though the New Model Army was the first regular British army, these men were by no means the first British soldiers. Where indeed are we to find the first British soldiers? The defenders of Maiden Castle and other prehistoric fortifications, the charioteers who fought so gallantly but so hopelessly against the legions of Caesar and Claudius, the Britons who served in the Roman army—all these were British soldiers. So too were the English who fought against Dane and Norman, the mail-clad knights who fought in Ireland and France and against the infidel at Lisbon and in the Holy Land, the Welsh and English archers whose longbows won victory at Falkirk and Crécy and Agincourt, the men of the Free Companies, such as that commanded by Sir John Hawkwood, most of whose life was spent in Italy and whose monument in Florence Cathedral describes him as the most skilful general of his age. But our knowledge of these men is limited; we must pass on to more articulate times.

When the Tudors were on the throne the Royal Navy was born. But it was a backward age as far as the army was concerned. There was no standing army and the shire levies were ill-armed, ill-trained and ill-disciplined. They were called out in 1588 to defend the realm against the dangers of invasion by the Duke of Parma's Spanish army, but it was fortunate for England that Drake and his ships defeated the Armada and so relieved the militia of its task. There were, however, two gleams of light in the darkness. Many London militia men laboured hard to keep themselves efficient and British soldiers were beginning to win a reputation for themselves in wars abroad. Shakespeare must have been familiar with the exercises of the London volunteers on St. George's Fields at Mile End. Falstaff and Justice Shallow in their youth "lay all night in the windmill in St. George's Fields," and Captain Dumain, according to Parolles, had at one time "the honour to be an officer at a place called Mile-end to instruct for the doubling of the files." The London trained bands were still efficient in the seventeenth century; here is what Clarendon says of their conduct in the first battle of Newbury: "they stood as a bulwark and rampire to defend the rest, and when their wings of horse were scattered and dispersed, kept their ground so steadily that, though prince Rupert himself led up the choice horse to charge them, and endured their storm of small shot, he could make no impression on their stand of pikes, but was forced to wheel about. Of so sovereign benefit and use is that readiness, order, and dexterity in the use of their arms which hath been so much neglected."

Volunteers from the London trained bands were included in the company commanded by Captain Thomas Morgan which left England in 1572 to assist the Dutch in their struggle for independence. These men were the first of a long succession of English, Welsh and Scottish soldiers who were to learn their trade in the Low Country wars. Elizabeth's favourites, Leicester and Essex, both fought in Holland, as did Sir Humphrey Gilbert and Sir Philip Sidney, who died gallantly at Zutphen in 1586. But the really great figures in these wars were the men whose only reputation was that which they won in fighting the Spaniard—Lord Willoughby and Sir John Norreys, Sir Roger Williams and Sir Francis Vere. English regiments remained in the Dutch service until the outbreak of the Second Dutch War in 1665, when most of the men returned home and were formed into the

By courtesy of the Provost and Fellows of Eton College

ROBERT DEVEREUX, EARL OF ESSEX, 1567-1601
Oil painting by an unknown artist

By courtesy of the Duke of Devonshire

GEORGE MONCK, DUKE OF ALBEMARLE, 1608-1670
Oil painting by Sir Peter Lely

Holland regiment. They had to change their buff jerkins for red coats, but were allowed to wear buff facings. The regiment, later numbered as the 3rd Foot, is still known as the Buffs.

Many officers on both sides in the Civil War, such as the Cavalier Goring and the Roundhead Skippon, had learned their profession in the Dutch service. Others had fought in Germany during the Thirty Years' War and the best of these had served under the great Swedish military reformer, Gustavus Adolphus. The bulk of the New Model Army, however, from Cromwell downwards, had no campaigning experience except that which they gained in the Civil War itself. More than half of its infantry in 1645 were pressed men and impressment remained the usual way of filling its ranks until 1652. The cavalry was from the first composed of volunteers. It was easy enough to get recruits, for, as Monk's chaplain wrote, "it was there a good employment for a gentleman, and as competent provision, to have near twenty shillings by the week, and live well and gentlemanlike, keeping themselves and their horses for some six shillings a week." The troopers were the aristocrats of the army since cavalry was then the decisive arm in battle. The horsemen advanced at a "pretty round trot" and "disputed it with sword and pistol" until they had broken the squadrons of the enemy and cleared them from the field. Cromwell then taught his horse to re-form and fall on the flanks of the infantry in the centre.

The foot-soldier, paid much less than the trooper, was armed either with a musket (usually a matchlock) or a pike. There were two musketeers to each pikeman, but the sixteen-foot pike was still regarded as the more honourable weapon, probably because the tallest and strongest men had to be detailed to carry pikes. In battle the infantry were preceded by a "forlorn hope" of musketeers, acting as skirmishers, who opened out to either flank when the regiment charged. In the attack the musketeers fired two volleys and the pikemen levelled their pikes and charged the enemy, the musketeers using their muskets as clubs. Battles were rarely decided by the infantry, although the battle of the Dunes in 1658 was virtually won as a result of the determined charge of the English foot against some of the best soldiers of Spain occupying a dominating position on an isolated sandhill. The real importance of the arm was to come later when the more efficient flintlock replaced the matchlock and the invention of the bayonet made the musketeer his own pikeman.

Although the New Model, with its rigid discipline, was an efficient army, it was never a popular one. Public opinion with a good deal of justice regarded it as the army of a religious and political faction rather than as the army of the nation. Cromwell's brief attempt to govern England through the Major-Generals and the intrigues which followed Cromwell's death implanted in people's minds a hatred of militarism and a suspicion of standing armies which was to have important consequences.

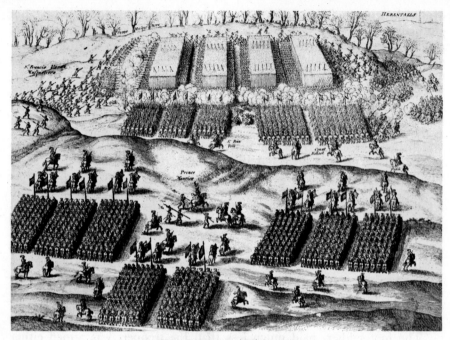

THE BATTLE OF NIEUPORT
Engraving from Sir Francis Vere's *Commentaries*, 1657

Sir Thomas Fairfax, "Black Tom," was the New Model's first commander. Only thirty-three years of age in 1645, his reputation was won
mainly in campaigns against the Royalists in the north of England, although
he had seen some service in Holland. From the beginning, however, he
was overshadowed by Cromwell, who created the New Model Army and
became its commander-in-chief in 1650. The soldiers sensed this fact, for
when Cromwell first rode into their camp just before the battle of Naseby
he was greeted "with a mighty shout" and the cry "Ironsides is come to
head us." Cromwell had never heard a shot fired in anger until the outbreak
of the Civil War, but he was a born organiser of victory, a brilliant leader
of cavalry and a shrewd strategist. The most typical soldier, however, among
the New Model's leaders was George Monk. At every stage in his career
he is the honest soldier of fortune, with a keen grasp of his profession and
a deep sense of loyalty to his paymaster of the moment. He was first a
volunteer and then an ensign in the expeditions to Cadiz in 1625 and the
Isle of Rhé in 1627. He was a captain in the Dutch army and a Lieutenant-
colonel in Charles I's service. When the first Civil War was over, he served
Cromwell loyally, especially as governor of Scotland. Cromwell dead, he

made the Restoration possible by insisting on the superiority of the civil power over the Army. His march from Scotland to London allowed the people of England to express its will and recall the King. He was to win new laurels and honours after the Restoration, but this sketch of his career may well end with the scene at Tower Hill on St. Valentine's Day, 1661, when men from Monk's own regiments were transferred to the royal service. They became the Lord General's regiment of Foot Guards, known also, from the place where Monk crossed the Border on his march to London, as the Coldstream Guards.

ROBERT DUDLEY,
EARL OF LEICESTER, 1532-1588
Armed for the tilt-yard

MARLBOROUGH

ON June 26th, 1650 Cromwell was appointed Captain-General of all the armies of the Commonwealth. A month before to the day, a third son was born to Winston Churchill, a Royalist and the squire of a small estate in Dorset. This son, John Churchill, later to be famous throughout Europe as the Duke of Marlborough, was a soldier from the age of seventeen to his death in 1722. He received his ensign's commission in the 1st Foot Guards, a regiment formed in 1661, with Royalists who shared Charles II's exile as its nucleus, and later given precedence over Monk's Coldstreamers. Before he was twenty he fought against the Moors while serving an attachment with the Tangier Regiment, specially raised to garrison this possession which had come to Charles II as part of his Queen's dowry. Back in Europe he served in campaigns against the Dutch, first under Monmouth and then as colonel of one of the English regiments in the army of the great French commander Turenne. His was the main responsibility for the defeat of Monmouth's rebels at the battle of Sedge-moor and for carrying the army over to the side of the Prince of Orange in the Glorious Revolution of 1688. Before falling out of William III's favour he led in person the charge of the Household Cavalry at Walcourt and distinguished himself at Cork and Kinsale.

It was thus no immature soldier who at the beginning of Anne's reign was appointed commander of both the English and Dutch armies. He had worked out ideas of his own on the conduct of war. At that time warfare was mainly a matter of sieges, since professional soldiers were too precious to be risked in battle, and wars were therefore long and indecisive. Marl-borough believed that humanity and economy alike demanded speed which could only be obtained by seeking the decision of battle. The difficulty of committing to battle not only his enemies but also his allies prevented Marlborough from realising his aim completely, but his reputation as a soldier rests on his great victories, beginning with the attack on the Schellen-burg and ending with the forcing of the Ne Plus Ultra lines. Marlborough was a statesman and diplomat as well as a soldier, but his qualities are seen at their best in the heat of action. With a very small staff and without any organisation higher than a brigade, the commander himself had to direct in detail the tactical conduct of the battle. At Blenheim every gun was sited by Marlborough himself. At Oudenarde, an encounter battle, the strain on the commander must have been exceptionally great; a Prussian officer reported back to his king, "Mylord Duke shone in the battle, giving his orders with the greatest sangfroid, and exposing his person to danger like the commonest soldier."

Marlborough was well served by his subordinates. Cadogan, his Quarter-master-general, was an invaluable staff officer. When he was captured by the French in 1706, Marlborough wrote to his Duchess, "Poor Cadogan is taken prisoner or killed, which gives me a great deal of uneasiness, for he loved me, and I could rely on him." So courteously were wars conducted then, however, that Vendôme at once released him and sent him back to Marlborough's headquarters. Marlborough had also some good fighting generals. Lord Cutts was nicknamed the "Salamander," because his element was fire, and he lived up to his name at the taking of Venloo and at Blenheim. Lord Orkney wrote home dry laconic letters showing a similar attitude to danger. At Blenheim he says, "I had the good luck not to be touched; only a horse shot under me." At Ramillies he commanded the British troops on the right and did not know that his attack was to be merely a feint. Marl-borough had great difficulty in getting him to abandon the attack. Ten aides-de-camp and Cadogan had to be sent before he could be persuaded

67

THE 34TH REGIMENT OF FOOT
A Soldier's stance before the 'heels together' position of attention was introduced
Coloured engraving, 1742

to withdraw: "we had a great deal of fire . . . both musquetry and
canon; and indeed I never had more shot about my ears, and I confess it
vexed me to retire." Such were the commanders; what of the men
they led?

That Marlborough could be called "Corporal John" is an indication of
how well he cared for the men under his orders. Serjeant Millner, of the
Royal Irish, tells in his journal how the troops were "animated by his grace-
ful presence and his inviting example." It is clear that the British troops
were the cream of his army. Certainly they thought so themselves. The
sternly religious Captain Blackadder of the Cameronians wrote in his diary
after the battle of Schellenburg, in which the British suffered more heavily
than their allies: "The British value themselves too much, and think nothing

215

can stand before them. We have suffered considerably on this occasion, and have no cause to be proud." But the British soldier's opinion of himself was confirmed by the orders given by Louis XIV to Villeroi in 1706 instructing him "to have particular attention to that part of the line which will endure the first shock of the English troops." At Ramillies in the same year Marlborough put his redcoats on the right in order to divert the French from the main thrust of the allied cavalry on the left.

The reputation won by the British troops seems a little curious when we remember how they were recruited. Recruiting in those days had an important effect on military operations. Campaigns were fought only in summer. It was then that the roads were fit for the movement of armies and the six months of winter were required to fill up the wastage in the ranks and exercise both old soldiers and recruits in the complicated drill that an eighteenth century battle demanded. Recruiting was a regimental matter, for the British army was little more than a collection of regiments each of them in a sense the property of its colonel. After a summer campaign in the Low Countries, a number of officers from each regiment would return to recruit, competing against each other with cajolery and bounties and helped only by the various Recruiting Acts which imposed conscription on certain classes—criminals, debtors and paupers. Only by iron discipline and unremitting care could such material be transformed into an effective army. Marlborough performed the miracle. He taught his cavalry to rely on shock, using the sword and not the pistol. His foot, armed with musket and ring bayonet, were taught to fire by platoons in directed volleys.

Not much is known about the men who fought and won Marlborough's battles, for those who wrote journals and books were hardly representative of their fellows. Serjeant Millner was more interested in routes and statistics than in human beings. Private Deane of the 1st Foot Guards was obviously a man of some education, while Matthew Bishop of Webb's, the 8th Foot, was a small landowner. But some of their sentiments must have been shared by the men in long, loose-fitting red coats and gaitered breeches, with cocked hats on their heads—the men of Marlborough's marching regiments. They would have understood Deane's complaints about the marches after Oudenarde when Marlborough was trying to bring the French to battle again; "we were continually fateagued and bugbeard out of our lives by those who had as much will to fight as be hanged." They no doubt shared the belief of Matthew Bishop "that every Ball that kills or wounds his man has his Commission before it is fired." Bishop has something to say about the food: "we got two three Bushels of Beans, and a Bushel of Wheat at a Time; so some days we had boiled Beans, and sometimes when we mounted the Trenches, we made ourselves Dumplings, which we thought extremely good Living."

Of the various regiments which took part in the War of the Spanish Succession, we have space for only one—the 34th Foot, now the Border

Regiment. It was raised in 1702 as Lucas's regiment, fought in Spain in 1705, and was sent to the Low Countries in 1709. It was not a particularly distinguished regiment, but it has interesting literary connections. Richard Steele, the essayist, was a captain in it and he has preserved for us in *The Tatler* what is either a genuine soldier's letter or a most skilful imitation. Serjeant Hall of the 1st Foot Guards writes in 1709 from the camp before Mons to his friend Serjeant Cabe of the Coldstreams "I have received a very bad shot in the head myself, but am in hopes, and please God, I shall recover . . . We had but an indifferent breakfast; but the mounseers never had such a dinner in all their lives." After the war was over among its ensigns appears the name of Roger Sterne, the father of the author of *Tristram Shandy*. In the pages of that book we get the best imaginative pictures of the soldiers who fought and defeated Louis XIV and "the exorbitant power of France." The memories of Uncle Toby and Corporal Trim may have been of King William's wars, of Namur and Steinkirk, but it is clear that the two old soldiers followed closely Marlborough's campaigns, including the detailed topography of the march to the Danube, and that their characters were drawn out of a mind whose earliest memories were bound up with the traditions of one of Marlborough's regiments.

THE STRUGGLE FOR EMPIRE

THE thirty years after the ending of the War of the Spanish Succession by the Peace of Utrecht in 1713 were a bleak period in the history of the army. The clamour against a standing army, never completely stilled by the almost constant warfare against France since the Revolution of 1688, broke out with fresh vigour. Regiments were disbanded, the establishment was drastically reduced, Parliament even shirked its responsibility for the small army that it reluctantly maintained. Control was in the hands of the Secretary-at-War, once a mere clerk to the Commander-in-Chief but now a politician with a seat in Parliament, where he consistently refused to account for his actions. In theory, one of the two secretaries of state was responsible to Parliament, but in practice, as was said in 1718, "our armies know no other power but that of the Secretary-at-War, who directs all their motions and fills up all vacancies without opposition and without appeal."

The soldier's life during these years of peace was a difficult one. In England itself regiments were usually split into detachments and quartered in ale-houses, because of Parliament's unwillingness to build barracks. When Howard's regiment, the 24th Foot, returned to England from Ireland in 1734, three companies were quartered at Dunstable, three at Woburn, two at Hitchin, and one each at Luton and Redburn. Such a system allowed few opportunities for training and created a situation full of potentialities of friction between soldiers and civilians, especially as the main employment of the troops was to assist the revenue authorities to suppress smuggling. Ireland, where there were barracks, had its own establishment, and troops were also employed in making Wade's strategic roads in the Highlands. Unhappy as the soldier's lot was in England, however, it was paradise to his lot abroad in the colonial garrisons—Gibraltar, Minorca, Nova Scotia or the West Indies. The West Indies in particular were detested as a station; desertions were frequent when a regiment was ordered there, because not only would disease carry off large numbers of the men, but there existed no organised systems of reliefs and a regiment's stay abroad would probably be a long one. Bad conditions and inadequate pay meant that only the dregs of the population were willing to enlist, and discipline among such recruits could only be maintained by severe and brutal punishments. It was not surprising that in 1733 General Wade could declare to the House of Commons that "the discipline of our army is already in a bad way."

Yet when a new series of wars against France broke out, the much maligned British soldiers soon showed the same quality as the men who had followed Marlborough; all that was lacking was leadership like Marlborough's. At Dettingen in 1743 an English king appeared for the last time on the battlefield. After the battle, Charles Russell of the Guards wrote home to his wife: "Our men and their regimental officers won the day, not in the manner of Hyde Park discipline, but our foot almost kneeled down by whole ranks, and so fired on 'em a running fire, making almost every ball take place . . . the English infantry behaved like heroes." Fontenoy, one of the few French victories in this long series of wars, was an even more glorious day for the British infantry. They won the admiration of the enemy commander, Marshal de Saxe, by their two attempts to attack the French prepared positions on a narrow front. Fontenoy is also

MARLBOROUGH AT THE BATTLE OF OUDENARDE, 1708
Tapestry presented to the first Duke of Marlborough

A MILITARY CAMP IN ST. JAMES'S PARK DURING THE GORDON RIOTS, 1780
Water colour by Paul Sandby

memorable because it was the first battle for the newly formed regiment of Highlanders, the Black Watch. Its initiation to battle was characteristic; even its chaplain, Adam Ferguson, later to be famous as a philosopher and as the friend of Sir Walter Scott, damned his commission and carried his broadsword into action. The battle of Minden in 1759 was another glorious day for the six regiments of British foot who took part in it. The defeated French commander wrote: "I have seen what I never thought to be possible, a single line of infantry break through three lines of cavalry ranked in order of battle, and tumble them to ruin." The glory of the day was somewhat dimmed by the disgraceful behaviour of Lord George Sackville, in command of the British and Hanoverian cavalry, whose failure to obey orders allowed the French to retire without being routed. The cavalry had its day, the following year, at Warburg when the Marquis of Granby, hatless and with his bald head shining in the sun, charged at the head of the Blues and with nine other British cavalry regiments put to flight a force of 20,000 French.

On the whole these were soldiers' battles. Lord Stair, who commanded at Dettingen, had learned some valuable lessons from his service under Marlborough, but in 1743 he was already seventy years of age. The Duke of Cumberland, George II's son, hardly distinguished himself as a commander in the field at Fontenoy, but he was a strict disciplinarian and a capable administrator and had much to do with raising the army from the state to which thirty years of neglect had reduced it. The infantry at Fontenoy were led by Sir John Ligonier, a Huguenot refugee who became Commander-in-chief and Pitt's principal military adviser in 1757. The Marquis of Granby was little more than a gallant leader of cavalry; he achieved immortality on the signs of the numerous inns which he set up for old soldiers of his beloved cavalry.

In this series of wars campaigning was not confined to the Continent of Europe. The East India Company had to fight for its position in India against the French. These campaigns were carried on mainly by English troops enlisted by the Company and native sepoys drilled and led by English officers. The Company's white troops were, in Clive's words, "the worst men of England," yet these sweepings of the seaport towns, even when raw recruits newly arrived in India, showed surprising steadiness in action at the taking of Chingleput in 1753. It was not until 1754 that a regular regiment, the 39th, was sent to India. It is no exaggeration to say that the English victory over the French was won by the initiative and ability of the English commanders. Stringer Lawrence, the real father of the Indian Army, was a captain in Clayton's regiment, the 14th Foot, when the Company appointed him to command its garrison at Madras. Clive, a born soldier, went out to India as a clerk and in 1757 won the battle of Plassey as a thirty-one year old lieutenant-colonel in the Company's Madras army. Eyre Coote, who completed their work, arrived in India as a company commander in the 39th.

SIR ROBERT CLIVE 1725-1774
Oil painting after Nathaniel Dance

Another theatre of operations was North America. Here the British soldier had to face a situation quite unsuited to his formal drill and red coat. In 1755, Braddock, on his way to capture Fort Duquesne, saw his men shot down by Indian marksmen hidden behind trees. He himself was mortally wounded. As he lay dying by the Monongahela River he said, "Another time we shall know better how to deal with them." Four years later Quebec was captured. Wolfe was only thirty-two when he died in the hour of victory as Braddock had died in the hour of defeat. He was a discovery first of Cumberland and then of Pitt, but he owed his discovery to his reputation in the army as a regimental officer. His *Instructions for young Officers*, drawn up when he commanded the 20th Foot, show the spirit in which he approached his work. Officers were to "make themselves acquainted with the men of the companies they belonged to; and as soon as possible with their characters, that they may know the proper subjects to encourage as well as those also whom it will be necessary to keep a strict hand over." Care for his men was the secret of Wolfe's success as a soldier. That explains why this frail, tubercular, somewhat neurotic young man could win such confidence from his troops, confidence crudely expressed in the verses of Serjeant Ned Botwood of Lascelles' regiment, the 47th, himself to fall in the taking of Quebec:

"And ye that love fighting shall soon have enough :
Wolfe commands you, my boys ; we shall give them hot stuff."

There were many changes in the army between 1739 and 1763, not all of them for the better. The profession of arms was still unattractive, for pay was still bad and discipline severe. German fashions in dress had been introduced by royal influence and the soldier had to fight in all the discomfort of a tight coat, powdered hair and a clubbed pigtail. On the credit side must be put the experimental light infantry corps raised for service in North America and the growing importance of artillery. The Royal Regiment was formed in 1722 and in the Westphalian campaigns of the Seven Years' War the British guns were said by a foreign observer to be the cleanest and most efficient in the whole allied army. The Militia Act of 1757, the work of Pitt, himself a former cornet of horse, was an attempt to revivify the old constitutional force by passing through it the whole able-bodied population of the kingdom. Boswell tells us that Dr. Johnson was once drawn to serve in the militia "and upon that occasion provided himself with a musket, and with sword and belt." However he did not serve in person and his biographer found the idea a laughable one. Yet another author, Edward Gibbon, who held a militia commission, was to feel "that the captain of the Hampshire grenadiers has not been useless to the historian of the Roman Empire."

THE AMERICAN REVOLUTION

THE British soldier may lose battles, but the only important war he has ever lost was the War of the American Revolution which began with shots on the village green at Lexington in 1775 and ended with the Treaty of Versailles in 1783 assuring the independence of the United States. But the defeat was hardly the soldiers' fault. It was rather due to the Navy's failure to maintain command of the sea, to the natural difficulties in fighting a war so far from home, and to the general inefficiency of the British administration. With Lord Sandwich, "Jemmy Twitcher," at the Admiralty and Lord George Germaine (the Lord George Sackville who had disgraced himself at Minden) as Secretary-at-War, the wonder was that in 1781 Washington could say, "We are at the end of our tether." It was of course no easy matter to arrange for the transport of large forces and their supplies across the Atlantic and the discomforts of the soldiers on the voyage were great. Serjeant Lamb of the 9th Foot embarked at Cork in the *Friendship* transport on 3rd April 1775 but did not arrive at Quebec until 29th

May. During the voyage one soldier tried to drown himself to escape punishment for stealing a comrade's shirt, a serjeant succeeded in doing so after a quarrel with his wife, and a recruit provoked by his fellows' mockery threw himself overboard and was lost. One of the Hessian troops employed in large numbers writes of the food supplied in the transports: "the ship biscuit was so hard that they sometimes broke it up with a cannon-ball, and the story was that it had been taken from the French in the Seven Years' War and lain in Portsmouth ever since."

Apart from the disasters at Saratoga and Yorktown, most of the engagements were British victories and the British soldiers showed in them all their old qualities. At Bunker Hill the most significant point is not so much the accuracy of the American fire or the severity of the British losses as the marvellous discipline which made the twice repulsed infantry obey the order to unbuckle their packs and attack for the third time with the bayonet. Their determined charge dislodged the Americans, now running short of ammunition, from their positions. It was magnificent, but it was hardly war. Gage, the British commander, had had plenty of experience in American warfare and ought to have known better than employ heavy infantry in a direct frontal attack.

At the beginning of the war the advantages in the irregular warfare which suited the country were all on the side of the Americans, many of whom had received their training in the British army during the Seven Years' War. The British light infantry corps raised for the conquest of Canada had been disbanded at the peace and the new light companies, added to each infantry regiment in 1770, had received little in the way of special training. It was not long, however, before the British light infantry and the much maligned Hessian Jägers showed themselves the superiors of the American skirmishers. The British troops who surrendered at Saratoga seem to have been of exceptional quality—they were "in a manner all light infantry," according to Ensign Anbury of the 24th—and Cornwallis's victory at Guildford Court House in 1781 was a striking tactical success over a much more numerous enemy in a chosen position. Earlier still, in 1778, there had been an even more convincing proof of the quickness with which the new tactics had been learned when a small force of 1,300 men under Colonel Meadows—the 5th Foot and the grenadier and light companies of eight regiments—inflicted 1,600 casualties on the French in the decisive battle for the West Indian island of St. Lucia.

With the possible exception of Benedict Arnold, who fought for each side in turn, the war produced no great commanders. But there was a fairly high level of ability among the British generals, although they were often unlucky and handicapped by interference from London. The unfortunate Burgoyne was a capable leader of men and it is greatly to his credit that he insisted on British soldiers being treated as "thinking beings." There was ability too among the leaders of the irregular corps—Tarleton,

THE FIRST REGIMENT OF GUARDS IN 1745
A Private, a Drummer and a Serjeant
Coloured lithograph after B. Clayton

the flamboyant commander of the British Legion, Simcoe, who led the mounted Queen's Rangers, and Patrick Ferguson, who invented his own breech-loading rifle but was overwhelmed by superior numbers at the battle of the King's Mountain.

Of the men they led we know much less. Except for a period of enthusiasm after the news of the surrender of Saratoga, recruiting was as difficult as ever. The pay was low, conditions were bad, and there were many influential people in England opposed to the war. But here and there we can trace the effects of the new attitude towards the soldier on the part of regimental officers. When Congress violated the terms of the Convention of Saratoga by separating the officers from their men, this separation seems to have been felt by the troops more hardly than their other privations and Serjeant Lamb at the end of his journal could write, "the friendship of the officer continues with the man who has fought under his command to the remotest period of declining years." Such a tradition, as well as the tactical lessons of the war, must have had their effect on the mind of young John Moore who saw his first service as an ensign in Maclean's Regiment at Penobscot Bay in 1779.

THE GREAT FRENCH WAR

IN introducing his budget in 1792 the younger Pitt assured the House
of Commons that "there never was a time in the history of this country,
when, from the situation of Europe, we might more reasonably expect
fifteen years of peace than at the present moment." On 1st February 1793
the revolutionary government in France began hostilities and for twenty-
two years until 1815, with only two slight breaks, we were at war. The condition of the army in 1793 certainly agreed with Pitt's expectation of a long
period of peace. A contemporary description has become famous: "Our
army was lax in its discipline, entirely without system, and very weak in
numbers. Each colonel of a regiment managed it according to his own
notions, or neglected it altogether; professional pride was rare; professional
knowledge still more so. Never was a kingdom less prepared for a stern
and arduous conflict." Some of the details of this gloomy picture are in-
correct. The War Office had recently taken out of the colonels' hands the
responsibility for paying and equipping troops. The government had begun
to build barracks, a policy which horrified an Opposition full of zeal for
the preservation of liberty but which gave the soldier a more suitable, if
not more luxurious, abode than the alehouse. And in 1792 Major-General
David Dundas won for himself the nickname of "Old Pivot" by writing
the first official drill book to win general acceptance in the army. Broadly
speaking, however, the army was too small and too ill-prepared for a
serious foreign war.

Its lack of readiness is clearly shown in the campaigns of 1793-4 and
in 1799 in the Netherlands, where the main reasons for failure seem to
have been lack of trained reserves and a proper system of supply and transport. To meet the threat of a French invasion of Holland in the first month
of the war the Government was able to send only three battalions of Guards.
The men marched to Greenwich, the head of the column sober enough
but those in the rear so drunk that they had to be carried in carts, and were
embarked in dirty Thames colliers, the only transports available. The de-
tachment helped to stop the French at Neerwinden and was soon joined
by a brigade of the Line. The reinforcements, however, were "undisciplined
and raw recruits," and two regiments out of three were found to be physically unfit for service. Private John Stevenson of the 3rd Guards went out
to Flanders in the spring of 1794. He had been in the army ten months,
but had received no training for active service. "This was the first time I
ever saw a tent pitched"; on the following day he was in battle. This same
soldier illustrates the inadequacy of the supply services. After his first engagement he tells how "we had no meat and but little bread in the last
two days, and we now look anxiously for the bread wagons. None came . . .
and so we were left to enjoy our rest unencumbered with an overloaded
stomach." In the 1799 campaign, Abercrombie was forced to remind the

AN OFFICER OF THE 10TH LIGHT DRAGOONS, A TRUMPETER AND TWO TROOPERS
Oil painting by George Stubbs, 1793

Cabinet that an army was helpless without wagons and horses. Small wonder that, in spite of some gallant fighting, both these campaigns ended in withdrawal. The severe winter of 1794-5 saw the British army retreating painfully from Holland to Bremen, with its rearguard commanded by Arthur Wesley, the young lieutenant-colonel of the 33rd. In 1799 the British army, hungry and ill-clad and suffering severely through sickness, was evacuated under a capitulation to prevent worse disaster in the winter.

One explanation of the Government's failure to provide sufficient men for these campaigns was Pitt's policy of "filching sugar islands" from the French in the West Indies, a policy approved by the mercantile class and to a certain extent justified later by Napoleon's insistence on the importance of these islands, but a policy which sent large numbers of British soldiers to almost inevitable death. For in the West Indies, the blacks were worse enemies than the French, and the yellow fever far worse than either. In 1796 the 57th lost in six months through fever 7 officers and 542 men; the 18th Royal Irish went to the West Indies in 1805 and saw no active service, but before its return in 1817 its two battalions had lost 52 officers and 1,777

227

other ranks. Dislike of West Indian service, more than anything else, made recruiting difficult in the first period of the war. In 1793 the recruiting bounty was ten guineas; in 1798 it had risen as high as eighty guineas.

In the first sixteen years of war the British army fought many other campaigns besides those in the Netherlands and the West Indies. There were expeditions to Toulon, Minorca, Corsica, the Cape, Egypt, Buenos Ayres, Copenhagen, Sweden and Italy, as well as raids on the French and Spanish coasts. There were rare gleams of success, but British soldiers showed their quality especially in Egypt in 1801 and at Maida in southern Italy in 1806. After so many reverses the capitulation of a more numerous French army in Egypt "revived," as a wise observer said, "confidence and an honourable pride in our military service." Much of the credit went to the commander, Sir Ralph Abercrombie, who died of wounds before the campaign was over. Not only was he considerate of his men and therefore popular with them, but he had learned from previous experience and was able to carry out successfully a carefully planned disembarkation in the face of the enemy. Maida, on the other hand, was a soldiers' battle. Success was mainly due to the resource and steadiness of the infantry and young John Colborne, who commanded the light infantry of the 20th had some excuse for his boast: "I now begin to think, as our ancestors did, that one Englishman is equal to two Frenchmen." Yet the victory could not be followed up for lack of cavalry and reinforcements, and the lesson of all these scattered campaigns was that the British army was badly in need of administrative reform and a better system of recruitment and training.

The Duke of York, George III's second son, had not distinguished himself as a commander in the field in either of the campaigns in the Netherlands. But as commander-in-chief he patiently and unobtrusively carried out a series of important reforms. He stopped the practice by which officers absented themselves from their regiments on "Secretary-at-War's leave"; from 1795 soldiers no longer had to powder their hair; in 1799 the establishment of a Royal Wagon Train gave the army a transport system under its own control. The problem of recruitment was to a large extent solved by Castlereagh's Militia Acts, which made the militia an efficient force for home defence and a reservoir from which the army could draw recruits. Most of the soldier-authors of this war began their service in the militia; Serjeant Cooper enlisted into the 7th Royal Fusiliers from the North York Militia and George Calladine was in the Derbyshire Militia before he joined the 19th Foot. Castlereagh not only has the main credit for persisting with the war in the Peninsula after the retreat to Corunna; his reforms provided the men who won it.

Sir John Moore was also unfortunate as a commander in the field; he never had a real chance to show his undoubted competence as a leader of troops. But as a reformer of training he was incomparable. When England was faced in 1802-4 with the possibility of an invasion by Napoleon's Grand

SIR JOHN MOORE 1761-1809
Oil painting by Sir Thomas Lawrence

Army, he commanded a brigade at Shorncliffe and exercised it in the light infantry tactics which had emerged in the American wars. His aim was "that not only the officers, but that each individual soldier, knows perfectly what he has to do." A disciplinarian, but a kindly one, he preferred that the officers should be "attached to the men, and the men to the officers." John Colborne, Moore's A.D.C. at Corunna, who was to command the 52nd, one of the Shorncliffe light infantry regiments, in the Peninsula and at Waterloo, says of his chief: "His life was spent among the troops." A few days before the battle of Corunna, in which Moore lost his life, Charles Steevens, then captain of the light company of the 20th, met him. "I thought that Sir John Moore made his enquiries and gave his orders in such a mild gentlemanly way, I was quite struck with his engaging manners, and so were my two subalterns; and I am sure the men of my company seemed, all of them to be equally pleased with him." Knowledge of his men and consideration for them were the foundation of Moore's success as a trainer of troops.

THE BATTLE OF CORUNNA, JANUARY 16, 1809
Coloured aquatint after W. Heath

WELLINGTON

THE purchase system enabled Arthur Wesley to become lieutenant-colonel of the 33rd Foot on the 30th April 1793 at the age of twenty-four, having spent nearly all the six years of his army life as aide-de-camp to the Lord Lieutenant of Ireland. At the age of thirty-nine, as Lieutenant-General Sir Arthur Wellesley, with a reputation won in Indian fighting, he was sent out to the Peninsula. On 18th June 1815, aged forty-six, as Field Marshal the Duke of Wellington he fought and won his last battle at Waterloo. Youth is a first and often forgotten characteristic of Wellington as a soldier.

Throughout his military life we find Wellington preoccupied with questions of supply and transport. The disastrous campaign of 1794 must have taught him this lesson at least; "I learned what one ought not to do, and that is always something." A good deal of his success in India was due to his talent for realistic administration. His despatches are full of detail about bullocks and wicker boats and in a very early memorandum he hit on the truth that "it is impossible to carry on a war in India without bullocks." The same care about supply is to be found throughout his Peninsular campaigns. While his troops are disembarking at Mondego Bay in the first days of August 1808, we find him on board H.M.S. *Donegal* writing memoranda for his commissary-general and laying down the exact number of mules and carts that will be needed for the supply of his army. In 1812 Captain

THE 79TH HIGHLANDERS AT THE BATTLE OF WATERLOO, JUNE 18, 1815
Coloured engraving published in 1816

Tomkinson of the 16th Light Dragoons is able to write in his diary that "the system of supplying an army by means of mules in Spain and Portugal is brought to the greatest perfection. There are about sixty mules to every cavalry regiment, for the purpose of supplying bread to the men and corn to the horses . . . The system though expensive was excellent, and the army continued its operations in countries where there was nothing to be had, and where any other army could not have remained." Bullocks in India and mules in Spain had much to do with Wellington's success. His meticulous attention to the details of commissariat gave him in the Peninsula a great advantage over an army ordered by its Emperor to live on a country which could not possibly support it.

Wellington often expressed his impatience of the making of detailed strategic plans—"I made my campaigns of rope; if anything went wrong, I tied a knot, and went on"—although it is only fair to remember that in 1809 he drafted for Castlereagh a *Memorandum on the Defence of Portugal* which forecast pretty accurately what was going to happen in the first phase of the Peninsular War. Wellington, however, was at his best in the field, youthfully energetic, apparently immune to enemy fire, seeing all and skilful in directing the tactical course of battle. At Argaum, in the Mahratta War, some of his sepoy regiments fell into a panic when the enemy artillery opened fire and Wellington wrote, "I am convinced that if I had not been near them, to rally them and restore the battle, we should have lost the day." An officer of the 53rd in a letter home describing the battle of Talavera

231

says: "Sir Arthur was on a hill in the centre of the line and saw every movement that took place; he sent down one of his aide-de-camps to say that a body of the enemy was moving down for the purpose of turning the right, and on our exertions depended the fate of the day." And at Waterloo it is no exaggeration to say that the day was won by Wellington's untiring minute-to-minute management of his troops, many of them raw recruits or unreliable foreigners. His own verdict on the battle is a just one: "it has been a damned nice thing, the nearest run thing that ever you saw in your life. By God, I don't think it would have been done if I had not been there." Well might the Rifleman Kincaid declare before Fuentes de Oñoro that "we would rather see his long nose in the fight than a reinforcement of ten thousand men any day."

Like all great commanders, Wellington was considerate towards his troops and sent them into battle as well-equipped and well-fed as he could. There was, of course, a good deal of hard campaigning in the Peninsula. In the campaign of 1809, writes Serjeant Cooper of the 7th Fusiliers, "tents we had none, nor yet blankets. We slept in the open air, and this was the mode: the great coat was inverted, and our legs were thrust into the sleeves; one half was put under us, and the other half above. The knapsacks formed our pillow. Thus arranged, with forage cap pulled over our ears, we bid good night to the stars, and rested as we could." Cooper had much else to grumble at—the hospitals (with much justice, although Sir James McGregor at Wellington's headquarters was doing his best to improve conditions), the dress, and the food. It is true that the British army often had to go on short commons, and that the men who won Talavera did not eat for two days, but its occasional sufferings were slight beside those of the French. The later campaigns of the war were fought by a well-fed army, and on the morning of Waterloo Serjeant Morris of the 73rd tells how "some commissariat wagons came to the field, with a supply of salt provisions and spirits, and two men from each company were sent for them." In matters of dress, Wellington had none of the Hanoverian precision and allowed both himself and his men considerable laxity. "Provided we brought our men into the field well appointed, and with sixty rounds of good ammunition each, he never looked to see whether their trousers were black, blue, or grey; and as to ourselves, we might be rigged out in all the colours of the rainbow if we fancied it;" such is the testimony of Lieutenant William Grattan of the Connaught Rangers. Another good illustration of Wellington's consideration is to be found in a postscript added to a letter in which Benjamin D'Urban was ordered to make a forced march with a mixed force: "if you make the Light Infantry march far, let some of your Dragoons carry their knapsacks."

Wellington's consideration for his men was never, however, the warm-hearted consideration of a Marlborough or a Wolfe or a Moore. He had no affection for his men, and they had not love but only respect for him.

THE SURREY YEOMAN CAVALRY, LATER 98TH FIELD BRIGADE, ROYAL ARTILLERY
Drawn and engraved by Charles Tomkins c. 1800

Throughout his life he remained a product of his class, the aloof Irish aristocracy of the Protestant Ascendancy, and the most serious flaw in his character was his scarcely veiled contempt for the men he led to victory. Napier ended his great account of the Peninsular War with this sentence: "thus the war terminated, and with it all remembrance of the veteran's services." Neglect of the veteran is not uncommon in our history, but Wellington must bear the blame for not calling attention to his merits and necessities. Yet it must not be forgotten that there was a foundation of truth in Wellington's strictures on his troops. He described them as "the scum of the earth; English soldiers are fellows who have enlisted for drink. That is the plain fact, they have *all* enlisted for drink." Even Napier has to qualify his eulogy of the British soldier with the words "notwithstanding his habitual excess in drinking." During the great retreats and after the storming of Badajoz and San Sebastian, Wellington could have found plenty of facts to back his opinion, and on one occasion, during the retreat from Madrid, Harry Smith of the Rifle Brigade tells how "every soldier" in the Light Division "staggered to their alarm posts" when the assembly sounded for an unexpected night march; "the good general [Vandeleur] had been at the shrine of Bacchus too, and was uncontrollable."

Such an army required rigid discipline; in Napier's opinion, it took three years to produce a completely disciplined soldier. It was discipline which enabled the British army to fight in the two-deep line which was able to produce such a shattering fire against the heads of the French attacking columns. For the French never varied their tactics. In April 1811 Wellington wrote, "But really these attacks in columns against our lines are very contemptible;" after Waterloo he told Creevey that the French "have always fought the same since I first saw them at Vimeiro." The discipline which Wellington forged in Spain showed brightest in France in 1815 when the good behaviour of the British army contrasted so forcibly with the excesses of the Austrians, Prussians and Russians. Wellington's sole recipe for good discipline was flogging and death; later in life he was to tell a Royal Commission that "he had no idea of any great effect being produced on British soldiers by anything but the fear of immediate corporal punishment."

Wellington's greatest mistake lay probably in his habit of generalising on the whole Peninsular army, a mistake which has its origin in the increasing difficulty of maintaining contact between his headquarters and the growing army in the field. He aroused great resentment by his general criticism of the regimental officers whom he held responsible for the breakdown of discipline on the retreat from Madrid in 1812. It was quite certain that some regiments had no breakdown in discipline at all, yet their officers were included in the general condemnation. And that all the rank and file were the scum of the earth is easily disproved by the fact that so many of them later published interesting and sometimes valuable accounts of the campaign. Some of his subordinates too, especially those trained in the school of Moore, had better ways of maintaining discipline than the lash.

Variety is the characteristic of Wellington's army and it is impossible to find an easy generalisation which will adequately describe it. The general officers included the warm-hearted and equable "Daddy" Hill, who was heard to swear twice only during the whole campaign; the Welshman

PIPER OF THE 93RD SUTHERLAND HIGHLANDERS
Engraving after B. Clayton

Picton, "a rough, foul-mouthed devil as ever lived"; the quick-tempered Crawford, the first commander of the Light Division, who was killed at the siege of Ciudad Rodrigo in 1812; and the Scottish gentleman, Graham of Balgowan, with his unrelenting hatred of the French. Among the regimental commanders were Colborne of the 52nd, whose flank attack at

Waterloo was the real turning point of the battle; Sydney Beckwith of the Rifle Brigade whose men would "follow him cheerfully through fire and water when the day of trial came, for they well knew he was the last man on earth who would give them unnecessary trouble, or, on the other hand, would spare either man or officer, when the good of the service demanded their utmost exertions;" Henry Walton Ellis of the 23rd Fusiliers, who was an ensign at birth and a captain at fourteen, and who was mortally wounded at Waterloo; and John Cameron of the Gordon Highlanders, "the finest soldier possible, but very strict." As for the regimental officers, the Rifle Brigade alone contained such diverse types as the gay and amusing Johnny Kincaid, Harry Smith, who married a young Spanish girl at Badajoz and carried her with him throughout the campaign, and the somewhat matter-of-fact George Simmons, who had been a militia surgeon before he joined the army to further "the interests of his family" out of his meagre pay. In the ranks were such men as William Lawrence of the 40th, who was flogged in 1809 for being absent from guard and who then reformed and became a serjeant in 1813; James Anton, the philosophic quartermaster-serjeant of the Black Watch; John Stevenson, private in the 3rd Guards and Wesleyan class-leader; and the anonymous private of the 71st, who joined the army as a result of the ignominious failure of his theatrical debut at Edinburgh. Divergency of character is to be found at every level in this army, for perhaps more than any previous army it was a mirror of the British people, fighting for a cause in which the majority of that people believed.

DRUM MAJOR OF THE ROYAL IRISH FUSILIERS,
THE 87TH REGIMENT
Lithograph by E. Hull, 1828

236

ARTHUR WELLESLEY, DUKE OF WELLINGTON, 1761-1852

Oil painting by Sir Thomas Lawrence

By courtesy of Maggs Bros., London

COMBINED NAVAL AND MILITARY FORCES, BURMA, 27TH MARCH, 1825

A Forerunner of the modern Commando

Drawn and engraved by Stothard and Prall after a sketch by Captain Thornton, R.N.

SMALL WARS

DURING the great wars and in the intervals between them, the British army still has its garrison duties to perform and its small wars to fight. The British soldier has fought in many parts of the world—on the dusty plains of India, in the mosquito-ridden jungles of Burma, among the rocky *kopjes* of the *veldt*, and in the rough and stony passes of the North-West Frontier. Among his enemies have been whirling Dervishes, treacherous Afghans, Maoris barking like dogs, and bloodthirsty Zulus. We can mention only a few of the small wars which the British army has fought and recall some of the occasions when British soldiers have paid, in suffering and blood, the price of Empire.

Very early on the morning of the 21st February 1805 a fourth assault was made on the great fortress of Bhurtpore, which General Lake was besieging in his campaign against the Mahrattas. Three previous assaults, the third on the day before, had failed. In the first two of them, the forlorn hope in front of the storming party had been led by Serjeant John Shipp of the 22nd. Wounded though he was, he volunteered to lead it again on this fourth attempt. Once more the attack failed. The breach was only wide enough for two men at a time and it could only be climbed by men using their bayonets as steps. Lake had to raise the siege—the only failure in his career—and it was not until 1826 that Bhurtpore was taken. John Shipp, who had been wounded again in the last attempt, received a commission as a reward and became a lieutenant in the 76th. Money difficulties forced him to sell out. He then enlisted in the ranks of the 24th Light Dragoons, rose to be regimental serjeant-major, and was then commissioned again in the 87th—the "Ould Fogs"—with whom he saw service in the Gurkha War and a second campaign against the Mahrattas. At last in 1825, after twenty-eight years' service, he went on half-pay to write a number of books, including his *Memoirs of an Extraordinary Military Career*.

From 1824 to 1826 British and Indian troops were employed in the First Burmese War. The Burmese, in spite of their skill at entrenchment, were easy enemies, but the casualties from disease—scurvy, cholera and malaria—were extremely heavy. Of the 3,738 men originally sent to Rangoon, 166 were killed in action and 3,160 died in hospital; of the 1,004 despatched to Arakan, none was killed in action, but 595 died in hospital.

George Bell, a lieutenant in the 45th, describes the assembly of the army at Rangoon at the end of the war: "I never saw such living skeletons." When he heard that his own regiment was to remain in Burma, he jumped at the chance of an exchange into the 2nd Royals, even though it would postpone the possibility of a captaincy. "I became the 22nd lieutenant of my regiment, with a poor chance of promotion; but released from Ava, and a grave under a talipot-tree, I was satisfied."

THE RIDGE AND FORT OF JYTOK ON THE INDIAN FRONTIER
Coloured aquatint from Fraser's *Himalayas*, 1820

In January 1849, Lord Gough had lost heavily in an indecisive battle at Chilianwala and, although the casualties of his Sikh opponents had also been heavy, he had been forced to withdraw. Something of a public outcry led to Gough's supersession in the command by Sir Charles Napier. But in the following month, with a reinforced army, before Napier had arrived, Gough brought the Sikh wars to an end at Gujerat. Gujerat was in the main an artillery battle. One by one the Sikh batteries were silenced by a three hours' cannonade from Gough's ninety-six guns, and the horse artillery joined the cavalry in the pursuit of the Sikhs who broke before our advancing infantry. A few days later the remnant of the Sikh army laid down its arms and before long the Sikhs had been transformed from tough enemies to staunch supporters of the British power in India.

In 1857 the greatly outnumbered white troops in India were faced with the mutiny of a considerable part of the sepoy army. This was one of the bitterest campaigns ever fought by the British soldier. Bitter enough at the start because many of the native regiments murdered their white officers, it was made bitterer still by the horrible massacres at Cawnpore. William Forbes Mitchell, then a serjeant in the 93rd Sutherland Highlanders, tells how after the attack on the Sikandarbagh at Lucknow the throats of the men were hoarse with shouting "Cawnpore! you bloody murderers." He goes on to tell how "the taste of the powder (those were the days when the

LORD ROBERTS 1832-1914
Water colour by Mortimer Menpes

muzzle-loading cartridges had to be bitten with the teeth) made men almost mad with thirst; and with the sun high over head, and being fresh from England, with our feather bonnets, red coats, and heavy kilts, we felt the heat intensely." There was much hard fighting and hard living before the Sepoy Mutiny was finally suppressed, but the threat was resolutely met by both Queen's and Company's troops and by leaders like John Nicholson, the stern young Ulsterman who was mortally wounded in the storming of Delhi, Henry Havelock, the defender of Lucknow who lived just long enough to see it relieved, the fiery but somewhat over-cautious Colin Campbell, and, greatest of all, Hugh Rose, who used both patience and mobility in the hunt for Tantia Topi.

The Ashantee campaign of 1873-4 did not involve a great deal of fighting but the hard marches called for endurance on the part of the British troops and for considerable organising ability on the part of the commander and his staff. Sir Garnet Wolseley, who had lately been Cardwell's principal military adviser at the War Office, was in command and with him were the famous "Wolseley Ring" of staff officers. The brigade of British troops employed wore a special issue of clothing; every officer and man in the 2nd battalion of the Rifle Brigade was provided with "two grey frocks, a pair of grey tweed trousers, a pair of white duck trousers, two flannel shirts, two flannel belts, a pith helmet with *puggaree* attached, and a pair of canvas gaiters." Transport was the main difficulty—everything had to be carried by native porters—but Wolseley successfully carried through the campaign in the short season in which white troops were able to operate. Not a man remained on the Gold Coast ten weeks after the arrival of the British brigade, but even so the deaths from disease were heavy enough.

In August 1880, through the hot days and cold nights of an Afghan summer, a force of ten thousand troops, just over a quarter of them white, marched the 350 miles from Kabul to Kandahar to relieve the beleagured garrison there and to avenge Maiwand, where the Afghans had cut to pieces General Burrows' brigade. Great heat during the day, choking dust storms, bad water, lack of sleep because of frequent picket duties were the main hardships of the march. Yet after the twenty-three days of the march the force was fit enough to scatter the Afghan army in the battle of Baba Wali Kotal. The credit for this success was rightly given to the force commander, Sir Frederick Roberts. He was not only a careful administrator able to make meticulous arrangements for supply and transport, but in battle he showed great personal courage and a keen eye for country which usually found a way of outflanking the positions taken up by the enemy. Above all, he was loved by the men he led. There probably never has been a more popular general in the British army than the "jovial Irishman."

> " 'E's the man that done us well,
> An' we'll follow 'im to 'ell—
> Won't we, Bobs ?"

The death of Gordon at Khartoum was left unavenged for thirteen years until the Dervishes were routed at Omdurman. Before the battle Kitchener had put in much patient work. He had to create an Egyptian army, the best elements in which were Sudanese prisoners of war, and he had to make sure of his supplies by pushing the railway up the Nile Valley. But the battle itself was the last of its kind. The account of an eye-witness, Lieutenant Winston Churchill with the 21st Lancers, shows us the infantry manoeuvring shoulder-to-shoulder in an almost coverless plain, often obscured by the powder smoke, and his own regiment charging masses of the enemy with lances levelled. At Omdurman the Fuzzy-wuzzy, who had "cut our sentries up at Suakim" and who had "broke a British square" at Abu Klea, had to yield to superior discipline and the greater fire-power of the new Lee Metford magazine rifle.

THE BATTLE OF QUATRE BRAS, JUNE 16, 1815
Coloured aquatint by S. Mitan

In these campaigns, and a score of others, the British soldier carried out his trade during the nineteenth century. At first very little attention was paid to his efforts; he usually fought and died unnoticed and unsung by those at home. But in the second half of the century a change can be detected. Memorials become less rare, campaign medals are awarded, private soldiers are decorated for gallantry, and not only officers are mentioned in despatches (this is especially true of those written by Roberts). The soldier, however, still remains a professional, fighting those " 'oom he is paid to kill" ; Tommy Atkins remains a man apart from the rest of the community.

THE NINETEENTH CENTURY

WHEN the Great War with France ended in 1815, the army was at once drastically cut down and for nearly forty years was almost completely neglected. The desire for economy was dominant and those who believed in the maintenance of an army seem to have felt that the only way to keep one at all was to hide most of it in India or the colonies.

243

THE ROYAL WELCH FUSILIERS
Coloured lithograph by Madeley c. 1849

The Duke of Wellington, who was either Commander-in-Chief or Prime Minister for much of this time, was resolutely opposed to army reform; he was as much a failure as an administrator in peace as he had been a success as a commander in war. In judging Wellington's apathy, however, it must be remembered that he hardly dared allow the army to be subjected to further economies, the usual result of calling attention to its deficiencies, and that in 1847 he told a private correspondent that he had tried to awaken the interest of several ministries in the army's weakness. But the House of Commons was always as it was in 1840, when it "spent on the army very little of its own time or of the nation's money." As a result the soldier continued to live in overcrowded barracks—these had been built during the Great War—and to spend the few coppers of his pay on the bad liquor supplied by the contractors who managed the canteens. The public rarely saw him unless he were called upon to suppress a riot, although in the troublous times after 1815 this unpopular work was usually done by the yeomanry and later the foundation of police forces made the employment of troops in this duty extremely rare. Altogether the calling of a soldier had few attractions and Alexander Somerville's reason for enlisting

THE RIFLE BRIGADE
Coloured aquatint by J. Harris after H. Martens, 1855

in the Scots Greys in 1831 was typical—he had no money and was unable
to get employment.

When war was declared on Russia in 1854 we were able to send a force
of only 26,000 men to the Crimea. This army was a mere collection of

THE BATTLE OF THE ALMA, SEPTEMBER 20, 1854
Coloured lithograph by W. Simpson

regiments with no experience of acting together in brigades or divisions
and with no organisation for supply or transport. The men had never been
taught the art of living in the field and had not even received much in the
way of musketry instruction. This did not matter a great deal as the British
army had just abandoned their old "Brown Bess" muskets in favour of
the muzzle-loading Minié rifle; while the army was encamped at Varna,
the men were given practice in the use of the new weapons, which, in fact,
were only issued to them on their arrival there. The British army was better
armed than the Russian, and it was better disciplined, but its crying weakness lay in its lack of trained reserves and in the absence of a proper commissariat system. Not all the gallantry shown at the Alma, Balaclava and
Inkerman nor all the resource of the regimental officers could prevent the
sufferings of the terrible winter in the trenches before Sebastopol. British
armies had often suffered the like or worse, but never before had the people
at home been told of their sufferings as they were this time by Mr. Russell
of *The Times*. The Crimean was the most senseless war we have ever waged.
Our commanders in the field are now almost forgotten and all we remember
is the gallantry and hardships of the regimental officers and men and the
devoted labours of Miss Florence Nightingale.

The conscience of the nation was aroused and the question of army
reform, if it could be effected with economy, became important in politics.

TANKS IN ACTION

Water colour by Charles Cundall

THE INVASION OF ITALY

Troops and vehicles embarking on invasion craft at "Charlie" beach near Santa Teresa di Riva, Sicily, Sept. 3rd, 1943.

Water Colour by Edward Ardizzone

THE DRESSING STATION AT LE BAC-DU-SUD ON THE DOULLENS-ARRAS ROAD, AUGUST 1918
Casualties from mustard gas
Oil painting by John S. Sargent

Between 1854 and 1904 there were no less than 567 committees and Royal Commissions on army administration. The tide of reform ran slowly at first but was accelerated by the fear first of Napoleon III and then of the new military power of Prussia. Most of the reforms and suggestions are of interest rather to the historian of the army, but round about 1870 Edward Cardwell, with Wolseley as his principal adviser, made changes which were to affect profoundly the lot of the officers and men in the service. The less important was the abolition of the purchase system. A cynic might easily say that the only result of this reform was that a subaltern could now wait for his promotion without the mortification of seeing his richer brethren soar quickly to high rank—but he still had to wait. Still the new system was fairer and it had the great advantage of putting an end to the constant transfer of officers between one regiment and another by exchange. More important was Cardwell's transformation of the army into a short-service army. The normal term for enlistment now became six years with the Colours and six with the Reserve. Unfortunately the need for economy meant that this change was accompanied by no increase in the rate of pay. A man might put up with low pay if he was sure of it for life, but low pay for six years only meant that the type of recruit obtained by the army was bound to decline in quality. The physical standards had to be lowered to obtain recruits at all and in the last decade of the century the army contained about 50,000 men unfit for active service or indeed hard work of any kind. In these years employment was good and wage rates were rising; therefore the army had to be content with the misfits and leavings of other employments—the "absent-minded beggars."

The South African War showed that much still remained to be done. The struggle against the Boers was at first looked on as one of the small wars with which the regular army was quite competent to deal. But it took 450,000 men three years to master 90,000 Boers. The actual fighting was the least troublesome part of the war. Our casualties in action were less than 6,000; we lost more than this through enteric fever. After the initial successes of the Boers, it did not take Lord Roberts long to defeat their field armies and occupy their capitals. His successor, Kitchener, was left with the more difficult task of guarding lines of communication and gradually wearing down the highly skilled Boer guerilla fighters. To the soldiers this meant "days of interminable and aimless trekking in the bushveldt," without leave and "in a permanent state of semi-starvation." Yet in the process the British army learned a new mobility and re-discovered the importance of marksmanship.

Between 1902 and 1914 great efforts were made, by politicians like Arnold Forster and Haldane and soldiers like Haig and Wilson, to profit by the lessons of the South African War and to prepare for the greater struggle that was clearly imminent. A General Staff was created to study the problems of possible future operations. The regular troops at home were formed into divisions as an Expeditionary Force, with the Old Militia, renamed the Special Reserve, to make good its wastage. The Yeomanry and Volunteers became the Territorial Force, ostensibly for home defence, but, in Haldane's conception, also to act as a reserve for the regular army. There was fairly general agreement that the special military needs of the Empire required a seasoned volunteer force and advocates of conscription were in a decided minority. But the problem of encouraging recruitment was hardly tackled at all by Haldane. Lord Roberts had done much to improve the soldier's lot. Kipling's verse had helped to change the nation's attitude to him. His pay, however, in spite of the small increase in 1904, remained low and it was clear that the regular army must continue to consist of officers dependent to a certain extent on the subsidies of their families and other ranks largely drawn from the lower levels of the artisan and agricultural labourer classes. Yet army reform of any kind between wars was a pleasing change in our normal policy and the B.E.F. that left England for France in August 1914 was certainly the best army we have ever had at the beginning of a serious war.

TWO GREAT WARS

THE South African War lowered the barrier between the army and the nation. More than half the troops used in the campaign were on regular enlistment, but the remainder consisted of militia and yeomanry and volunteers, as well as the "five-bob colonials." The barrier was removed completely by the Great War of 1914-18. While the regular army was sacrificing itself at Mons, Le Cateau and Ypres, a new army of volunteers, "Kitchener's army," was being trained under great difficulties in England, and from 1915 onwards a steady stream of the manhood of Britain

THE ROYAL TANK REGIMENT: TOOL INSPECTION
Oil painting by Henry Lamb, 1941

flowed across the Channel. In November 1918, when the armistice was
signed, there were over three and a half million men in the British army.
Never before had there been so many British soldiers. Voluntary recruitment alone could not supply such vast numbers and the semi-compulsion
of the Derby scheme, which invited men to register in age groups, had to
be followed in 1916 by a Military Service Act making all men in Great
Britain between the ages of 18 and 41 liable to be called up.

The man-power situation would have been even worse but for the response of the Empire. The Indian Army had often been called on to fight
outside India and Indian troops were used in almost every theatre of war.
In the Boer War thirty thousand colonial troops arrived in South Africa
before hostilities were over. In the Great War however, the response from

251

the Dominions and colonies was on a far greater scale. Gallipoli and Villers-Bretonneux will always be associated with the Australians and New Zealanders, Vimy ridge with the Canadians, and the brilliant campaigns in Germany's African colonies with the South Africans. In the Boer War the officering of the colonial contingents had been a difficult problem. There was no such difficulty in the Great War and John Monash, an Australian militiaman, became a successful Corps commander in France, with the probability of still further promotion if the war had lasted longer.

As always in our great wars British soldiers had to fight all over the world—in Africa and Mesopotamia, in Palestine, at Gallipoli and in the Balkans and Italy. But the great increase in the size of the army was made necessary by the incessant demands of the Western Front. For the first time in its history the army was committed to a large scale continental kind of warfare completely at variance with its old traditions. After the first few months the power of manoeuvre was lost and a long period of almost static trench warfare set in. When in 1918 this phase came to an end the army had almost lost the secret of mobility. Endurance was the main quality that trench warfare demanded in soldiers, the ability to stick discomforts and to hold the line, and it was a quality displayed in the same measure by the early regulars and the later conscripts. It was not the fault of the soldier that the infantry which had dominated Peninsular battlefields became the P.B.I. of the Somme and Passchendaele.

In the main it was a soldier's war from which the generals were oddly detached. The increased size of the armies had created a gap between the troops in the line and the headquarters and no commander ever learned the art of bridging it. Haig for all his faults had great gifts, an invaluable tenacity of purpose and mental powers of a high order, but circumstances and a certain shyness of temperament prevented him from exercising that magnetism which is the mark of the great commander; only once, when on October 31st 1914 he rode at the head of his staff among the shell fire on the Menin road, can we detect the Marlborough touch. It was no accident that the commander with the greatest direct influence on his troops should have been Allenby, for in Palestine he had a theatre of war where manoeuvre was possible and the art of generalship could be exercised.

The Great War was a landmark in the development of warfare because of the great strides made in technical invention and the increasing strain which combat placed on a country's industrial resources. Aircraft were used for reconnaissance, bombing and strafing, and before the war was over the Royal Flying Corps, developed in 1912 out of the Air Battalion of the Royal Engineers, had become the Royal Air Force, a separate service and no longer a mere part of the army. Artillery became more important than ever before and the supply of munitions for vast concentrations of guns was a critical problem in the conduct of the war. The machine gun, no longer the almost permanently jammed Gatling of earlier colonial cam-

A STATION SCENE IN WAR-TIME
Oil painting by William Roberts

paigns, was mainly responsible for the static conditions of trench warfare. To cross trenches in spite of the hail of machine gun fire there was developed the tank, an armoured and tracked vehicle, first used, in a small way, in the battle of the Somme in 1916. Nearly two years later at the battle of Amiens, "the black day of the German Army," Rawlinson's Fourth Army had well over four hundred tanks, supported by two thousand guns and seventeen squadrons of aircraft. The machine age of warfare had arrived.

The Second World War has seen further developments in the application of invention to war. The soldier can now drop by parachute from the skies to assault key-points or to capture landing-grounds for large bodies of troops transported in troop-carrying aircraft or gliders. Tanks have become faster, their armour is heavier and they carry guns of larger calibre; and the Royal Armoured Corps which operates them has successfully combined the new tradition of the armoured fighting vehicle with the old tradition of the cavalry. The modern soldier, to be effective, requires the co-operation of the other services—specially designed landing craft and constant air cover. The importance of the machine has transformed the army into a force of skilled craftsmen—gunners, sappers, signallers, tank crews, the men of the Royal Corps of Electrical and Mechanical Engineers. The infantry, with their Bren guns, mortars, carriers and anti-tank weapons, have had to acquire skills which would have seemed fantastic a hundred years ago. There is no arm which is not now a technical arm, and a highly organised Department for the Selection of Personnel is required to allocate men according to their individual aptitudes.

The increased use of machines and the greater speed of modern warfare calls for greater endurance on the part of the men who fight and demands from every soldier the disciplined use of his own initiative. Men found themselves flung at once, without any gradual introduction, into total warfare. To meet this situation a new system of battle training has been devised, consisting partly of inoculation for battle in as realistic conditions as possible, and partly of learning beforehand drills to perform the various tasks which may have to be done on active service. Battle drill has restored drill to its rightful and traditional place as a preparation for combat, and it is intended to ensure that men will know what they have to do as part of the team to which they belong. The ideal aimed at in the training of the army as a whole is now that of the special service troops or commandos, men physically fit, skilled in the use of their weapons, able to work harmoniously together. In spite of the machine, personality is triumphant, and the development of transport and communications has restored to generals the possibility of direct personal command of their troops, a chance which has been eagerly seized by men like Wavell, Alexander, Montgomery and many others.

In a world war the British soldier often finds himself in places where his predecessors have been before. The 1939-45 war saw our fourth campaign in Burma. The East Indies brings back memories of Robert Rollo Gillespie, reputed in his day to be the bravest man in the British army, and his adventures in Java. We had fought the Senussi in the Western desert in 1915; we have entered Damascus both in 1918 and in 1941. We occupied Sicily during the Great War with France and fought a campaign in southern Italy. France and the Low Countries are old fighting grounds for the British soldier. Throughout this last war he has been walking in the shadow of the past.

EPILOGUE

SIXTEENTH century writers were fond of making epigrammatic comparisons between the military characters of the principal nations of Europe and they would hardly understand my hesitation at attempting to sum up in a word or two the main characteristics of the Briton as soldier. Neither popularity nor perfection will be among them. Until recently the British soldier has not been a popular figure with the nation and many people can still remember when it was considered a disgrace for a man to "go for a soldier," and it would be idle to pretend that there

THE HARBOUR OF TOBRUK
Water colour drawing by Edward Bawden 1940

were no stains on the record of the British army. The British soldier has sometimes given way to panic, his discipline has sometimes crumbled as it did during the retreats in the Peninsula, he has sometimes indulged in excesses, as he did at Badajoz and on occasions during the Mutiny. In fairness, however, it must be made clear that such blots are rare. Throughout his long history the British soldier has been on the whole a clean, courageous and well-disciplined fighting man.

What then are the positive qualities which distinguish him from the soldiers of other nations? We may perhaps find them in the outward grumbling which conceals an inner cheerfulness, in a sense of humour which has always been rather ribald (it shocked Blackadder in the seventeenth century), and in the power which the British soldier has always had of making friends with the civil population of the country where he is fighting, even though they are his enemies. The popularity of the British troops in the Rhineland after the last war had been paralleled by the reception of Wellington's army in France after it had crossed the Pyrenees.

In battle, the British soldier may not have the *élan* of the French, although he has always had a reputation for aggressive bayonet charges. At any rate the Russians in Sebastopol were reported to have been exercised in bayonet fighting and included in their course was the characteristic British cheer. One of the most memorable of British charges was that of the Gordon Highlanders at Dargai in the Tirah campaign of 1897 when the wounded piper Findlater continued to play as the highlanders "cheering like mad" rushed up the precipitous slope. The British soldier too has always had a reputation for marksmanship, whether with the "Brown Bess" or the later rifle. At Mons in 1914 the rapid fire of the British infantry was found so "murderous" by the Germans that they attributed it to machine guns rather than rifles. And from Blenheim to El Alamein the reputation of the British gunners has been high.

The British soldier, however, is at his best and has performed his most memorable feats when he has been faced with the greatest odds. Essentially his main characteristic is his discipline and his long story is full of actions when he has fought, often hopelessly, against superior numbers, without thought of retreat. Elliot's defence of Gibraltar in the War of the American Revolution, the 44th at Gundamuck in 1842, the "thin red streak" at Balaclava, the defence of Lucknow, Rorke's Drift, the Devonshires at Bois des Buttes, the defence of Calais in 1940—these are strands in the weaving of the British military tradition. A foretaste of it can be found in the oldest battle poem in our language. In the year 991 at Maldon on the Blackwater the Danes defeated the shire levy of Essex. A fragment of a poem describing the battle is extant. Towards the end of it, Byrhtwold, an old English warrior, exhorts the survivors in these words: "Thought shall be the harder, heart the keener, courage the greater as our might lessens. Here lies our leader all hewn down in the dust. I am old in age; I will not hence, but I purpose to lie by the side of my lord, by the man so dearly loved."

BRITAIN
IN THE AIR

BY

NIGEL TANGYE

PREFACE

ON a quiet summer's evening early in 1808, an English squire watched what appeared to be a large white bird fly from a hill top to the valley below. The squire was Sir George Cayley and the bird was a glider of his own construction. To the onlookers —if indeed there was one other than the squire—there was nothing to mark the event as being one of any importance. True, the contraption flew, but it quickly lost height and could not be compared with the majestic achievements of Messieurs Blanchard and Lunardi in their balloons. The fact was that this successful flight confirmed the theory of Cayley that heavier-than-air flight could be achieved on the principle that a stream of air directed on to an inclined plane gave it 'lift.' This successful approach to the problem—an English attainment be it noted—led the way to the aeroplane as we know it to-day ; but a hundred years were to pass by before the problems of control and the means for sustained flight were solved. In those hundred years, the researches and experiments of other British men, notably John Stringfellow and William Henson, went far towards providing the data which made possible the first controlled, power-driven flight by the Wright brothers.

On December 17th, 1903, at Kitty Hawk, North Carolina, Orville Wright took off in an heavier-than-air machine and flew it under control for twelve seconds. This was the first occasion in the history of the world on which, as Wright put it, "a machine, carrying a man, had flown freely into the air under its own power in a horizontal direction without slackening speed and landed again without being wrecked." In other words, controlled flight had been achieved. Man had mounted the first step into a world of which he had dreamed ever since he had seen his first bird winging through the air.

Other steps have been mounted since then in quick succession. Continents have been contracted into counties, oceans into lakes. It takes no longer to-day to cross the Atlantic than it took to cross the North Sea fifty years ago. The vast immensity of the world, its arrogant display of space, uncharted seas, un-mapped tracts imposing almost unscaleable barriers between the free intercourse of men, has been pricked by the wit and ingenuity of a handful of scientists and pioneers. Between these men has been produced the aeroplane, a vehicle that disdains to differentiate between mountains and plains, between oceans and seas. It mounts majestically into the free air and cares not what lies beneath the skyway.

And all this achievement took place in a few years, in a tiny fraction of man's life on this earth. For at the beginning of this century there were no more than a few bulbous shapes groping around the skies, unwieldy balloon gas-bags carrying men in wicker baskets trying ineffectively to control their erratic flight from place to place.

Obstacles are the stimulus to man's invention. Without obstacles there would be no human effort. "The human race," wrote Professor Macneile Dixon, "turns wearily and dejectedly away from the easy and the obvious, and delights in its exertions and its pains. If you would make human beings happy, give them a task and a cause, and the harder the better. They rise to their full stature only when challenged. . . . It is when the gods call them that men rise to the crest of their powers."

The challenge to fly was thrown. And men, by 'blood, toil and sweat,' shaped wings and flew.

> Oh ! I have slipped the surly bonds of earth
>   And danced the skies on laughter-silvered wings ;
> Sunward I've climbed, and joined the tumbling mirth
>   Of sun-split clouds—and done a hundred things
> You have not dreamed of—wheeled and soared and swung
>   High in the sunlit silence. Hov'ring there
> I've chased the shouting wind along, and flung
>   My eager craft through footless halls of air.
> Up, up the long, delirious, burning blue
>   I've topped the wind-swept heights with easy grace
> Where never lark, nor even eagle flew—
>   And while with silent, lifting mind I've trod
> The high, untrespassed sanctity of space,
>   Put out my hand and touched the face of God.
>
>   *J. B. Magee*

BEGINNINGS

For the early beginnings of the story of flight, one must delve into the realms of mythology. The legend of Daedalus and Icarus affords the proof that the art of flying had captured the hearts of men in the earliest times. In every story of this type it is not surprising to find that the secret of flight was thought to be in the materials comprising a bird's wing, and this was the cause of many a man's death or discomfiture.

In England, one of the earliest recorded attempts to fly was made by King Bladud, reputed founder of Bath, in the middle of the ninth century. 'Recorded' is perhaps too precise a word, for the tale of the king's attempt to fly and resulting death is legendary. But it has its importance in that he was a patron of the arts of magic and necromancy, and right up to the beginning of the sixteenth century any man who interested himself in flying was liable to be called a necromancer, a dealer in black magic, and one to be avoided ; and his efforts almost invariably aroused the antagonism of the Church. All flying pioneers seem to have been doomed to be handicapped in their efforts by official indifference or active hostility, and the Church's antagonism in the pre-Renaissance period was but a foretaste of Government disregard that has been so very apparent in our own century. The contempt in which the courageous efforts of Bladud, of Oliver Malmesbury in the eleventh century, and of John Damian in the beginning of the sixteenth, were held, is seen to have been but a forerunner of what was to come. It was John Damian who endeavoured to overtake an embassy recently despatched to France by James IV of Scotland by flying from Stirling Castle. Needless to say he got no further than the foot of the castle wall. History does not relate whether James IV could claim to be the first enlightened sovereign to subsidise an aviation exploit by royal patronage, or whether the attempt was a private venture.

Alongside these actual attempts to fly were the more serious gropings by thinkers to fathom the theory of flight. Roger Bacon was probably the first Englishman, according to Hodgson, "to write on the subject in any mechanical or scientific sense—certainly his are the oldest extant speculations." And here we have that curious union of opposites that persists to the present day—the Bacons who adventure in the world of aeronautical thought, and the Damians who pioneer and fly at any cost ; the Mitchells who design that most beautiful of machines (the Spitfire) and never fly, and the test pilots who leap into the air with whatever they may be given ; the one content to design the aircraft he never wishes to fly, the other content to fly aircraft he has not the capacity to design. "As the child is born of two parents, so is the flying machine of two opposites."

Though the greater part of the eighteenth century failed to contribute anything towards a solution of the problem of flight, it did produce two

'DIVERS PROJETS SUR LA DESCENTE EN ANGLETERRE'
Early nineteenth century engraving

far-seeing prophecies which are of great interest at the present time. The
first is taken from Gray's *Luna Habitabilis* written in 1731 and published
in Cambridge :

> The time will come when thou shalt lift thine eyes
> To watch a long-drawn battle in the skies,
> While aged peasants, too amazed for words,
> Stare at the flying fleets of wond'rous birds.
>
> England, so long mistress of the sea,
> Where winds and waves confess her sovereignty,
> Her ancient triumphs yet on high shall bear,
> And reign, the sovereign of the conquered air.

And then, later on, in 1759, Doctor Johnson contemplated the impli-
cations of flying in his "Dissertation on the Art of Flying" in *Rasselas* :
"What would be the security of the good," he wrote, "if the bad could at
pleasure invade them from the sky ?"

The end of the eighteenth century saw the first successful flights by
men. On October 17th, 1783, the Montgolfier balloon rose into the air.

260

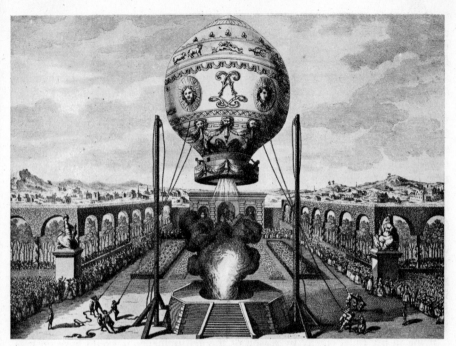

THE MONTGOLFIER BALLOON, 1783
French engraving by Desrais

The aeronaut, Pilâtre de Rozier, made this captive ascent from the Jardin Réveillon on the Faubourg St. Antoine. He rose to a height of eighty feet and remained in the air just over four and a half minutes.

The success of this captive ascent proved the soundness of the Montgolfier brothers' ideas. The balloon was filled with hot air by placing the orifice at the base of the envelope above a large fire. Around this orifice was hung a wicker basket in which the aeronaut stood. As the bag, or envelope, filled, so the 'lift' made itself felt and the balloon had to be held down until the moment of release. Once released, the buoyancy caused the balloon to rise, but with the passage of time, the hot air cooled, the buoyancy was reduced and the balloon would begin to lose height. Such was the principle of this successful experiment.

Triumph was complete when five weeks later, on November 21st, 1783, de Rozier, with the Marquis d'Arlandes as passenger, made the first free flight in the history of the world. The two aeronauts rose to a height of some 300 feet and were carried across Paris by the wind for a distance of five and a half miles. They landed after a flight of twenty-five minutes. Lighter-than-air flight had been achieved.

Leonardo da Vinci applied his versatile talent to the theory of mechanical flight in the early sixteenth century. His manuscripts reveal that he accurately evolved the basic theory for a winged flying apparatus, for the helicopter, and even for the parachute, but we cannot consider in detail, within the confines of this book, the drawings and theories contained in the *Codex Atlanticus* and the *Codice sul Volo degli Uccelli*.

After the Renaissance, men's minds in England were able to dwell on the problems of flight without their being charged with black magic. Francis Bacon, John Wilkins and Robert Hooke, the latter two being successive Secretaries of the Royal Society, each interested himself in the fascinating theory during the seventeenth century. It was Wilkins who first conceived the idea of the lighter-than-air principle based as it is, of course, on the physical law of Archimedes governing the flotation of bodies in fluids. His friend, Robert Hooke, carried on the work by probing and extending the theories in greater detail.

There followed in England a barren hundred years in which enthusiasm, both of scientists and would-be flying men, suffered an eclipse. Indeed, the subject became one for ridicule. Addison must take some responsibility for this. In 1713, he wrote a letter to *The Guardian* in which he showed his polite but satirical contempt for those who treated flying seriously. The following is an extract from this letter :

"... (I am) resolved so far to discourage it, as to prevent any person from flying in my time, chiefly by reason of the evil influence it would have on love affairs. It would fill the world with innumerable immoralities, and give such occasions for intrigues as people cannot meet with who have nothing but legs to carry them. You should have a couple of lovers make a midnight assignation upon the top of the monument, and see the cupola of St. Paul's covered with both sexes like the outside of a pigeon house. Nothing would be more frequent than to see a beau flying in at a garret window, or a gallent giving chase to his mistress, like a hawk after a lark."

I have already remarked on the curious lack of desire on the part of designers to taste the fruits of their labours themselves. One would think that the Montgolfier brothers would have wished to round off their triumph by being themselves the first men in the world to fly. But no ; they were the thinkers who evolved the machine and, as many others after them were to do, evinced comparatively little interest in the practical side of flying. Such men prefer adventures of the mind to those of the body, and are content to fashion the instruments for others to employ. Their fill of satisfaction is reached at the point where that of the flying man begins.

An exception to this tendency was the successful flight of Professor Charles, a French physicist, who, within two months of the Montgolfier triumph, had not only thought of the advantage to be gained by filling the envelope with hydrogen, but had evolved an apparatus to do it, had supervised the construction of the balloon, and had flown in the balloon

himself on its trial flight. However, he found the experience so alarming that it is said he never flew again. But this distinguished scientist, by taking advantage of Henry Cavendish's discovery of the weight of hydrogen, by applying his own ingenuity and by his courage, achieved a feat surpassing in importance that of de Rozier's hot-air balloon flight.

England was intrigued to know what all the fuss on the Continent was about, and it was not long before Vincent Lunardi, a gentleman of obscure nationality, rose in his 'Globe' from the Artillery Ground at Moorfields before the eyes of incredulous townsfolk who had paid prices ranging from five shillings to one guinea to get a good view from within the ground. This ascent—which ended successfully at Ware in Hertfordshire—was made on September 15th, 1784, and was the signal for every charlatan in England to take advantage of the enthusiasm of the public for the new wondrous art. Public subscriptions were opened to support budding aeronauts, and milliners took advantage of the fashion by creating Lunardi bonnets and Lunardi garters. But amid a welter of commercialism there were serious minds who turned their attention to the possibilities opened up by these successes, and who applied themselves to developing them.

Within a short time, the Montgolfier brothers had improved their balloon so as to enable a fire to be suspended beneath the orifice within

THE DEPARTURE OF BLANCHARD AND JEFFRIES FROM DOVER CASTLE, JANUARY 7TH, 1785
Engraving in the Norman Collection

stoking-reach of the aeronaut. This prolonged the flight by keeping the air hot within the envelope. But such an expedient had obvious dangers, and it was not long before it was realised that the hydrogen balloon was the 'balloon of the future.' In point of fact, the free balloon was destined virtually to have no future because all efforts to find a method of directing it, of rendering it independent of the caprice of the winds, failed. Two flights in free balloons do, however, stand out from innumerable unimportant adventures and call for permanent recognition. One of these is the flight of Blanchard and Jeffries across the English Channel, and the other a courageous scientific ascent by Coxwell and Glaisher in 1862.

Ask anyone to give the date of the first cross-Channel flight and he will almost certainly reply, "about 1910 or '11." The first flight across the Channel was actually made on January 7th, 1785, by Blanchard and Jeffries—the one a Frenchman, the other an American. This feat was achieved one hundred and twenty-five years before Blériot's infinitely more significant flight.

The other balloon flight worthy of record was the ascent in 1862 by Coxwell and Glaisher, two British scientists, who rose to 37,000 feet. Their purpose was the advancement of knowledge by venturing, with a multitude of scientific instruments, higher into the upper air than any

man before. Indeed, some eighty years were to pass before flights to this altitude could be considered free of an element of pioneering. The remarkable fact about this flight was its accomplishment by the aeronauts without oxygen. The unknown hazards that these two men voluntarily faced called for great courage. Their feat ranks side by side with the greatest British voyages of exploration. Here is an extract from the report of the flight by Glaisher. It is as unsensational a record of adventure as ever was told by a true explorer :

"We reached the elevation of four miles at 1h. 40m. ; the temperature was 8 degrees, the dew point minus 15 degrees, or 47 below the freezing point of water. Discharging sand, we attained in ten minutes the altitude of five miles . . . Up to this time I had taken observations with comfort, and experienced no difficulty in breathing, whilst Mr. Coxwell, in consequence of the exertions he had to make, had breathed with difficulty for some time . . . I then looked at the barometer and found its reading to be 9¾ in., still decreasing fast, implying a height exceeding 29,000 feet . . . As in the case of the arms, so all muscular power was lost in an instant from my back and neck. I dimly saw Mr. Coxwell, and endeavoured to speak, but could not. In an instant intense darkness overcame me, so that the optic nerve suddenly lost power, but I was still conscious, with as active a brain as at the present moment while writing this. I thought I had been seized with asphyxia, and believed I should experience nothing more, as death would come unless we speedily descended . . .

"Whilst powerless, I heard the words 'temperature' and 'observation,' and I knew Mr. Coxwell was in the car, speaking to and endeavouring to rouse me, therefore, consciousness and hearing had returned . . . I heard him again say, 'Do try, now do.' Then the instruments became dimly visible, then Mr. Coxwell, and very shortly I saw clearly. Next I arose in my seat, and looked around as though waking from sleep, though not refreshed, and said to Mr. Coxwell, 'I have been insensible,' he said, 'You have, and I too, very nearly.' I then drew up my legs, which had been extended, and took a pencil in my hand to begin observations. Mr. Coxwell told me that he had lost the use of his hands, which were black, and I poured brandy over them."

One should also mention another English exponent of the art of ballooning. Charles Green, in 1807, was the first to use coal gas as the lifting medium. It was heavier than hydrogen but cheaper and easier to obtain. He also invented the "guide-rope" which he suspended from the basket and which was of a length up to 1,000 feet. When the end of the rope touched the ground, the part of its weight approximating to that of the length on the ground was taken from the balloon. This checked the descent of the balloon automatically without the need of discarding ballast, and the effect was to enable the balloon to adjust itself to fairly level flight. Alternatively if the aeronaut was intending to land, the device enabled the rate of descent automatically to be reduced as the ground was approached.

The balloon survives to-day only in the form of media for meteorological observations, and for certain military purposes. In neither case is it a man-carrying vehicle. But a development of it can be seen in the airship which, after a period of some promise, particularly between the two wars, has declined before the onslaught of aeroplane development. In only certain limited military roles does it survive. It is, however, quite possible that it may be revived as a specialised freight-carrying vessel at some future date.

Aeronautical development is marked by two separate but complementary approaches to the subject. One can be termed the progressive approach, and the other the cautionary approach. Those subscribing to the progressive approach are the men who seek performance above all else, performance in their eyes entailing the utmost in speed, weight carrying capacity and, indeed, all that is spectacular. They force the pace regardless of personal danger ; and without their energy and courage progress would be restricted. Those subscribing to the cautionary approach are the men who smooth off the rough edges of rapid development and render it pliable and safe for universal use. They are the men who say, "Not so fast, there. Ease up a bit and get this thing straight first before you rush on to the next." Theirs is the unspectacular and, to some, unenviable rôle, but without them the aeroplane would not be the reliable machine it is to-day.

The first practical disciple of the cautionary approach can be said to be Garnerin. No sooner had the first balloon made its ascent from the Faubourg St. Antoine than Garnerin was struck by the problem, "How can the lives of the aeronauts be saved should the balloon burst ?" He applied his mind to the problem and constructed the first parachute. This, of course, was a long way from the folding parachute we know to-day, but it was a beginning. It consisted of a concave frame of light wooden sticks, the whole covered with a linen material and from which was suspended a basket. The parachute was suspended from beneath the basket of a balloon. Garnerin's first drop was made successfully in France in 1793. The parachute is not a modern invention but one which was first thought of by Leonardo da Vinci and which was first tried out a century and a half ago.

The first descent in this country was made in 1802, by Garnerin. This was followed by periodical descents by others many of which were for commercial reasons, but some were serious attempts at development. These latter led up over the years to the first free drop by Irving in 1919. Since then, many thousands of airmen have been saved by the parachute, the life-belt of the air.

We have seen the first high hopes that the balloon was to prove the answer to the age-old quest for flight soon discarded, and the balloon relegated to the level of an entertainment for the populace. Navigation through the air—the controlled flight from one defined place to another—still eluded the grasp of men. The inability of the balloon to

AN ASCENT BY CHARLES GREEN, SEEN FROM THE HIGH STREET, LEWES, SUSSEX
Coloured lithograph after a drawing by T. Henwood, 1828

fulfil this condition directed men's minds back to the original idea, the heavier-than-air principle. In the forefront of this new attack was Sir George Cayley, one of the great names in aeronautical history. Hodgson writes of him thus: "He deserves to stand among the great pioneers of aviation and in the direct line of descent between such names as Leonardo da Vinci and John Stringfellow."

Cayley was born in 1773 and died in 1857. He owned estates in Yorkshire and Lincolnshire, but throughout his life devoted his energies towards the attainment of controlled flight. He was quick to approach the subject along the right lines by recognising that the solution lay in the fact that an inclined plane was given 'lift' if a stream of air was directed on to it. Cayley, from this observation, deduced that flight would be achieved if the inclined plane was drawn through the air by some application of power, the motion forward creating the wind required to strike the plane, thus producing the 'lift.' So confident was he with his theory that even in the early days of his experiments he visualised transporting "passengers and goods more securely by air than by water, and with a velocity of from 20 to 100 miles per hour."

'THE FIRST AERIAL SHIP, *THE EAGLE*'
Coloured engraving in the Norman Collection

He was, of course, handicapped by the lack of an engine, but he built many gliders (the 'motive power' being provided by gravity) which confirmed his theory of flight though none of these was intended to carry a man. Describing the flight, in 1808, of one of his gliders, Cayley wrote :

"It was very beautiful to see this noble white *bird* sail majestically from the top of the hill to any given point of the plain below it, according to the set of its rudder, merely by its own weight, descending in an angle of about 18 degrees with the horizon."

The glider he was referring to was a large one with a wing area of 300 square feet. Cayley's description of its flight, quoted above, is of particular interest as it is the first authentic account of the flight of a heavier-than-air aircraft.

Cayley's work came to a full stop, since the engineers of the first half of the nineteenth century failed to provide him with an engine. But his theoretical and practical work was of immense value to those who came after him. It will be observed that though he constructed large gliders for experiments, Cayley was one of those designers whose interest in the science of flight did not include a burning desire to try and fly. He was certainly capable of designing and constructing a glider to carry a man, but he probably desisted on logical grounds knowing that he had yet to solve the problem of stability. A few hops down the valley, borne on the wings of luck as much as his glider, would not appeal to this great man. He chose the cautionary approach. "Solve the problem first. Eschew the temptation of premature spectacle."

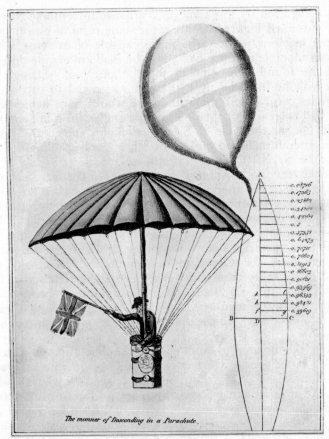

The manner of Descending in a Parachute.

DESIGN FOR A PARACHUTE, C. 1802
Coloured engraving in the Norman Collection

Cayley's line of thought was taken up and developed by John Stringfellow, one of the great names in aeronautical technical history. Stringfellow was the owner of a lace factory in Somerset, but at an early age he was attracted to the problem of flight. With the aid of William Henson, he carried out experiments that led to the first power-driven model aeroplane flight. This was in 1848. The model measured ten feet from wing tip to wing tip and, together with the steam engine, weighed only nine pounds. Both the model and the engine were constructed by Stringfellow. Henson had ceased his partnership with him at the time of the successful flight, but had been responsible for much preliminary work which Stringfellow brought to fruition.

It was recognised by this time (mid nineteenth century) that in order to achieve sustained flight, not only must some form of power be applied to a winged machine for it to be made capable of carrying a man, but also that considerable advance had yet to be made in engine design before one could be found light enough for the purpose. Stringfellow was successful with his model only because it was asked to carry no weight other than its own. It is doubtful if he would have achieved success even if he had been able to obtain a suitable engine for a full size machine, for he had not, at the time of his model flight, solved the problem of making the aircraft stable in flight. In other words, the method of safely controlling the aircraft in flight was still lacking.

The belief that the attainment of controlled flight was held up owing to the late arrival of the internal-combustion engine is therefore not wholly a true one. It was not until Otto Lilienthal's experiments from 1890-1896 with gliders that the true foundation of flight by men was laid. It was he who, in experiments in Germany which ultimately cost him his life, evolved the broad principles of control in the air which the Wright brothers took as their basis for successful development. Lilienthal's machines were made of no more than sticks and shirting, materials that had been at hand to Man for centuries. It is intriguing to contemplate how long it took before a man was found who could fashion these simple materials into a shape which enabled him to glide as much as five hundred yards.

Although the honour of finding this basic solution to the problem of controlled flight goes to Germany, it was England who bred such men as Cayley, Henson and Stringfellow, men who paved the way for Lilienthal's success. And it is Britain who has been in the forefront of aeronautical design and achievement ever since. Had it not been for a fatal accident, the honour of the first powered flight might have fallen to Britain instead of to America. In 1894, a British Naval Officer, Percy Sinclair Pilcher, bought from Lilienthal one of his gliders and started experiments on his own account. He soon built his own glider and evolved the method of launching that is still practised to-day. He made some good flights—one of seventeen seconds—and the degree of control he obtained is illustrated by his account of one of them :

"Once when sailing fast I saw I was going to land in a big bush, so getting back a little in the machine I was able to rise a little and pass quite clear of the Bush (although it was quite calm at the time) ; and I have also been able to steer sideways to a limited extent by moving the weight of my body towards the side to which I wanted to turn. This is the first machine in which I have had any wheels, which are a great convenience for moving the machine about, and often save the framework from getting broken if one lands clumsily."

To Pilcher then, we owe the initial design of aeroplane undercarriages as we know them to-day. He was the first man to fit landing-wheels to

SIR GEORGE CAYLEY, 1773-1851
Oil painting by H. P. Briggs

an aircraft for landing and taking off. By 1899 he had constructed a
new machine. He planned to carry out the trial flight on September 30th,
1899, in the grounds of Stanford Hall, Market Harborough, where he
was staying with Lord Braye. The weather proved too bad for a first
flight, so he made two flights in an old glider of his to pass away the time.
On the second flight, one of the wires of the tailplane snapped. The
machine turned over in the air and Pilcher, fatally injured, died two days
later. His pioneer spirit lives on to-day in the deeds of the pilots of the
Royal Navy, the Service to which he belonged.

273

In 1903, there burst upon the world the cataclysmic triumph of the Wright brothers. Man, at last, could fly.

> And then I stood erect and cheered,
> Ay ! shouted into the sky;
> I filled the vast semicircle round
> There was only the Sun and I,
> The round, red, glittering, blazing Sun
> And a fluttering human fly.
>
> *W. J. Turner*

FIRST APPLICATIONS

Probably because she was leading in the realm of internal-combustion engine development, France proved to be the country where the Wright brothers' achievement was seized upon with most avidity. Ferber, Voisin, Farman, Dumont, these were the names that led the way in Europe. All met with varying degrees of success ; but in 1908, Wilbur Wright came over to France, and he and his aircraft eclipsed all that the French had so far attained. The degree of superiority that he enjoyed was decisively shown when he flew, on December 31st, 1908, for 2 hours 30 minutes, covering a distance of 77 miles. Blériot, only two months before, had created a record by flying 17 miles, and this with two landings.

But the spectacular performances in France should not be allowed to obscure the quiet but remarkable work of an Englishman, J. W. Dunne, a man who was later destined to become world famous with his book *An Experiment with Time*. Of Dunne's early work on the problems of heavier-than-air flight, Davy writes : "His investigation of the subject of inherent (automatic) stability was a brilliant work, the full value of which is probably not even yet realised." In 1906, the War Office granted him £5,000 to help him pursue his experiments.

Though the flying movement was slow to start in England, it received a big impetus when the *Daily Mail* offered a prize of £1,000 for the first flight in an aeroplane across the Channel. As all the world knows, this was won by Blériot in July 1909 ; but Hubert Latham, a Frenchman with an English father, might well have forestalled him if fortune had been on his side. He had made one attempt, and was ready for another on the very day that Blériot was successful but, the story goes, his servant forgot to call him and he overslept. A month later, the first flying meeting in the world was held at Rheims. Records were made by Farman with a duration flight of three hours, by Blériot with a speed of 47 miles an hour, and by Latham who attained a height of 508 feet. These modest performances represented the best attainable in 1909.

By courtesy of "Country Life" and the Executors of the late Sir John Lavery

AN AERODROME IN 1918

Oil painting by Sir John Lavery

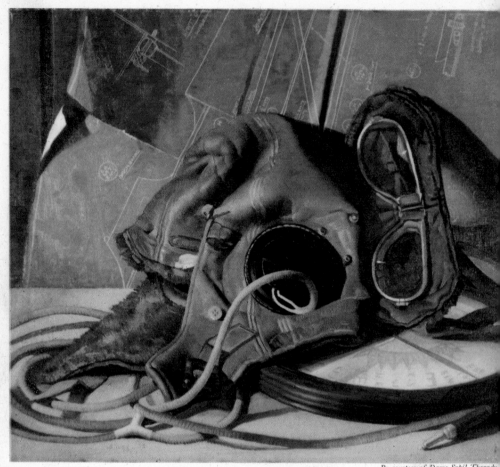

AIRMAN'S EQUIPMENT, 1932
Oil painting by E. A. Harvey

A few individuals were in the meantime experimenting with airships. As early as 1900, Dr. Barton had flown over London from Alexandra Palace.

In 1904 Mr. E. T. Willows, of Cardiff, designed a dirigible in which were certain patents subsequently purchased by the Government. In 1909, Mr. Willows flew from Cardiff to London in ten hours, and the following year flew across the Channel. The Government showed its interest in the possibilities of the airship by instructing the Government Balloon Factory to build a dirigible. In 1907, the factory produced the *Nulli Secundus II* which flew successfully but crashed at the Crystal Palace after a flight from Farnborough. Later, in 1911, the Admiralty built the ambitious *Mayfly*, a dirigible 510 feet in length powered with two 200 h.p. engines. She broke her back while being taken out of her hangar for her trial flight. These early experiments and failures were made worth while by the success of the coastal "Blimps" which did great work during the First World War as patrol craft over the North Sea and English Channel.

British aviation, in the modern sense, really began the year before this. In 1908, Mr. A. V. Roe built his own aeroplane. It was a biplane, but so underpowered that he had to enlist the aid of motoring friends to help him into the air by towing him until he was airborne. This aeroplane was followed by a triplane fitted with a 9 horse-power engine which he flew from Lea Marshes, much to the disapproval of the local police.

The difficulties of A. V. Roe in his relations with the police officers of the Crown were symbolic of the antagonism, or indifference, destined to be displayed by officialdom towards flying enterprise for a long time to come.

By 1939, much had been achieved in British air line and military development, but what was attained was in spite of, rather than because of, official and public attention, and was, in scope, but a fraction of what was due to the Empire from the mother country.

By good fortune, throughout those thirty years, there were British airmen, British air line operatives, British technicians, who refused to be overcome by public apathy. And, to those who have more recently come to know the noble, far-seeing qualities of his leadership, it will not be a surprise to learn that Winston Churchill played a vital part in laying the foundations of British aviation. Only one instance, an immensely important one, of his vision in this connection can be related here.

In 1913, the aeroplane had advanced sufficiently for it to be accepted by the War Office and the Admiralty as a potential weapon of significance. British aeroplanes were then few and far between and were designed and constructed by a handful of pioneer individuals who lived on little else but enthusiasm. The War Office decided to adopt one type of aeroplane from one designer from which to develop a military machine. They did this in pursuance of the ideal of standardisation of weapons. The chosen designer was Geoffrey de Havilland.

The First Lord of the Admiralty was Winston Churchill. He directed the able chief of his Air Department, Captain Murray Sueter, to "spread" his orders, on the grounds that aeroplane design was in its infancy and to standardise at that stage would have the effect of stifling the child of aviation at its birth. The effect of this policy—a policy that was criticised inevitably as a squandering of public money—was that the men from whom have descended the Hurricane, Typhoon, Stirling, Sunderland, Lancaster and many other famous aircraft, were financially sustained in their early efforts and enabled to develop their ideas. The men who were given orders for their aeroplanes by Churchill were the Short Brothers, Sopwith, Blackburn and A. V. Roe.

"On first going to the Admiralty," wrote Churchill, "I resolved to develop and extend the naval air service by every means in my power. . . I thought it would be a stimulus to progress generally if I, as First Lord, participated to some extent. . . Accordingly early in 1912 I took my seat in a seaplane piloted by Commander Spencer Grey, and resigned myself to what was in those days at once a novel and thrilling experience . . . Once I had started flying from motives in which a sense of duty, as well as excitement and curiosity, played its part, I continued for sheer joy and pleasure. . . I soon became ambitious to handle these machines myself, and took many lessons at the Naval and Military Schools. Dual control machines were developing fast in 1912, and I had one made where pilot and passenger could sit side by side and take control alternately. As I began to know more about flying, I began to understand the enormous hazards which beset every moment of the airman's flight . . . and I noticed on several occasions defects in the machine in which we had been flying—a broken wire, a singed wing, a cracked strut—which were the subject of mutual congratulation between myself and my pilot once we had returned safely to terra firma. However, having been thoroughly bitten, I continued to fly on every possible occasion when my other duties permitted."

By the time of the outbreak of the First World War, the aeroplane had already earned its spurs and had proved by its achievements that it possessed much that could be applied to the service of mankind. The English Channel had been crossed in 1909, the North Sea had been crossed in July, 1914, and already the possibility of crossing the Atlantic was being seriously contemplated.

For these successful examples of first applications of the new principle of transportation, it is right to acknowledge the stimulus to airmen provided by the *Daily Mail* in the form of large money prizes to encourage aeronautical attainment. The encouragement afforded by this newspaper was invaluable, and was continued in many forms during the period between the two wars. Other newspapers subsequently emulated its enthusiasm, to the lasting benefit of British aviation. Patronage, in the form of sub-

WILBUR WRIGHT, 1867-1912
Oil painting by A. J. Hervé-Mathé, 1908

stantial financial help to aviation projects, was also subsequently offered
by private individuals, without whose help British pioneers would have
been impotent. Lord Wakefield was to help many record pilots ; Lady
Houston made Britain's outright winning of the Schneider Trophy possible, with its legacy of the Spitfire and the Rolls-Royce Merlin engine ;
and Lord Rothermere gave a private order to the Bristol Aeroplane
Company for what was to be the forerunner of the Blenheim bomber
solely to show the Government what British designers could produce in
the form of high performance aircraft if given the opportunity.

It was private enterprise and private generosity that nurtured the
child of British aviation. Successive Governments and, I fear, the British
public, were apathetic and did little or nothing to help.

PRELUDE TO PROGRESS

The urgent demands of war call inexorably on the national genius to turn from positive goals. Men are called on to devote themselves to the negative task of devising and wielding weapons of destruction of complex ingenuity with which to surprise and annihilate the enemy. Civilised progress is checked, and civilisation itself ebbs back into the ocean of time until the tide turns and peace rides in on the waves. Yet the challenge that the aggressor throws in the faces of men of peace is an opportunity as well as a tragedy ; for to meet the challenge, nature endows men with resource and courage and nobility, which leave men with lasting dignity and a faith in the values of life. War can therefore be said to strengthen the foundations of peace, and to lead to better living, to act as a prelude to progress.

This sense of urgency, born of the will to survive, results naturally in war being the forcing ground of technical development. But it is unnatural development and is largely limited in its application to peaceful pursuits. The First World War was responsible for aircraft performances developing at a rate that would have taken four times as long in peace time ; but these performances were obtained with a disregard of the economic factor and consequently much of the development could not be adapted to civil aviation.

In 1914, the Royal Flying Corps and the Royal Naval Air Service had between them perhaps 300 aeroplanes. An average aircraft could fly at 80 miles an hour and reach a height of little more than 8,000 feet. Four years later, the Royal Air Force, which came into being as an independent Service on April 1st, 1918, had over 20,000 aeroplanes on charge. Maximum speeds had risen to 150 miles an hour, and some aeroplanes had reached heights approaching 30,000 feet. Such are the results of national concerted effort.

These improvements in performance were obtained by improved engine design rather than airframe design. The weight of an engine of

POSTER SHOWING TYPES OF BRITISH AND GERMAN AIRCRAFT, 1915

the same horse-power had been halved, but aeroplanes remained a mass of wires and struts which impeded their passage through the air, thus preventing improved engine performance being exploited to the full. The job was thus only half done. Due, perhaps, to the urgent need for

AN 'H.12' FLYING BOAT RESCUING A SEAPLANE'S CREW FROM THE NORTH SEA, 1918
Water colour by C. R. Fleming-Williams

rapid production, designers tended to concentrate on improving existing airframes rather than designing new machines with better aerodynamic qualities embodied as a basic factor.

There was one outstanding exception to this generality. On Christmas Day, 1914, the head of the Naval Air Department, Captain Murray Sueter, backed by the ever progressive Winston Churchill, gave an order to Mr. Handley Page for four of the heaviest aircraft ever built. The aircraft, the O.400, was to be four times the weight of the contemporary type. During the process of design, this order was increased up to 40, so confident was the Admiralty in the Handley Page design. Eventually there were several hundred of these aircraft built and used for night bombing. The aircraft was a great success and led to a machine of very considerable interest when viewed in the light of our bomber policy in the Second World War. This was the Handley Page V.1500, a huge aircraft with four engines designed to take 1,000 lbs. of bombs to Berlin. The Armistice intervened before it could be used. This aircraft weighed 30,000 lbs., had a wing area of 2,880 square feet and a span of 126 feet. Compare this with the Handley Page Halifax, designed some twenty years later, which has a weight of 63,000 lbs., a wing area of 1,250 square feet, a span of 99 feet, more than double the speed and a bomb load capacity of 8 tons. The value of the aeroplane to each side during the war necessitated,

THE FIRST BRITISH RAID OVER MANNHEIM, DECEMBER, 1917
Water colour by Bertram Sandy

as we have seen, a tremendous expansion in the size of the Air Services. This created one very important element in the foundations of progress to be attained in the ensuing years of peace, an element which has not been fully recognised. The war in the air brought forth thousands of pilots who otherwise would never have been attracted to the air, and, in consequence, added much to the then forming tradition of airmanship. Further, the sum of experience of these men contributed to the development of the technique of flying at a rate very much faster than would have been the case if there had been no war.

THE WINGED WORD

East to the dawn and southward to the sun,
  Borne on aloft by Man's great gift of wings
To legend lands that make the pulses run
  And towns that leap with names of ancient Kings.

Gandar Dower

The British Commonwealth of Nations, spread-eagled across the face of the globe, segregated by ocean and desert, by mountain and forest, provides at once an inspiration and a challenge to its members to solve the problems of swift inter-communication. Thus can the spiritual links that bind the Dominions and Colonies to the mother country be vitalised by ever closer contact. Already the development of air transport has shrunk the time scale of world travel from weeks to days, and in this development Great Britain has played a major part.

"East to the dawn and southward to the sun." Pioneer airmen through the years have opened the eyes of the world to the possibilities that lie within the grasp of man, possibilities that may not be neglected if mutual understanding and tolerance between nations are to be won ; for, together with the magic of the radio, it is the aeroplane which has the power of eliminating the geographical barriers between nations and which, by destroying these barriers, can let the light into the counsels of men.

This conception would have been considered an idealist's generality a few years ago, but the reality of it has been exemplified during the Second World War. Who can deny the debt we owe to air transport for the part it has played in making the term "United Nations" the living thing it is ? Without air transport Britain, the United States, Russia and China must inevitably have remained remote from one another, separated by vast oceans and continents demanding weeks of travel which statesmen and military staffs could not afford to set aside. It is the aeroplane that has made possible this meeting together of the Allied leaders and the resulting mutual understanding only to be reached by human intercourse. Throw open the gates ! Let the aeroplane penetrate the farthest corners of the earth ! Let it create, unhindered, free channels of swift communication between nations ; and its success for the Allies during the war can be expanded to embrace the whole world after the war.

No less important than the carriage of passengers in the attainment of this success is the swift transport of documents and mail. Indeed, under conditions of peace, the major purpose of air transport may be said to be the delivery of mails. The vast majority of men are necessarily restricted in their freedom of movement. But all require the services of the Post Office ; and the Post Office, ever seeking ways for the swifter delivery of letters, has become the chief patron of the air line. So air line companies have come to regard the creation of air services for the carriage

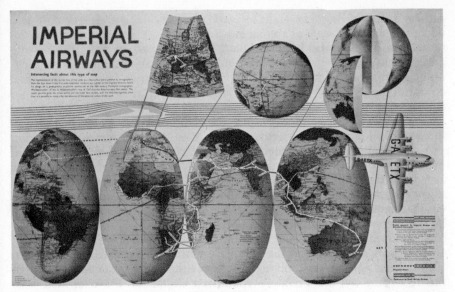

IMPERIAL AIRWAYS
A pre-war poster

of mails as their most fruitful aim. A passenger demands comfort and breathing space. A mail bag can lie in a dark hold. The passenger is therefore the more expensive of the two to carry ; and it is the mail bag that pays for part of the passenger.

Britain was quick to see the potentialities of air lines spreading across the Empire, the benefits that the winged word would bestow on the British Commonwealth of Nations. But though much to be proud of had been achieved before the outbreak of the Second World War a minority of men was responsible for what was attained. The British Government throughout the period between the two wars put the financial factor in air transport before the social. The power that comprehensive British air lines would possess to enhance British prestige was largely neglected because air lines overseas could not pay for themselves. From time to time Government spokesmen would speak pretty words about the great work being done by Imperial Airways along the Empire routes, how their services strengthened the bonds of Empire and such like ; but those services were less frequent than they should have been, slower than they could have been, and less comprehensive than they might have been.

In entrusting Imperial Airways, on its formation in 1924, with the development of European and, later, Empire services, the British Government directed that it should aim at being a non-subsidised concern at the earliest possible moment and, by way of inspiring encouragement, laid down a decreasing scale of annual subsidy that the Company was to expect to receive. The subsidy to be paid was £137,000 in 1924, decreasing gradually to £32,000 in 1934. One could hardly imagine a more depressing, unimaginative initial approach. The men of Imperial Airways, then, had an uphill task. They were judged by the public on results, on the number and extent of their services as compared with the heavily subsidised companies of other nations. They were forced to shape their plans to the diminishing scale of subsidy, instead of to the requirements of Britain and the Empire. The inauguration, in 1937, of the Empire Air Mail Scheme by which a half-ounce letter could be sent by air to Australia or South Africa, or anywhere else along the route, was a milestone in the history of the winged word of which Britain may be proud. But the vision displayed by the Government on that occasion—mainly inspired by the vigorous, buoyant Sir Kingsley Wood when Postmaster General— cannot efface the memory of its long indifference to the potentialities of air transport as an asset in the Empire's moral and material development. Throughout those years, progress was maintained by the inspiration of the few, and by the privately sponsored flights of brave airmen who showed by their example how close were the Dominion territories to one another when bridged by the aeroplane.

The first official Post Office experiment in air-mail service took place in 1911 when an impractical but spectacular service was established between Hendon and Windsor. The occasion was the celebration of King George V's coronation. Souvenir letters and postcards were provided, and these had to be posted in special letter boxes in London. The letters were then taken out to Hendon for transport by aeroplane to Windsor. More than 100,000 letters and postcards were delivered in this way. The experiment was instituted for effect rather than for practicability ; but it yielded an impressive speed record for those days. On one windy day, Gustav Hamel averaged 100 miles an hour between Windsor and Hendon. The first serious air mail service was operated by the Royal Air Force immediately after the First World War. The R.A.F. Communication Wing, based at Kenley, was engaged in transporting passengers and mail to and from Paris in connection with the Peace Conference. By the time the Peace Treaty was signed the Wing had carried 1,382 passengers and 710 bags of mail. At the same time the Wing was also engaged in flying mails and passengers to and from the Army of Occupation in Cologne. This section of the Wing was based at Hawkinge, near Folkestone.

Early in 1919, British civil aviation gained a powerful ally. Major General Sir Sefton Brancker had had a distinguished war career. At the outbreak of the war he was a Major G.S.O.2 at the War Office. In four years he had risen to the rank of Major General and was one of the

BRITISH SCOUTS LEAVING THEIR AERODROME ON PATROL OVER THE ASIAGO PLATEAU, ITALY
Oil painting by Sydney W. Carline, 1918

acknowledged leaders of the new Service, the Royal Air Force. The King had conferred on him the honour of knighthood. At the peak of his Service career he decided to resign. The explanation of this action can be found in a lecture given to the Royal Aeronautical Society at the beginning of 1917. In this lecture he said :

"I am looking forward to post-war aviation even in the midst of my own tremendous war effort. The War has been the making of aviation and we must look to it that we develop its fruits."

And then, in an article published in the *Daily Mirror* on March 25th, 1919, he wrote :

"The League of Nations may or may not be about to accomplish great things ; one fact is certain, however—it will enforce the reduction of armaments and so curtail the military power of Europe.

"The wisely-governed nation, while cordially supporting a measure which will prevent much unproductive expenditure will foster commercial aviation by all possible means, realizing that in the future the nation with the greatest aerial commerce, backed by the most efficient and extensive aircraft industry, will be able to protect its interests and preserve its honour, fearlessly and with confidence; for aerial strength will mean everything in the next great war."

From 1919, when he resigned from the Royal Air Force, to 1930, when he was killed in the R.101 airship disaster, Sir Sefton Brancker devoted his untiring energy and zeal to the furtherance of British civil aviation.

On the signing of the Peace Treaty, the R.A.F. Communication Wing was disbanded, leaving the way for private civilian enterprises to develop air services under Government control (but not with Government financial aid). The first British commercial air service was opened, between London and Paris, on August 25th, 1919, and was operated by Air Transport and Travel Ltd. This company had been formed by Mr. Holt Thomas who almost immediately invited Sir Sefton Brancker to help organise it. A week later, Handley Page Transport Ltd. opened with services to Paris and Brussels. Air Transport and Travel Ltd. started well. Its aircraft were converted military de Havilland 4's and de Havilland 9's. They carried two passengers in an enclosed cabin, the pilot sitting in an open cockpit. The fare for the journey was £21 and the scheduled time for it was two hours and a quarter.

After two months' operation, during which 135 out of 139 journeys had been successfully completed without accident, the company was granted a six months' monopoly to carry express air mail. The surcharge to the public was 2s. 6d. for a 1-oz. letter of which the company received 2s. This was too high a price for success in the first commercial air mail service, and it was soon apparent that a subsidy was necessary so as to reduce the cost of the service to the public. But Brancker, at this stage, was not disappointed. The practicability of the air mail, the era of the winged word, was an accomplished fact, and the small beginnings of his London-Paris service led him to write at this time :

"The point which is significant is that such an express air service, planned on these lines, can be instituted in almost every other part of the world ; and in happier climates the length of the stages can be increased somewhat. When eventually, real organisation on the ground is undertaken, and routes are marked, lighted, and fully equipped with wireless, and when plenty of emergency landing places are provided, flying by night will be almost as easy as by day. It is easy to realize, therefore, that with definite, well-appointed aerodromes, it becomes quite feasible—indeed advisable—to establish quite soon a commercial air service between, say, Calcutta and Cairo."

"Quite soon" wrote Brancker. It was, in fact, ten years before the Government instituted a service between India and Egypt.

I have dwelt at some length on the circumstances surrounding Brancker's entry into civil aviation because it should be recorded that the talent and initiative of British pilots and operatives had shown itself as

By courtesy of The de Havilland Aircraft Co. Ltd.

DEFIANTS EN ROUTE TO DUNKIRK, MAY 1940

Oil painting by Frank Wootton

SEPTEMBER, 1940

Oil painting by John Armstrong

early as 1919. These men, too, saw the tremendous potential value of air commerce to Britain and the British Empire. They had confirmed their faith by starting and operating the first "over the sea" air line. Yet the Government remained disinterested, apathetic. Indeed, its indefensible attitude was defined when, in October, 1920, intensive efforts by Air Transport and Travel Ltd. to obtain a subsidy to keep going finally failed, and the company was allowed by the Government to die. Handley Page Transport was also forced to close down but later gallantly got going again. This official attitude towards British air transport development persisted, in essence, right up to the Second World War. Recognition in official quarters of its potentialities was forever lacking, and although British air lines stretched across the Empire by 1939, the services operated were far fewer than they should have been ; and what had been achieved was virtually the result of courageous enthusiasts battling against official indifference, a battle more exhausting than any against the elements. Britain had a tremendous opportunity in 1919 and 1920. It was not taken. "It is never likely to recur" wrote Macmillan. "The direct loss to our aircraft industry, and to our revenue, from the yearly augmenting invisible exports of commercial air transportation, will become increasingly more noticeable as aviation grows in importance in the world." It proved distressingly noticeable on the outbreak of the Second World War when we found ourselves with but a handful of transport aeroplanes in our possession, and a high proportion of the best that we had were of American manufacture or powered by American engines.

The British public is now awake to the value of air transport. Let them resolve that the barren outlook in the years between the two wars shall never be repeated, and let them give the lead in air transport development themselves rather than rely on the doubtful inspiration of future Governments.

The Royal Air Force was the first British organisation to operate air mail services along Empire routes. Much good work was done by pilots and ground staffs in preparing the way for subsequent civil air services. But the employment of the R.A.F. in these duties, with quite unsuitable aircraft for economic operation, was misplaced. It can be seen now as one more example of the failure of the Government of the day to appreciate the potentialities of air transport. "I feel very strongly," wrote Brancker in 1921, "that it is absolutely wrong in principle to employ military aircraft on commercial aviation ; either military aircraft and their crews should be too busy on their own duties or there must be too many of them. Unless our private enterprise is allowed to start now, we shall be very seriously behind the rest of the world in a few years' time." The first R.A.F. mail service was short lived. It was a weekly one between Karachi and Bombay and survived no more than six weeks early in 1920. A much more significant service was instituted in 1921 between Baghdad and Cairo. This was operated weekly until 1927 when it was handed over to Imperial Airways. Its influence on air transport development was limited because Service operational conditions were totally different to civilian. The Service type of aircraft, designed as a war machine, was quite unsuited commercially to air line work and, furthermore, there was only a limited supply of them.

In October, 1921, the Government announced that a total sum of £200,000 per annum for three years would be allocated between British air line companies operating cross-Channel services. This step was taken by the Government because the incursions of heavily subsidised foreign companies could no longer be ignored. But although the decision on the surface appeared an encouraging sign of official awakening, it was eclipsed by the inference that for three years at least not a penny was to be spent on Empire civil air line development.

By 1924, there were four British companies (Handley Page Transport Ltd., Daimler Airways Ltd., Instone Air Line Ltd., and British Marine Air Navigation Co. Ltd.) operating services to the Continent in addition to the more heavily subsidised foreign companies that were operating along the same routes. It was apparent that the individual British companies were not strong enough to hold their own against the increasing competition from the foreign lines. Accordingly, the Government decided to combine them together into one organisation to operate the British European services and, later, to develop Empire services. The merger was completed on April 1st, 1924, and on this date Imperial Airways Ltd. came into being.

Within the limits imposed upon it by the Government's unimaginative policy, Imperial Airways did great work. The pilots, the technicians and operations staffs proved themselves over the years that were to follow to be second to none. The executive, on the other hand, suffered from the parsimonious patronage of the Government and the feeling of untroubled security that the company's position of "chosen instrument" was inevitably to foster. There was no other rival to set the pace. Instead, therefore, of pursuing a vigorous progressive policy in competition with rival companies, Imperial Airways tended to become aloof, untouchable, an edifice that stretched higher and higher into the air—and ever further from the ground. But if, as a result, the company developed air services slowly and without the imaginative impetus that the task called for, one must not lose sight of the patient spade work that it carried out, or begrudge it praise for the thousands of miles of routes over wild and desolate country that it established.

Something akin to a bombshell shook the imposing edifice of Imperial Airways Ltd., chosen instrument of the Government, sole recipient of subsidy, in the summer of 1933. A Mr. Edward Hillman, a motor-coach operator, was impudent enough to challenge the giant by starting an

BRITISH BIPLANES, D.H.9a's, BEATING OFF AN ATTACK BY FOKKER TRIPLANES
Oil painting by G. H. Davis, 1919

unsubsidised daily service between London and Paris at fares considerably lower than those of Imperial Airways. In this he was eminently successful. Hillman had a profound and invigorating influence on British aviation. It was the country's loss when he died in 1934, but he lived long enough to infuse new standards into air transportation and by his competing example, a new stimulus into Imperial Airways who viewed the activities of this motor-coach owner first with disdain, then with alarm, and finally with respect. The British Overseas Airways Corporation, which has done such sterling service under conditions of great difficulty during the Second World War, owes almost as much to British Airways Ltd. (which was a development of Hillman's Airways) as to Imperial Airways. The B.O.A.C. is the result of the amalgamation of the two companies. The Corporation has now come commonly to be known as British Airways, a point of not unimportant significance.

Imperial Airways in the early 1930's was the staid, respectable conservative concern loyally intent on carrying out to the letter the terms of that pernicious point in its charter, namely, to shake itself free of subsidy as soon as possible. In stark contrast was Hillman's Airways, and Hillman himself, intent on providing the public with air services within its means by dispensing with all the trappings and concentrating on speed and frequency of service. He set himself a tremendous task, none other than

A HANDLEY-PAGE AEROPLANE BOMBING NABLUS BY NIGHT, 1918
Oil painting by Stuart Reid

to compete with the huge national company which held the monopoly of subsidy and air mail traffic. But, as so often happens, his courage was rewarded and a month before his death his company was granted its first mail contract for the route London-Belfast-Glasgow. In October, 1935 Hillman's Airways combined with three other small companies operating internal air lines and formed British Airways. The company swiftly gained prestige. By February, 1936, it had been granted an air mail contract for a service between London and Scandinavia. Later it secured the contract for carrying the night mail between London and Berlin. In 1937, the company was selected by the Government to operate a South Atlantic service to South America. Though the route was surveyed, it was not opened before the Second World War put a temporary stop to such ambitions.

Throughout the life of the Hillman-influenced British Airways, the company pursued a progressive policy in regard to its fleet of aircraft. It started life with the simple and extremely economical (though with low speed) de Havilland biplane Dragon, an aircraft that was built especially to Mr. Hillman's specification and which revolutionised the

'NIGHT WORK'—HURRICANES IN 1940
Oil painting by Frank Wootton

cheaper form of air transport in all parts of the world. The fleet was then augmented by the addition of a four-engined type de Havilland biplane, the D.H.86, and later, the D.H.89. In 1936 it took delivery of its first Lockheed Electra, an American type of aircraft faster than any other in operation on European routes. And then, shortly before the war, it obtained Lockheed 14's, the prototype of the Lockheed Hudson with which the Royal Air Force Coastal Reconnaissance squadrons were subsequently equipped so effectively and for so long. It was a sad commentary on Government policy that the neglected British aircraft industry was unable to offer any aircraft to compete with these American aircraft for British Airways Ltd.

Imperial Airways was all this time extending its Empire services. Owing to the comparatively limited funds allocated for the purpose, the surveying of proposed routes was a slow business. Another obstacle that had to be overcome, and largely out of the control of the company, was the conciliation of the various countries through which the routes lay and the formulation of agreements with them. The Royal Air Force helped considerably towards the preliminary surveying of routes. But it is to Sir Alan Cobham that chief credit is due. This airman, quietly and unostentatiously, undertook hazardous flights of exploration with always in his heart the burning ambition of seeing the early establishment of British air routes as a parallel to British sea routes. He, like Brancker, saw the value of air commerce to Britain and the Empire, and for many years worked laboriously, courageously and with infinite patience in the face of disappointments, building the foundations on which the air routes could be laid. Without detracting from the epic achievements of such pilots as Hinkler, Amy Johnson, Mollison, Scott and the many others who made record Empire flights in the years between the wars, it was Cobham who, more than anyone, laid the practical foundations of the Empire routes. The value of those other record flights was in the visions they inspired, the standards they set for the air lines to follow.

Imperial Airways' first Empire task was to take over from the R.A.F. the running of the air mail service between Cairo and Baghdad. This was in 1927. In 1929 the service was extended eastward to Karachi, westward across the Mediterranean to Europe. By progressive stages, stages which involved lengthy political negotiation for their accomplishment as well as technical and material problems to be overcome, the route was extended to Australia in 1934. The section Singapore-Brisbane was operated by an Australian associated company, Qantas Empire Airways Ltd. A year later, a branch line was opened from Penang, this junction afterwards being changed to Bangkok. The great route southward to Cape Town was opened in 1932, and another route subsequently was opened westward from Khartoum to the British Colonies in West Africa. This section was to prove of the utmost strategic value during the Second World War when, the Mediterranean being closed to us, and before North Africa was occupied, it formed the only means of reinforcing the Middle East Forces. It was a controversial but bold decision on the part of Imperial Airways to change from land planes to flying boats for the operation of the Empire services. Many critics of the move at the time remain unconvinced of the wisdom of the decision to this day. It was made as an economic expedient and finance, it was claimed by many, should not have been allowed to influence so vital a service. In the event, the economy of using open waterways instead of improving airfields could hardly be said to have balanced the greatly increased cost in maintaining a fleet of flying boats. Be that as it may, the flying boats—and certain sectional landplane services—carried the Empire mail from England to Egypt, on to Iraq and India, Singapore and Australia. And on the southern route the mail was carried to the Sudan and East Africa. A half-ounce letter with a $1\frac{1}{2}$d. stamp on it and posted in an ordinary letter box automatically was sent by air to any place served by these services. In this long-distance postal air service with no surcharge, Britain provided an example to the world.

AIRSHIP 9
Oil painting by A. E. Cooper, 1918

BETWEEN THE TWO WARS

The period of twenty years between the two wars was distinguished chiefly by the inauguration and development of commercial air transport, the goal to which pioneers had been striving from earliest times. The previous chapter was confined to this aspect of British achievement in the air. Concurrently with this specialised development, there was progress in other spheres of aviation naturally enough, progress that showed itself particularly in a more scientific approach to airframe and engine design. At the end of the First World War Britain possessed over twenty thousand aeroplanes all designed for military use regardless of operating cost. No possible use in civil aviation could be found for the great majority of these machines, but the larger type of bombers did lend themselves in general outline to the carriage of freight and passengers instead of bombs, provided certain modifications were made to their structure and provided the cost of operation was not considered.

The Royal Air Force had little use for this huge fleet of war machines. With the signing of the Peace the Royal Air Force was allowed to shrink to a size most dangerously small. "Broadly speaking," wrote Sir Hugh Trenchard, "the principle has been to reduce Service Squadrons to the minimum considered essential for our garrisons overseas with a very small number in the United Kingdom as a Reserve, and to concentrate the whole of the remainder of our resources on perfecting the training of our officers and men." This policy adopted by the Air Staff of concentrating on supreme quality if quantity was to be denied them was to prove the saving feature of our mistakes when, in 1936, the R.A.F. started to expand at a forced pace far in excess of what would have been possible without the core of high quality which had been maintained and was there to build on.

Two statements by Ministers in the House of Commons will suffice to show the degree of shrinkage the Royal Air Force had to accept. On November 26th, 1920, Mr. Churchill, the Secretary of State for Air, stated that as at October 1st, the strength of the R.A.F. was 2,812 officers, 23,862 men. The Air Force had thus by then been reduced to one-tenth of its war time strength. Three and a half years later, another Secretary of State, Sir Samuel Hoare, informed the House that "to-day we have 371 first line machines as compared with 3,300 in November, 1918." The pace of subsequent expansion is best realised when we recall that even in 1934 we had only 850 first line aircraft at home and overseas. Only a very small proportion of these aircraft were larger than light single-engine biplane bombers ; a high proportion were single-engine fighters. By 1942 the Metropolitan Air Force bomber squadrons alone were sufficiently numerous to despatch two raids over Germany, each of 1,000 multi-engined bombers, within three days of one another.

Throughout this period of tribulation for the Royal Air Force, the technical quality of aircraft and the skill of aircrews were fortunately maintained at a high pitch. This was achieved by the Air Staff, from time to time, encouraging the personnel by authorising assaults on world aviation records. The world records of Long Distance, Height and Speed —the three most coveted prizes of aeronautical technical endeavour— were each attained more than once by Royal Air Force crews and aircraft. The annual Displays at Hendon were another means of providing pilots and ground crews with a positive aim during the years of neglect between the two wars.

The Royal Air Force overseas during this period was based on Egypt, Iraq, Aden, India and Singapore. In India it was of great help to the Army in maintaining order on the frontier. In Iraq, until Britain resigned her mandate, and in Aden, the R.A.F was virtually responsible for maintaining order. Much ignorant criticism was made of the British policy of 'police bombing' recalcitrant tribes. Steps had to be taken to prevent a stronger tribe robbing a weaker, to prevent raids on the caravan routes across the desert, and to punish such lawlessness when it occurred. In the old days this was done by the Army undertaking a punitive expedition which invariably was costly in lives to both sides. The R.A.F.'s method,

RUNWAY PERSPECTIVE

Water colour by Eric Ravilious, 1941

A SERVICE STATION—SEAPLANES
Oil painting by Charles Cundall

SHORT STIRLING HEAVY BOMBERS PREPARING FOR A NIGHT RAID
Drawing by Frank Wootton

on the other hand, involved the minimum of bloodshed and, incidentally, saved the taxpayer in aggregate an immense amount of money. Recalcitrant tribes were never bombed themselves. They were first told that they must pay up a fine commensurate with the particular act of lawlessness. If the sheik refused, he was told that his village would be bombed at a given hour on a given day and that none who valued his safety should be at home at that time. Full warning was in this way given, and only on the most rare occasion was anyone killed. Faced with the partial destruction of his village, the offending sheik generally used to pay. In undertaking this duty overseas, the R.A.F. acted essentially as policemen, the representatives and purveyors of law and order.

The strength of the Royal Air Force during this period was augmented by the Air Ministry enlisting the help of the civil population. In 1923 the Reserve of Air Force Officers was formed. This included all those who served as pilots in the R.N.A.S., the R.F.C. or R.A.F. during the war, and also qualified civil pilots who volunteered to be included. Later the Auxiliary Air Force was formed by civilians who trained for and operated their own squadrons in their spare time and reached a standard of efficiency that proved invaluable when hostilities were re-opened in 1939. In 1937, another organisation for volunteer pilots was formed—

8 a.m. PARADE, R.A.F., 1942
Oil painting by Alan Sorrell

the R.A.F. Volunteer Reserve. The Fleet Air Arm, slow in starting due to the Admiralty's reluctance to appreciate the significance of Air Power, was, by 1939, a small but invaluable component of British Sea Power.

For some time after the 1918 Armistice, the Air Ministry undertook experiments with a view to developing the airship. These experiments were continued until the disaster to the R.101 which crashed at the outset of a flight to India in 1930 with Lord Thompson, Secretary of State for Air, and Sir Sefton Brancker, Director of Civil Aviation on board. We have since come to regard the achievements of Germany to be paramount in the world of airship development. But it was Britain who was in the van in the years immediately following the First World War. The most remarkable achievement was the crossing of the Atlantic by the airship R.34 in 1919. On July 2nd, with a crew of twenty-nine under the command of Major G. H. Scott, R.34 left Scotland and arrived at

302

MORNING ON PARADE
Water colour by Eric Ravilious

Mineola, Long Island, on July 6th with fuel left for only another forty minutes' flying. Before landing, and while the airship hovered over the airfield, the hundreds of spectators were horrified to see a man fall from the gondola. Relief followed when it was seen that he had a parachute. It was Major G. Pritchard who explained to the American officers who ran to him that he had come a bit ahead of the rest of the crew in order to help with the landing operations. Later, the R.34 accomplished the return flight to England.

A few days before this successful flight of the R.34, the Atlantic had been crossed non-stop by air for the first time. Piloted by John Alcock, with Arthur Whitten Brown as navigator, a modified Vickers Vimy bomber crossed the ocean from St. John's, Newfoundland, and landed in Ireland at Clifden, Co. Galway. The flight took 15 hours 57 minutes and was accomplished at an average speed of 118 miles an hour. The courage of these two airmen, who were each knighted by the King for their achievement, remains unsurpassed to this day. Somehow the solo flight of Lindbergh across the Atlantic eight years later caught the imagination of the world more than that of Alcock and Brown with the result that many people quite erroneously credit Lindbergh with the honour of being the first to cross the Atlantic non-stop. He was the first to fly the ocean solo—an impractical refinement.

The flight of Alcock and Brown was the first of those many epic flights by pioneer airmen who gallantly faced unknown hazards during the period between the two wars. It is of this company of modern adventurers that Alfred Noyes might have been thinking when he wrote :

> Feeble the wings, dauntless the soul !
> Take thou the conqueror's laurel crown ;
> Take—for thy chariot grazed the goal—
> The imperial garland of renown ;
> While those young eyes, beyond the sun,
> See Drake, see Raleigh, smile 'Well done.'

Many governments encouraged their airmen to undertake record flights by financing attempts and providing appropriate aircraft. The British Government left private airmen to make their own arrangements and remained virtually indifferent to the gallant failures and successes of British airmen and airwomen. Fortunately there were men such as Lord Wakefield and Lord Rothermere, who saw value in these flights, and the stimulant they provided for air transport development ; and these men, with others, financed the ventures and turned the courage of British hearts to practical account.

Many were the British men and women whose names momentarily hit the front page while they flew against time to the ends of the earth— Scott, Campbell Black, Clouston, Ken Waller, Henshaw, Mrs. Markham and many others—but two of them will be remembered with especial admiration not only for their brilliant flights but for their gallant failures. Amy Johnson and Jim Mollison, these two ; these two who, both individually and together, made attack after attack on the hazards that were an integral part of record-breaking flights over continents and oceans in frail craft with 'feeble wings.' Amy Johnson's most famous flight was, of course, her first out of England. In 1930, as a girl of twenty-two, she flew her Moth to Australia in twenty days. During those three weeks she endured tremendous trials, and the world held its breath as she surmounted them. Amy was untouched by the adulation that was showered upon her. She, being a serious minded person, forthwith prepared for her next adventure. At the same time, Jim Mollison was also preparing a series of record flights. During the years that followed, these two startled the world with their achievements, Mollison showing a curious predilection for flying the Atlantic, which in those days was the most dangerous challenge that could be thrown to an airman. And then,

ASSEMBLING A HAWKER-HURRICANE
Oil painting by E. D. Hewland

finally, in 1933, the two flew the Atlantic together in an attempt to fly to
New York from England.   They failed to be the first to do so by just
forty miles ; but they were successful in making the first direct flight
from Great Britain to the United States.   Amy Johnson died in the service
of her country in 1940 while acting as a ferry pilot delivering aircraft to
the Royal Air Force.   Her attainments, her gallantry, her tenacity of
purpose, her indifference to material rewards, her humility, her profound
sincerity—all these ensure her being remembered among the truly great
aviators.

There were, during the period under review, two international air
races, in each of which British entrants were successful.   One of these
was the last of the Schneider Trophy races in 1931, the other was the
England-Australia race for the "McRobertson" Trophy in 1934.   Private
generosity was responsible for our successes.   The Government had no
intention of entering for the 1931 Schneider Trophy race, on the score
of expense.   Fortunately for Britain, Lady Houston came to the rescue
and put up £100,000.   With this backing, the Air Ministry got busy and

W

instructed Mr. R. J. Mitchell, the Supermarine Aircraft Company's chief designer, to design a winning machine. The outcome was the Supermarine Rolls-Royce S.6.B. When the time came, the opposing Italian team withdrew, so that it was only left for the British entrant to fly over the course to claim the Trophy. This was successfully accomplished. Later the same day, the S.6.B. won the World's Speed Record at 378.05 miles per hour and three days later, its engine running on special fuel, raised the figure to 407.5 miles per hour.

The day's achievements were satisfactory; but they were as nothing to the lasting significance of the work of Supermarines and Rolls-Royce in producing the S.6.B. A direct and clear-cut consequence of the production of this machine was the Spitfire and the Rolls-Royce Merlin engine. The invaluable achievements of the Spitfire in the Second World War need no emphasis, but what is not so generally known is the fact that the performance of many other British military aircraft, including the Hurricane which played so vital a part in the Battle of Britain, depended on the outstanding qualities of the Merlin engine. More countries than Great Britain owe much to Lady Houston.

The de Havilland Aircraft Company designed and built an aircraft of novel wooden construction for the England-Australia race for which Sir Macpherson Robertson had offered a prize of £10,000. The race was won by this machine, the Comet. Piloted by C. W. A. Scott and Tom Campbell Black it flew to Melbourne from Mildenhall in 70 hours and 59 minutes. The direct descendant of the Comet was the Mosquito, the most successful machine of its type in the Second World War. The outcome of these two races demonstrates beyond all doubt the national importance of participation in international air races. It is to be hoped that the lessons will not be lost on future governments.

Behind the façade of these international events, British aviation was developing quietly and with modest success. In 1926, the first Light Aeroplane Club was formed, and with every year that followed, more of these clubs came into being. The movement enabled thousands of people to learn to fly and proved a considerable national asset when, on its foundations, the Civil Air Guard was built in 1938 as the clouds of war were forming on the horizon. Gliding clubs also flourished, and several British pilots, notably Philip Wills, made soaring flights approaching the best of Germany, the nation which led the way in this art. By September, 1939, Britain was beginning to become air-minded, beginning to be conscious of the significance of air development, beginning to realise that her future rested in the air as much as on the sea. Her pulses were quickening for the coming great trial in which the freedom of Europe was to be won largely through the activity and courage of her airmen.

LIST OF ILLUSTRATIONS
PLATES IN COLOUR

BRITISH MERCHANT ADVENTURERS

BRITISH POLAR EXPLORERS

BRITISH MOUNTAINEERS

BRITISH SOLDIERS

BRITAIN IN THE AIR

BLACK AND WHITE ILLUSTRATIONS

BRITISH MERCHANT ADVENTURERS

The illustration on p. 27 is reproduced by courtesy of the Curators of the Bodleian Library and the Oxford University Press ; on p. 51, by courtesy of Horace Marshall & Son Ltd.

BRITISH POLAR EXPLORERS

BRITISH MOUNTAINEERS

Illustrations on pp. 107, 139 are reproduced by courtesy of Maggs Bros. London; on p. 125, by courtesy of J. Howard Whitehouse, Esq., and the Director of the Victoria & Albert Museum; on p. 123, by courtesy of the Royal Institution ; on pp. 127, 131, by courtesy of the Trustees of the British Museum ; on pp. 140, 141, by courtesy of "The Times" ; on pp. 143, 155, by courtesy of F. S. Smythe, Esq.

BRITISH SEAMEN

Illustrations on pp. 159, 161, 191 are reproduced by courtesy of the Trustees of the British Museum ; on p. 171, by courtesy of the Curators of the Bodleian Library ; on p. 187, by courtesy of the Parker Gallery, London ; on p. 197, by gracious permission of H.M. The King ; on p. 261, by courtesy of N. Sotheby Pitcher, Esq.

Illustrations on pp. 207, 212 are reproduced by courtesy of the Curators of the Bodleian Library ; on pp. 215, 230, 231, 243, 246, by courtesy of the Parker Gallery, London ; on pp. 222, 229, by courtesy of the Trustees of the National Portrait Gallery ; on pp. 225, 233, 236, 244, by courtesy of the Walker Galleries, London : on p. 227, by gracious permission of H.M. The King ; on p. 240, by courtesy of Maggs Bros., London ; on p. 249, by courtesy of the Imperial War Museum ; illustrations on pp. 251, 253, 255, Crown copyright reserved

BRITAIN IN THE AIR

Illustrations on pp. 257, 279, 280 are reproduced by courtesy of the Royal Aeronautical Society ; on pp. 260, 269, by courtesy of James Falcke, Esq. ; on p. 261, by courtesy of the Director of the Science Museum, South Kensington ; on pp. 263, 264, 270, 271, from the Norman Collection, by courtesy of the Comptroller General of Patents, Designs and Trade Marks ; on p. 273, by courtesy of Sir Kenelm H. E. Cayley, Bt. ; on p. 281, by courtesy of H.M. Stationery Office ; on pp. 282, 283, 291, 293, 294, 297, by courtesy of the Imperial War Museum, London ; on p. 285 by courtesy of British Overseas Airways ; on pp. 295, 301, by courtesy of The de Havilland Aircraft Co., Ltd. ; illustrations on pp. 302, 303, 305, Crown copyright reserved

SHORT BIBLIOGRAPHIES

BRITISH MERCHANT ADVENTURERS

Ralph Fitch: Merchant-Traveller *fl.* 1583-1611. *Early Travels in India*, by William Foster, c.i.e., 1921.—*Purchas His Pilgrimes.* Hakluyt Society. Vol. X.—Sir Thomas Roe: Merchant-Ambassador 1580-1644. *Memoirs of Jehangir,* translated by A. Rogers, 1909.—*Embassy of Sir Thomas Roe to the Court of the Great Mogul,* edited by W. Foster, c.i.e., 1899, for the Hakluyt Society.—Samuel White : Merchant-Interloper 1650-1689. *Siamese White,* by Maurice Collis, 1936.—Robert Clive : Merchant-Soldier 1725-1774. The authorities for Clive are too numerous to quote here. Macaulay's *Essay* may be cited as still the best short account.—Mungo Park : Merchant Explorer 1771-1806. *The Travels of Mungo Park.* Everyman's Library.—Stamford Raffles : Merchant-Administrator 1781-1829. The best account is *Raffles,* by R. Coupland, 1926

BRITISH POLAR EXPLORERS

South with Scott by Admiral Sir E. R. G. R. Evans. Collins.—*The Conquest of the South Pole* by J. Gordon Hayes. Thornton Butterworth.—*The Home of the Blizzard* by Sir Douglas Mawson. Hodder & Stoughton.—*The Great White South* by Herbert G. Ponting. Duckworth. —*The Geographical Journal.* Royal Geographical Society.—*Southern Lights* by John Rymill. Chatto & Windus.—*The Voyage of the Discovery* by Capt. R. F. Scott. Murray.—*The Polar Record.* The Scott Polar Institute, Cambridge.—*South* and *Heart of the Antarctic* by Sir Ernest Shackleton. Heinemann.—*Sea Adventurers of Britain* by Commander Taffrail. Collins.—*The Life of Sir John Franklin* by H. D. Traill. Murray

BRITISH MOUNTAINEERS

Scrambles amongst the Alps, 1871, by Edward Whymper (6th edition, Murray, 1936).—
The Playground of Europe, 1871, by Sir Leslie Stephen. Longmans (reprinted, Blackwell, 1936).—*My Climbs in the Alps and Caucasus*, 1895, by A. F. Mummery. Fisher Unwin (reprinted, Blackwell, 1936).—*On High Hills*, 1927, by G. Winthrop Young. Methuen.—
Everest 1933, 1937, by Hugh Ruttledge. Hodder & Stoughton.—*The Mountain Way—an Anthology*, 1938, by R. L. G. Irving. J. M. Dent

BRITISH SEAMEN

Memoirs of Admiral the Right Hon. the Earl of St. Vincent, G.C.B., 1844, by Jedediah Stephens Tucker.—*Lord Nelson's Letters and Dispatches*, 1844-46, edited by Sir N. H. Nicolas.—*Life of Nelson*, 1897, by Rear-Admiral A. T. Mahan, U.S.N. Sampson Low (reprinted in Penguin Books, 1942).—*The Royal Navy : A History*, 1897-1903, edited by W. Laird Clowes. Sampson Low.—*Drake and the Tudor Navy*, 1898, by Julian Corbett. Longmans.—*Memoirs of Admiral the Right Hon. Sir Astley Cooper Key, G.C.B.*, 1898, by Vice-Admiral P. H. Colomb. Methuen.—*Samuel Pepys*, 1933-38, by Arthur Bryant. Cambridge University Press. —Publications of the Navy Records Society

BRITISH SOLDIERS

A History of the British Army, 1899-1930 (Macmillan), and *Wellington*, 1925 (William & Norgate), both by Sir John Fortescue.—*The Great Boer War*, 1902, by A. Conan Doyle. Smith Elder.—*Wellington's Army*, 1912, by Sir Charles Oman. Edward Arnold.—*The War Office Past and Present*, 1914, by Owen Wheeler. Methuen.—*The Wars of Marlborough*, 1921, by Frank Taylor. Blackwell.—*Cromwell's Army*, 1921 (3rd edition), by C. H. Firth. Methuen.—*Sir John Moore's System of Training*, 1925, by J. F. C. Fuller. Hutchinson.—
A History of the World War, 1914-18, 1934, by B. H. Liddell Hart. Faber.—*Outline of British Military History*, 1660-1936, 1936, by D. H. Cole and E. C. Priestley. Sifton Praed.
—*A History of the Uniforms of the British Army*, 1940-41, by Cecil C. P. Lawson. Peter Davies.—*The Defence of Calais*, 1941, by Eric Linklater. H.M.S.O.

EVERY REGIMENT HAS ITS HISTORY, AMONG THE BEST BEING :

The Life of a Regiment : the History of the Gordon Highlanders, 1901-3 (reprinted 1929) by C. Greenhill Gardyne. Medici Society.—*History of the Royal Dragoons, 1661-1934*, 1934 (Maclehose), and *The South Wales Borderers, 1689-1937*, 1937, both by C. T. Atkinson.—
The Scots Guards, 1645-1914, 1934, by Sir Frederick Maurice

OF SOLDIERS' OWN BOOKS SOME OF THE BEST ARE :

Journal of Occurrences during the American War, 1809, by R. Lamb. Dublin.—*A Journal of the Campaign in Flanders, 1708*, 1846, by J. M. Deane, edited by J. B. Deane.—*Forty-one Years in India*, 1897, by Lord Roberts. Macmillan.—*Autobiography*, 1901, by Sir Harry Smith. Murray.—*Adventures with the Connaught Rangers, 1809-1814*, 1902, by William Grattan. Edward Arnold.—*A Private in the Guards*, 1919, by Stephen Graham. Macmillan (reprinted 1928 in the Travellers' Library, Heinemann).—*Listening for the Drums*, 1944, by Sir Ian Hamilton. Faber

BRITAIN IN THE AIR

The History of Aeronautics in Great Britain, 1924, by J. E. Hodgson. Oxford University Press.—*Sefton Brancker*, 1935, by Norman Macmillan. Heinemann.—*Interpretative History of Flight*, 1937, by M. J. B. Davy. H.M.S.O.—*The Air*, 1940, by Edgar B. Schieldrop. Hutchinson.—*A History of the Air Ministry*, 1940, by C. G. Grey. Allen & Unwin.—
British Aviation, 1940, by F. A. de V. Robertson. Longmans.—*Battle of Britain* (1941), *Bomber Command* (1941), *Coastal Command* (1942), *Fleet Air Arm* (1943). H.M.S.O.

INDEX

318

323